A LEXICAL STUDY OF THE SEPTUAGINT
VERSION OF THE PENTATEUCH

SOCIETY OF BIBLICAL LITERATURE
SEPTUAGINT AND COGNATE STUDIES SERIES

Edited by
Harry M. Orlinsky

Number 14

A LEXICAL STUDY OF THE SEPTUAGINT VERSION
OF THE PENTATEUCH

by
J. A. L. Lee

A LEXICAL STUDY
OF THE SEPTUAGINT VERSION
OF THE PENTATEUCH

by
J. A. L. Lee

Scholars Press
Chico, California

A LEXICAL STUDY
OF THE SEPTUAGINT
VERSION OF THE PENTATEUCH

by

J. A. L. Lee

Library of Congress Cataloging in Publication Data
Lee, J. A. L.
A lexical study of the Septuagint version of the
Pentateuch.

(Septuagint and cognate studies ; no. 14) (ISSN 0145–
2754)
Includes index.
1. Bible. O.T. Pentateuch. Greek—Versions—
Septuagint. 2. Bible. O.T. Pentateuch—Criticism, Textual.
I. Title. II. Series.
BS744.L43   222'.1048   82-5460
ISBN 0-89130-576-9   AACR2

Printed in the United States of America

PREFACE

The present work was submitted as a doctoral dissertation at the University of Cambridge in 1970, and the text is reproduced here without revision, apart from the addition of indexes. I am conscious of the drawbacks this entails. No subject, not even that of LXX lexicography, stands still for ten years: references to more recent work could certainly be added. In addition, like most dissertations, this would in any case benefit from revision or expansion in a number of places. Nevertheless I believe it has a useful contribution to make in its present form, and to delay publication until a thorough revision could be undertaken seemed certain to mean that it would remain unpublished.

In two places the existing discussion has been superseded by a fuller treatment I have published elsewhere: ἀποσκευή (pp. 101-7) is dealt with in *JTS* XXIII (1972) 430-7, and μέρος (pp. 72-6) in *Antichthon* VI (1972) 39-42.

It remains to repeat the thanks expressed in my original preface, first to those scholars in Cambridge who so readily welcomed and advised an unknown Australian with out-of-the-way interests: Barnabas Lindars S.S.F., my supervisor, patiently guided me throughout; Dr. J. Chadwick gave valuable advice on many matters, especially lexicographical methods; Dr. S.P. Brock kindly shared with me his unrivalled knowledge of the LXX; and Mr. S.J. Papastavrou gave assistance with Modern Greek.

Thanks are due also to Pembroke College, for general support and encouragement during my years in Cambridge.

Finally I owe my greatest debt to the late Professor G.P. Shipp (1900-1980), of the University of Sydney. He set me an example of scholarship which, though an unattainable goal, has been constantly before me. More especially, it was he who, in 1964, introduced me to Koine Greek and provided the basis of all my later work.

J.A.L. LEE
University of Sydney
December, 1981

CONTENTS

ABBREVIATIONS

AELex	Μέγα ῞Αγγλο-'Ελληνικὸν Λεξικόν, 'Αθῆναι, [1968], ed. Θ.Ν. Τσαβεας.
Anz, *Subsidia*	H. Anz, *Subsidia ad cognoscendum Graecorum sermonem vulgarem e Pentateuchi versione Alexandrina repetita* (Diss. Phil. Halenses XII. 2), Halle, 1894.
Archiv	*Archiv für Papyrusforschung.*
Barr, *Semantics*	J. Barr, *The Semantics of Biblical Language,* Oxford, 1961
Bauer	W.F. Arndt & F.W. Gingrich, *A Greek-English Lexicon of the New Testament and Other Early Christian Literature* (A transl. & adaptation of W. Bauer's *Griechisch-Deutsches Wörterbuch zu den Schriften des Neuen Testaments und der übrigen urchristlichen Literatur,* 4 ed., 1952), Chicago & Cambridge, 1957.
BDB	F. Brown, S.R. Driver, & C.A. Briggs, *A Hebrew and English Lexicon of the Old Testament,* Oxford, 1907.
Bl.DF	F. Blass, A. Debrunner, & R.W. Funk, *A Greek Grammar of the New Testament and Other Early Christian Literature,* Cambridge & Chicago, 1961.
BP	C.D. Buck & W. Peterson, *Reverse Index of Greek Nouns and Adjectives,* Chicago, 1944.
Brooke-McLean	A.E. Brooke & N. McLean, *The Old Testament in Greek,* Cambridge, 1906-40.
BZAW	*Beihefte zur ZAW.*
Chantraine, *Formation*	P. Chantraine, *La formation des noms en grec ancien,* Paris, 1933.

Daniel, *Recherches*	S. Daniel, *Recherches sur le vocabulaire du culte dans le Septante* (Études et Commentaires LXI), Paris, 1966.
Deissmann, *BS*	G.A. Deissmann, *Bible Studies* (transl. by A. Grieve of *Bibelstudien,* 1895, & *Neue Bibelstudien,* 1897), 2 ed., Edinburgh, 1909.
Deissmann, *LAE*	G.A. Deissmann, *Light from the Ancient East* (transl. by L.R.M. Strachan of *Licht vom Osten,* 4 ed., 1923), New York, 1927.
ET	*The Expository Times.*
Frisk	J.I.H. Frisk, *Griechisches Etymologisches Wörterbuch*, Heidelberg, 1954-.
HDB	*Dictionary of the Bible* by J. Hastings, 2nd ed., revised by F.C. Grant & H.H. Rowley, Edinburgh, 1963.
Helbing, *Gramm.*	R. Helbing, *Grammatik der LXX: Laut- und Wortlehre*, Göttingen, 1907.
Helbing, *Kasussyntax*	R. Helbing, *Die Kasussyntax der Verba bei den Septuaginta*, Göttingen, 1928.
HTR	*Harvard Theological Review.*
HUCA	*Hebrew Union College Annual.*
ICC	*International Critical Commentary.*
Jannaris	A.N. Jannaris, *A Concise Dictionary of the English and Modern Greek Languages as Actually Written and Spoken*, London, 1895.
JAOS	*Journal of the American Oriental Society.*
JBL	*Journal of Biblical Literature.*
Jellicoe,	S. Jellicoe, *The Septuagint and Modern Study*, Oxford, 1968.

JNES	*Journal of Near Eastern Studies.*
Johannessohn, *Präpositionen*	M. Johannessohn, *Der Gebrauch der Präpositionen in der Septuaginta (MSU* III.3), Berlin, 1926.
JTS	*Journal of Theological Studies.*
KB	L. Koehler & W. Baumgartner, *Lexicon in Veteris Testamenti Libros*, Leiden, 1958.
Kiessling	E. Kiessling, *Wörterbuch der griechischen Papyrusurkunden* IV: 1, Berlin, 1944; 2, 3 Marburg, 1958, 1966.
Kiessling Suppl.	E. Kiessling, *Wörterbuch der griechischen Papyrusurkunden* Suppl. I (1940-1966), Amsterdam, 1969.
Lex. Pr.	Λεξικὸν τῆς ᾽Ελληνικῆς γλώσσης (Published by Athens newspaper ᾽Πρωΐα'), Athens, 1933.
LSJ	H.G. Liddell, R. Scott, & H.S. Jones, *A Greek-English Lexicon*, 9 ed., Oxford, 1940.
LSJ Suppl.	H.G. Liddell, R. Scott, & H.S. Jones, *A Greek-English Lexicon: A Supplement*, ed. E.A. Barber, Oxford, 1968.
Mayser, *Gramm.*	E. Mayser, *Grammatik der griechischen Papyri aus der Ptolemäerzeit*, Berlin-Leipzig, 1906-38.
MM	J.H. Moulton & G. Milligan, *The Vocabulary of the Greek Testament Illustrated from the Papyri and Other Non-Literary Sources*, London, 1914-30.
Moule, *Idiom Book*	C.F.D. Moule, *An Idiom Book of New Testament Greek*, Cambridge, 1953.
Moulton, *Proleg.*	J.H. Moulton, *Grammar of New Testament Greek: I Prolegomena*, 3 ed., Edinburgh, 1908.

Moulton-Howard, *Gramm.* II	J.H. Moulton & W.F. Howard, *Grammar of New Testament Greek: II Accidence & Word-Formation,* Edinburgh, 1929.
Moulton-Turner, *Gramm.* III	N. Turner, *Grammar of New Testament Greek: III Syntax,* Edinburgh, 1963.
MSU	*Mitteilungen des Septuaginta-Unternehmens der Akademie der Wissenschaften in Göttingen.*
MT	Massoretic Text.
NTS	*New Testament Studies.*
OLD	*Oxford Latin Dictionary,* Oxford, 1968-.
PAAJR	*Proceedings of the American Academy for Jewish Research.*
Palmer, *Gramm.*	L.R. Palmer, *Grammar of the Post-Ptolemaic Papyri: Part I The Suffixes,* London, 1946.
Preisigke	F. Preisigke (& E. Kiessling), *Wörterbuch der griechischen Papyrusurkunden* I-III, Berlin, 1925-31.
Psichari, *Essai*	J. Psichari, 'Essai sur le grec de la Septante', *Revue des Études juives* LV (1908) 161-208.
Rahlfs	A. Rahlfs, *Septuaginta,* Stuttgart, 1935.
REG	*Revue des Études grecques.*
Schleusner	J.Fr. Schleusner, *Novus Thesaurus philologicocriticus, sive Lexicon in LXX,* Londini, 1829.
Schnebel, *Landwirtschaft*	M. Schnebel, *Die Landwirtschaft im hellenistischen Ägypten: Bd. I Der Betrieb der Landwirtschaft,* München, 1925.
Schwyzer, *Gramm.*	E. Schwyzer, *Griechische Grammatik,* München, 1959-60.

SOED	W. Little, H.W. Fowler, J. Coulson, & C.T. Onions, *The Shorter Oxford English Dictionary,* 3 ed., Oxford, 1944.
Swanson	D.C. Swanson, *Vocabulary of Modern Spoken Greek,* Minneapolis, 1959.
Swete, *Introd.*	H.B. Swete, *An Introduction to the Old Testament in Greek,* Cambridge, 1900.
Thackeray, *Gramm.*	H.St.J. Thackeray, *A Grammar of the Old Testament in Greek according to the Septuagint: I Introduction, Orthography and Accidence,* Cambridge, 1909.
Thumb, *Hellenismus*	A. Thumb, *Die griechische Sprache im Zeitalter des Hellenismus,* Strassburg, 1901.
Th.Z	*Theologische Zeitschrift.*
TWNT	*Theologisches Wörterbuch zum Neuen Testament,* ed. G. Kittel & G. Friedrich, Stuttgart, 1933-. Cited by vol. & p. of Engl. transl. by G.W. Bromiley & F.F. Bruce, Michigan, 1965-.
VT	*Vetus Testamentum.*
ZAW	*Zeitschrift für die Alttestamentliche Wissenschaft.*
ZNW	*Zeitschrift für die Neutestamentliche Wissenschaft.*

Names of ancient authors and their works, books of the LXX and *NT*, and titles of papyrological and epigraphical publications are abbreviated as in LSJ and Suppl., with a few minor variations. Attention may be drawn to one or two of LSJ's abbreviations that are perhaps liable to confusion, or not easily recognized: A. = Aeschylus, Ar. = Aristophanes, Arist. = Aristotle; Hdt. = Herodotus, Herod. = Herodas; Hp. = Hippocrates, Hyp. = Hyperides. *PPetr.* is mostly cited by volume and text

number, not, as in LSJ, by volume and page number. In references to *PCair.Zen.* the digits 59(00) are omitted, as in LSJ:
thus 2 = 59002.

In references to papyri and inscriptions the following are
to be noticed: (i) The line cited for a given word is usually
that in which the word itself occurs or begins, though the
passage actually quoted may extend over a number of surrounding
lines (as MM, p. xxx). (ii) Dates given to texts are strictly
those assigned by the editors. (iii) Symbols used in the
published text (brackets, dots, etc.) are not always reproduced
in full: I have omitted them where the reading seems beyond
doubt or where they have no bearing on the point under discussion. For these symbols see E.G. Turner, *Greek Papyri* 179-180.

In giving dates, lower-case Roman numerals indicate the
century, Arabic numerals the year: e.g. iii B.C. = the third
century B.C.

The LXX text cited and quoted is that of Rahlfs (Stuttgart, 1935). Rahlfs' numeration alone is given. Rahlfs is
followed in the matter of accents and breathings on proper
names.

In giving the original Hebrew the sign '=' has been
avoided. Occasionally the swung dash (~) is used, as an abbrevi-
ation for 'corresponds to'. The portion of MT quoted is usually
only that to which the Greek word under discussion corresponds,
not the whole MT passage corresponding to the whole LXX passage
quoted.

CHAPTER I

INTRODUCTORY

The chief purpose of this study is to demonstrate as far as possible the affinities, in the sphere of vocabulary, between the language of the Septuagint version of the Pentateuch and the vernacular Koine Greek of its time. It is intended that in so doing it should form a contribution specifically towards (i) the solution of the general problem of LXX language, i.e. the question of its relation to the Greek language proper; and (ii) the lexicography of the LXX.

The language of the LXX is plainly not normal Greek in many places. The question whether it is nevertheless to be regarded as belonging to the main stream of the Greek language has still not been satisfactorily settled. Deissmann, followed by Thumb, Thackeray, Moulton, and other older scholars, considered, and gathered evidence to show, that the language of the LXX translators was essentially the Greek of their time. According to this view the peculiarities of LXX Greek are to be explained chiefly as a result of the translation-techniques employed. This view was and still is accepted by many, probably by most, scholars. It has however been maintained by others that we have in the LXX a specimen of a form of Greek actually spoken by the Jews in Egypt, a Greek so extensively contaminated by Semitic usage as to be an entity separate from the normal Greek of the time. The case for this has recently been argued afresh especially by H.S. Gehman, with support from N. Turner.

It is to this debate that the present study is designed to contribute, in support of the earlier view. The general question of the nature of LXX Greek will first be discussed in more detail, in Chapter II. There the main arguments already advanced, and certain new points, will be considered. The bulk of the study will consist of a detailed examination of certain portions of the Pentateuch vocabulary. The words and uses selected for study are chiefly those that are new in the Koine and are attested in documents contemporary with the translators.

1

2

My purpose in examining them will be to support the thesis that
the language of the LXX translators was essentially the Greek of
their time. The study will thus be in the main a continuation
of Deissmann's work and methods. Since his time a large quantity of papyrological evidence has accumulated and has been
little explored for the light it throws on LXX vocabulary. The
present study aims at making the fullest possible use of this
material.

My main concern will be with the everyday, non-theological,
vocabulary of the Pentateuch, but in attempting to show affinities between it and the vocabulary of 'secular' Greek I have no
wish to deny the distinctive character of some parts of the LXX
vocabulary, notably its religious terminology. It is hardly
possible to doubt that the translators, and the Alexandrian Jews
generally, introduced *some* novel features into their vocabulary,
in all three ways available to them: by borrowing words from
Hebrew or Aramaic, by forming new words in Greek, and by giving
special significations to some current Greek terms. Similarly
no-one would wish to deny that the translators' Greek has been
strongly influenced in every respect by the Hebrew of the
original text.[1]

As is well known, the lexicography of the LXX is a subject
that has been seriously neglected for some time. The only lexicon of the LXX is that of Schleusner, dating from the 1820s.
This work, though in some respects still valuable, is now definitely obsolete. The gap is only partially filled by the more
modern lexicographical tools, LSJ, Bauer, and MM, which give
little more than incidental treatment to the LXX.

There have of course been numerous studies in the field of
LXX vocabulary apart from what is found in the lexicons, but
only a small part of the whole vocabulary has yet been adequately treated. All these studies (of which more will be said

---

1. I see no reason to disagree with C.F.D. Moule's 'word of
caution', *Idiom Book* 3f.: 'The pendulum has swung rather too far
in the direction of equating Biblical with "secular" Greek; and
we must not allow these fascinating discoveries to blind us to
the fact that Biblical Greek still does retain certain peculiarities, due in part to Semitic influence...'.

below) have been limited in extent, and the important older ones
by Deissmann and Anz are now in need of re-appraisal and supple-
menting with new evidence. Much recent study has been limited,
especially in that it has tended to concentrate on words of
theological interest, and then often with the chief object of
elucidating the language and ideas of the *NT*.

The evidence of the papyri, although generally recognized
as important for LXX lexicography, has yet to be thoroughly investigated. As many of the examples in this study will show,
there is still a great deal to be discovered about LXX usage
from this source. Much that is important for the LXX vocabulary
has not been noted by any of the standard dictionaries.

An up-to-date lexicon of the LXX, embodying the results of
a thorough re-examination of its vocabulary and taking full
account of the papyrological evidence, is clearly a pressing
requirement.[2] There is at the present time an increased interest in providing such a work, but the task will be a difficult
and lengthy one, and it is clearly desirable that as much pre-
liminary study as possible should be undertaken for it.

It is intended that the present study should make a
contribution in this direction, not only by its examination of
individual words and uses but also by offering a number of observations relevant to LXX lexicography generally. In particular we shall observe how important a full investigation of the
non-Biblical evidence can be in deciding the meaning of a word
in the LXX.

In any study of the LXX one encounters at the outset the
problem of the uncertainty of our text. We may distinguish
three separate questions on which there is still some measure of
uncertainty. They are: (i) Is it possible to speak of a single
original LXX translation? (ii) To what extent is an ancient
translation preserved in our MSS? (iii) If such a translation
does survive, at what date was it made? The present study is
not directly concerned with solving these problems. It will

---

2. G.B. Caird *JTS* XIX (1968) 453, Jellicoe, *SMS,* 359. Already
in 1909 Deissmann spoke of the 'clamant need' of a lexicon,
BS 73 n.3.

proceed on the hypothesis that it *is* possible to speak of a single original version of the Pentateuch; that this version is preserved essentially unchanged in our major MSS; and that it dates from around the middle of the third century B.C. The opinion of most scholars today appears to be in agreement with this view. Certainly it is generally accepted that, as Aristeas relates, a translation of the Pentateuch was undertaken in the third century; and on the other points the present position of LXX textual study suggests that there is every likelihood of recovering an original Alexandrian version. This is especially so in the case of the Pentateuch, which presents fewer problems than other parts of the LXX.

This study is not, however, seriously affected by these uncertainties. Lexical study of the LXX can, and indeed ought to, proceed alongside of textual study, even though many textual problems remain unsolved. Deissmann was clearly right in saying that 'the knowledge of the lexical conditions is itself a pre-liminary condition of textual criticism'.[3]

Nevertheless, lexical study itself affords evidence that may be used to test the age of our text. To begin with, of course, the fact that the Pentateuch is written in Koine Greek is an indication of date. But this allows too wide a span of time to be useful. It is possible however to find evidence for dating within this range by studying particular features of vocabulary. Some of these will be examined in Chapter VIII. The conclusion to which they lead is that our text must be older than about the middle of the second century B.C. Although this is not as narrow an indication of date as we should like, it is nevertheless of some value. Moreover, it is of interest to establish such a method of dating. It could, I believe, be use-fully applied to other parts of the LXX. And there is a possi-bility of making it more accurate by investigating more features of the same kind as those that will be studied here.

Rahlfs' text of the LXX will be taken as a basis on which to work. Variant readings (in the notation of Brooke-McLean)

---

3. *BS* 73 n.3. Daniel, *Recherches* 12, makes the same point.

will be noticed where they seriously affect the point under
discussion. I have however tried as far as possible to avoid
using examples that might be vitiated by uncertainty of the
text. In the majority of cases the words examined occur without
important variants and more than once. If it should turn out
that some of my examples must be set aside because of the fault-
iness of the text used, the bulk of them is nevertheless sufficient to ensure that the general picture is not affected. In
some instances the lexical study itself provides evidence that
will be helpful in choosing between variants.

Previous study of the LXX vocabulary

It is natural to begin with the fundamental researches of
Deissmann.[4] As is well known, it was he who made the discovery
of the similarities between the language of the papyri and that
of the *NT* and LXX, a discovery that has been of the greatest
significance for subsequent study. Deissmann's detailed studies
of examples are also valuable today. Many of these can be
supplemented with papyrus evidence that has since come to light,
but in only a few cases does it substantially alter the picture.
However, Deissmann dealt with only a small part of the LXX
vocabulary. He was concerned more with the *NT* than the LXX, and
in any case was not attempting to examine more than a sample of
their vocabulary. The examples he considered were those that
most clearly illustrated his point.

For the *NT* vocabulary Deissmann's researches have been
taken to their natural conclusion by Moulton and Milligan,[5] but
no such systematic enquiry into the papyri has so far been

4. G. Adolf Deissmann, *Bible Studies* (transl. by A. Grieve of
Bibelstudien 1895 and *Neue Bibelstudien* 1897), 2 ed., Edinburgh,
1909; *Light from the Ancient East* (transl. by L.R.M. Strachan
of *Licht vom Osten* 4 ed. 1923), New York, 1927.

5. J.H. Moulton and G. Milligan, *The Vocabulary of the Greek
Testament Illustrated from the Papyri and other Non-literary
Sources,* London, 1914-29.

undertaken for the LXX.[6]

One work published before Deissmann's discoveries, that by Anz, is still worth attention today.[7] Anz treated the LXX as a useful source for furthering our knowledge of the Koine generally. He examined 289 verbs in *Genesis* and *Exodus*, tracing their occurrences elsewhere in Greek, primarily in order to see what conclusions could be drawn about the origins of the Koine vocabulary and the various elements in it. In carrying out this examination he collected a good deal of useful and accurate material from Koine writers and the limited documentary evidence then available.

Other older works are for the most part of little value now.[8] Although they may contain useful observations on one point or another, they were unable to take account of the evidence which, as Deissmann discovered and as I hope further to demonstrate, is of such importance for the study of the LXX vocabulary.

In the years since Deissmann's work appeared there have been numerous studies of particular words or groups of words in the LXX. Mme Daniel's examination of the cultic vocabulary, which recently appeared, is one of the most important, both for the detailed study of the words and for the general conclusions that emerge.[9] Also important is Repo's exhaustive examination

---

6. Attention has been drawn to the links between the two by Orsolina Montevecchi, 'Continuità ed evoluzione della lingua Greca nella *Settanta* e nei papiri', *Actes du Xe Congrès Internat. de Papyrologues,* 1964, 39-49. This is a general survey, with extensive lists, but no detailed study of examples. My material has been gathered independently.

7. H. Anz, *Subsidia ad cognoscendum Graecorum sermonem vulgarem e Pentateuchi versione Alexandrina repetita* (Diss. Phil. Halenses XII.2), Halle, 1894.

8. H.A.A. Kennedy, *Sources of New Testament Greek*, Edinburgh, 1895; E. Hatch, *Essays in Biblical Greek,* Oxford, 1889; H.Guil.J. Thiersch, *De Pentateuchi versione Alexandrina,* Erlangae, 1841. There is much good sense in F.Guil. Sturz,*De dialecto Macedonica et Alexandrina,* Lipsiae, 1808; even at that early date Sturz made use of the small amount of documentary evidence available. I have been unable to see K. Hartung, *Septuaginta-Studien,* Bamberg, 1886, which, according to Helbing, *Gramm.* p.ii, contains a certain amount of lexical material.

9. S. Daniel, *Recherches sur le vocabulaire du culte dans le Septante* (Études et Commentaires LXI), Paris, 1966.

of ῥῆμα in the Greek of the LXX and *NT*.[10]

There are many minor studies, especially of words of theological interest. For example, ἱλάσκεσθαι and related words have been examined by Dodd,[11] ἅγιος by Gehman,[12] verbs of praise by Ledogar,[13] ψυχή and related words by Lys.[14] In many other instances an investigation of the LXX evidence forms the background to a study of some aspect of the *NT* vocabulary. The outstanding work of this kind is the well known *Theologisches Wörterbuch zum Neuen Testament,* edited by G. Kittel.[15]

Most of the works just mentioned deal with words that are significant theologically. Indeed, this applies to the majority of studies of the LXX vocabulary. This preoccupation is understandable, but it has meant that much of the ordinary vocabulary has been neglected. Moreover, it is unfortunately true that many studies concerned with theologically significant terms are marred by unsound linguistic methods.[16] On the whole, as Mme Daniel remarks, 'les recherches proprement philologiques ont été jusqu' à maintenant plutôt négligées'.[17]

There are, however, one or two other works to be noticed. There is useful incidental treatment of vocabulary in the studies of Helbing[18] and Huber,[19] and in Thackeray's *Grammar.*

---

10. E. Repo, *Der Begriff "Rhema" im Biblisch-Griechischen: eine traditionsgeschichtliche und semasiologische Untersuchung,* 2 vols., Helsinki, 1951 and 1954.

11. C.H. Dodd, ''Ιλάσκεσθαι, its Cognates, Derivatives, and Synonyms in the LXX', *JTS* XXXII (1931) 352-60.

12. H.S. Gehman, ''Άγιος in the Septuagint, and its Relation to the Hebrew Original', *VT* IV (1954) 337-48.

13. R.J. Ledogar, 'Verbs of Praise in the LXX Translation of the Hebrew Canon', *Biblica* XLVIII (1967) 29-56.

14. D. Lys, 'The Israelite Soul according to the LXX', *VT* XVI (1966) 181-228.

15. A recent example of the same type of study is D. Hill, *Greek Words and Hebrew Meanings,* Cambridge, 1967.

16. J. Barr's far-reaching criticisms of *TWNT* in this respect are well known.

17. *Recherches* 8.

18. R. Helbing, *Die Kasussyntax der Verba bei den Septuaginta,* Göttingen, 1928.

19. K. Huber, *Untersuchungen über den Sprachcharakter des griechischen Leviticus* (Diss. Zürich), Giessen, 1916.

Ziegler's examination of the LXX of *Isaiah* includes a comparison of the book's vocabulary with that of the papyri.[20] Also to be noted is Barr's discussion of words for time, which includes a valuable study of these words in the LXX.[21]

In an article published in *Textus*, Gehman deals briefly with a number of LXX words and uses.[22] The contribution of these notes to LXX lexicography is however very limited. Gehman examines only Hebraistic uses, many of which have been noted before,[23] and the discussion of them is sketchy, and unreliable in some points of detail.

Further mention must be made of the standard lexicons, which of course also form contributions to the study of the LXX vocabulary.

LSJ includes a large amount of LXX material, but as is mostly well known, is often in error.[24] A particular fault is its tendency to equate the LXX word with the Hebrew it translates when there is no good reason to do so. In some instances the meaning given seems to be adopted directly from one of the English versions of the *OT*. Less obvious, but just as serious, is its frequent omission of important matter.

Bauer's excellent lexicon of the *NT* is of course of great value for the study of the LXX. It can be relied on for accurate and up-to-date treatment of the *NT* vocabulary, and it also

---

20. J. Ziegler, *Untersuchungen zur Septuaginta des Buches Isaias* (Alttestamentliche Abhandlungen XII 3), Münster, 1934.

21. J. Barr, *Biblical Words for Time* (Studies in Biblical Theology, 33), London, 1962.

22. H.S. Gehman, 'Adventures in Septuagint Lexicography', *Textus* V (1966) 125-32. Gehman says, *ib.* p.125, that he began some years ago to compile a dictionary of Septuagint Greek, with the help of his graduate students, and that most of the work completed is now deposited on microfilm in the Speer Library of the Princeton Theological Seminary. I have no knowledge of this material. Nor have I been able to accompany Gehman on his 'Rambles in Septuagint Lexicography', *Ind. Journal of Theology* XIV (1965) 90-101.

23. See e.g. Thackeray, *Gramm.* 39ff.

24. See G.B. Caird, 'Towards a Lexicon of the Septuagint', I, *JTS* XIX (1968) 453-75; II, *JTS* XX (1969) 21-40, chiefly corrections of LSJ's errors in the treatment of LXX vocabulary. The recent *Supplement* to LSJ, ed. E.A. Barber, Oxford, 1968, contains many similar errors: see my article in *Glotta* XLVII (1969) 234-42.

gives frequent references to the LXX. However, the vocabulary
that the LXX and *NT* have in common is less than is often supposed. In particular it is to be noted that words common to
both often vary considerably in regard to their uses.

In the same way MM, although an indispensable storehouse
of information, does not treat all LXX words and uses. It can
moreover be supplemented even in the case of a number of those
it does treat.

As to Schleusner, there is little to be added to what was
said above. It is true that Schleusner's work is 'sober and
learned throughout',[25] and from time to time offers suggestions
that are still useful today. But from a lexicographical point
of view it must be regarded as quite obsolete.[26]

It is convenient to mention here certain other lexicons
and indexes that are not directly concerned with the LXX, but
are essential tools for the study of the Greek vocabulary.

For the papyri there is the well-known *Wörterbuch* of
Preisigke.[27] This work however is out of date, a fact that
seems often to be forgotten. The last part appeared in 1927,
but it does not cover much papyrological material later than
about 1921. A supplement by Kiessling, itself rapidly going out
of date, reached Εἰρ- in 1966. Kiessling has recently published
(1969) a further supplement for the whole alphabet in the form
of an index, which apparently covers material published between
1940 and 1966. Although these works cover the bulk of the
material, the only sure way to investigate the papyri is to
check the indexes of the individual papyrus publications themselves. I have drawn attention to these points because they may
not be generally known to students of the LXX,[28] and it is important that none of the available papyrus evidence should be

---

25. H.M. Orlinsky, *HUCA* XXVIII (1957) 71.

26. Jellicoe, *SMS* 335, 359, seems to me to overrate Schleusner.

27. For the full titles of Preisigke and other works mentioned
see Abbreviations and Bibliography.

28. Jellicoe, *SMS* 335, discussing the tools available for
lexical study of the LXX, lists Preisigke without comment, and
does not mention Kiessling's supplements either there or in the
Bibliography.

overlooked in LXX lexicographical study.

Indexes to Greek authors, which are indispensable ad-
juncts to LSJ, are too numerous to mention individually here. I
would draw attention however to the lexicon to Polybius now in
progress. This author has, I believe, much to contribute to
the understanding of the LXX vocabulary.

CHAPTER II

THE NATURE OF LXX GREEK

It is evident that the Greek in which the books of the
LXX are composed contains many features that cannot be normal
Greek. It is clear moreover that these features are due prin-
cipally to the influence of Hebrew. They are usually spoken of
as 'Hebraisms', or 'Semitisms'. Examples of such constructions
and uses have long been noted, and are familiar to all readers
of the LXX.[1] We need only observe one or two well-known
examples: υἱός of age, corresponding literally to Hebrew בן ,
as in Σημ υἱὸς ἑκατὸν ἐτῶν (Ge.11.10); τίς δώσει or τίς δῷη
translating מי - יתן , 'would that ...'; δίδωμι in the sense of
'make' (~ נתן). In such cases it cannot be doubted that there
is an abnormality from the point of view of Greek and that it is
due to the influence of Hebrew.

There are of course a number of difficulties which at
once arise. These we shall notice briefly, but not go into
here. To begin with, there are many uncertainties involved in
the use of the terms 'Hebraism' and 'Semitism'. Precisely how
they are to be defined and applied is a very difficult matter.
Also, it is practically impossible to arrive at a quantitative
assessment of their extent. Another difficulty is that LXX
Greek is not homogeneous. The type of Greek used and the extent
of Hebrew influence vary from book to book. Strictly speaking,
therefore, the term 'LXX Greek', implying the consistent use of
a certain type of Greek, is unsatisfactory. But for the purpose
of discussion the term will be used here, it being understood
that there is considerable variety within LXX Greek. The main
point however is clear. It is beyond question that the majority
of the books of the LXX exhibit, to a greater or lesser extent,
features that are abnormal for Greek and must be due to the

---

1.   See the examples collected e.g. by Thackeray, *Gramm.* 29-55,
Psichari, *Essai* 193ff., Huber, *Untersuchungen über den
Sprachcharakter des griech. Leviticus* 98ff., Gehman *VT* I (1951)
81ff., *VT* III (1953) 141-8. Cf. also Helbing, *Kasussyntax*
IXf.

influence of a Semitic language. On this there is general agreement.

Where opinions differ is over the explanation for the presence of these foreign elements. We have a choice between two main types of explanation. On the one hand it can be argued that the Hebraisms of LXX Greek have arisen chiefly because the work is a translation of a Hebrew original, executed according to methods which frequently led to the reproduction of Hebrew idiom in the translating language. According to this view the Greek spoken by the translators was by and large the vernacular Egyptian Greek of the time.

This, as is well known, was Deissmann's opinion.[2] For him the fact that the LXX is a translation is of fundamental importance in understanding its linguistic character. In attempting to turn a Semitic text into Greek the translators undertook a difficult and unprecedented task. 'Over the Hebrew, with its grave and stately step, they have, so to speak, thrown their light native garb, without being able to conceal the alien's peculiar gait beneath its folds. So arose a written "Semitic-Greek" which no one ever spoke, far less used for literary purposes, either before or after' (*BS* 67). The Hebraisms of the version 'permit of no conclusions being drawn from them in respect to the language actually spoken by the Hellenistic Jews of the period' (*ib*. 69). In this view Deissmann has been followed by the majority of scholars.[3]

On the other hand, it may be argued that the peculiarities of LXX Greek are largely independent of the fact of translation. The Greek spoken by the translators, and by the Egyptian Jewish community generally, was (it is said) already extensively

---

2. See especially *BS* 66ff; also *Philology of the Greek Bible* (transl. L.M. Strachan), London, 1908, 48ff.

3. E.g. Thumb, *Hellenismus* 120-6, 174-85, Moulton, *Proleg*. 13, Thackeray, *Gramm*. 25ff., Psichari, *Essai* 175ff., R. Meister, 'Prolegomena zu einer Grammatik der LXX' *Weiner Stud*. XXIX (1908) 238ff., Helbing, *Kasussyntax* VI, Meecham, *The Letter of Aristeas* 43f., F. Büchsel, 'Die griechische Sprache der Juden in der Zeit der Septuaginta und des Neuen Testaments', *ZAW* XIX (1944) 132ff., cf. Daniel, *Recherches* 8, Bauer xviii.

influenced by a Semitic language before the translation was made;
when the translation came to be made the translators used an
already-existing form of Greek. In other words, according to
this view, the LXX is a specimen of a living dialect of Greek,
an Alexandrian 'Jewish-Greek'.

This view is an old one,[4] but in the years following
Deissmann's discoveries was seldom advocated. It has however
been put forward again recently by Gehman,[5] with support from
Turner.[6] Gehman's argument, which we shall return to later, is
essentially as follows: since the LXX presumably 'made sense' to
its audience, the language used in it must have been a form of
Jewish-Greek already familiar to them. 'If the LXX made sense
to Hellenistic Jews, the translation was understood because its
idiom corresponded to a familiar *Denkart*.'[7] And again: 'if the
LXX made sense to Hellenistic Jews, we may infer that there was
a Jewish Greek which was understood apart from the Hebrew language.'[8] The existence of a 'Jewish-Greek' in some sense in *NT*
times is also accepted in the *Grammar* of Blass-Debrunner-Funk,[9]
and by some other *NT* authorities.[10]

The question of the nature of LXX Greek is of course a
complex one, involving many factors. There is an extensive
literature on it and on matters that have bearing on it, and

---

4. E.g. Swete, *Introd.* 9, 299. Cf. Deissmann, *BS* 68 on Wellhausen.

5. H.S. Gehman, 'The Hebraic Character of Septuagint Greek',
VT I (1951) 81-90.

6. N. Turner, 'The Unique Character of Biblical Greek, *VT* V (1955)
208-13; 'The "Testament of Abraham": Problems in Biblical Greek',
NTS I (1954-5) 219-23; 'Second Thoughts - VII Papyrus Finds', *ET*
LXXVI (1964) 44-8; *Grammatical Insights into the New Testament*,
Edinburgh, 1965, 174ff.; and cf. Moulton-Turner, *Gramm.* III 4ff.
    Gehman's view seems to be accepted by Hill, *Greek Words and
Hebrew Meanings*, Cambridge, 1967, 16.

7. *Op.cit.* 87.

8. *Op.cit.* 90

9. §4: 'there was certainly a *spoken Jewish-Greek* in the sense
that even his *secular* speech betrayed the Semitic mind of the Jew.'

10. Knopf-Lietzmann-Weinel, *Einführung in das Neue Testament* (5
ed.), Berlin, 1949, 18; M. Black, 'Second Thoughts. IX. The Semitic
Element in the New Testament', *ET* LXXVII (1965-6) 20-3 . See
also E. Norden, *Die antike Kunstprosa* (5 ed.), Stuttgart, 1958,
Nachtr. 2-3.

there are many differing shades of opinion. It seems to me,
however, that the central issue involved is as I have outlined
above. Essentially the question that faces us is: in order to
account for the undoubted peculiarities of LXX Greek, is it
sufficient to refer to the fact that the LXX is a translation,
or is it necessary to assume the existence of a living 'Jewish-
Greek' dialect?

It must be said at the outset that we do not have sufficient evidence to establish beyond doubt the answer to the question. Various arguments can be brought to bear on it, but after
a certain point further argument is fruitless and the answer remains a matter of opinion. In my view, however, the available
indications are definitely against the existence of an Alexandrian 'Jewish-Greek' dialect.

We may begin by noticing one of the arguments put forward
by Deissmann[11] and Thackeray.[12] They pointed to the contrast
that can be seen between Jewish writings composed originally in
Greek and those that are translations of Semitic originals. The
extreme form of Semitic Greek is confined to the latter. This is
difficult to explain if one maintains (as Gehman does) that
Hellenistic Jews spoke a 'Jewish-Greek' like the Greek we find
for example in the Pentateuch. If that was the language they
spoke we should expect it to be used more consistently than it
is. Why is 'Jewish-Greek' not used by the writers of 2-4 *Maccabees* and the *Epistle of Jeremiah,* for example? Especially
difficult to explain is the difference between the prologue to
Sirach and the translation itself. As Deissmann said, 'whoever
counts the Greek Sirach among the monuments of a "Judaeo-Greek",
thought of as a living language, must show why the translator
uses Alexandrian Greek when he is not writing as a translator.[13]

This argument is on the whole a sound one, though certain
points of difficulty must be noticed. A large amount of evidence
is involved, and it is difficult to generalize. The evidence of
the *NT* is particularly complicated. There are some 'Semitisms',

11. *BS* 69 n.1, 76, cf. 296.
12. *Gramm.* 27 f. Similarly Psichari, *Essai* 176 f.
13. *BS* 69 n.1.

and other features peculiar to Biblical Greek, in the books
originally composed in Greek, as well as in the parts that are
thought to be translated from Aramaic originals.[14] Moreover,
the Semitic originals of those parts of the *NT* generally supposed to be translations are not extant. The evidence for regarding them as translations consists chiefly of presumed
examples of Semitic influence occurring in them. The same difficulty is found with certain books of the LXX, such as *Tobit*
and 1 *Maccabees*. In addition there are problems both in deciding exactly what constitutes a Semitism and in estimating the
extent of the Semitic element in a given book.

It seems to me, however, that the essential point remains.
The kind of Greek found, for example, in the Pentateuch is confined to books that are known to be translations, or are generally thought to be translations. Jewish works composed
originally in Greek show nothing like the same degree of Semitic
influence.[15] Clearly this leads to the conclusion that the
supposed 'Jewish-Greek' is a result of translation, and did not
exist as a spoken language.

This argument has not, as far as I know, been answered by
advocates of 'Jewish-Greek'.[16]

A more serious objection to the hypothesis of a spoken
'Jewish-Greek' is that it does not take into account the fact
that there are two Semitic languages involved in the question,
not one.

It is quite clear that the Greek of the LXX translation is
heavily influenced by Hebrew idiom and usage; and according to

---

14. Cf. Moulton-Turner, *Gramm.* III 4 f.

15. The application of certain tests has revealed a sharp distinction between translated and non-translated books: see R.A.
Martin, 'Some Syntactical Criteria of Translation Greek', *VT* X
(1960) 295-310 (relative frequency of prepositions); J. Merle
Rife, 'The Mechanics of Translation Greek', *JBL* LII (1933) 244-52
(word-order). Cf. I. Soisalon-Soininen, *Die Infinitive in der
Septuaginta*, Helsinki, 1965, 157.

16. In addition Deissmann, *BS* 68, pointed to a number of Jewish
papyri, whose language shows none of the peculiarities seen in
the LXX. Similarly Bickerman, *PAAJR* XXVIII (1959) 24 n.53.
A systematic study of this evidence would be valuable.

Gehman's hypothesis it was that kind of Greek that was spoken by
Egyptian Jews. In other words, if there was a 'Jewish-Greek',
it was a form of Greek that has been influenced by Hebrew.

But it is generally agreed that the everyday language of
the Egyptian Jews before they adopted Greek was Aramaic, not
Hebrew.[17] Papyri, ostraka, coins, and grave inscriptions all
witness to this.[18] There are, besides, a number of indications
to this effect in the LXX itself. Certain words appear in forms
that must be derived from Aramaic: e.g. γειώρας from Aramaic
גיורא , not Hebrew גר ; πάσχα < פסחא πάταχρα < פתכרא
σάββατα < שבתא .[19] It is especially significant that the words
for the Sabbath and the festival of the Passover, terms which
must have been in constant use among Jews, are Aramaic in form.
Also, the translators occasionally take a word in its Aramaic
sense instead of its Hebrew sense.[20]

It follows that if the Greek spoken by Egyptian Jews was
affected by the idioms of a Semitic language, that language must
have been Aramaic. Although Hebrew was the language of the *OT*
and was no doubt still understood by some, it had never been the
spoken language of Egyptian Jews generally. It is therefore
unlikely that it could have exerted a significant influence on
their Greek at any stage. 'Jewish-Greek', if it existed, would

---

17. See e.g. L. Fuchs, *Die Juden Ägyptens in ptolemäischer und
römischer Zeit*, Wien, 1924, 114ff.; F. Büchsel, *ZAW* XIX (1944)
133-8; R.A. Bowman, *JNES* VII (1948) 80f., 86; V. Tcherikover,
Corpus Papyrorum Judaicarum I 30; L. Delekat, *VT* VIII (1958)
225ff.

18. For a summary of the evidence see Delekat, *ib.*

19. Thackeray, *Gramm.* 28, Büchsel, *op.cit.* 137, Bickerman, *op.
cit.* 22, L.H. Brockington, *ZAW* XXV (1954) 84, Bl. DF §141.3; cf.
already Thiersch, *De Pentateuchi versione Alexandrina*, Erlangae,
1841, 29. But Bl. DF, *ib.*, following Schwyzer, *KZ* LXII (1935)
10f., take σάββατα as Hb. שבת + α 'to make it pronounceable in
Greek': this I find unconvincing.

20. Examples have frequently been noted. See e.g. Brockington,
loc.cit.; J. Ziegler, *Beiträge zur Ieremias-Septuaginta* (*MSU* VI),
Göttingen, 1958, 18f.; J. Barr, *Comparative Philology and the
Text of the Old Testament*, Oxford, 1968, 54f., and references
there.

have been a form of Greek that had been influenced by Aramaic.[21]

It is to be remembered that, although they have much in common, Hebrew and Aramaic are different languages.[22] To take a particular example: in Hebrew there is a construction combining the 'infinitive absolute' of a verb with another part of the same verb. In LXX Greek this idiom is often imitated by the use of the finite verb with its participle (φεύγων φεύγω) or with the dative of the cognate noun (φευγῇ φεύγω).[23] It is clear that the translators' Greek is influenced at this point by Hebrew idiom[24] (though it is worth noticing that these constructions have some links with normal Greek).[25] Yet the 'infinitive absolute' construction is not usual in Aramaic.[26] It is difficult to see, therefore, how this idiom could have been current in the Greek spoken by Jews, since it could not have been derived from the Semitic language that they had spoken prior to the adoption of Greek. It is much more likely that this 'Semitism' in LXX Greek arose through the translators' attempt to reproduce an idiom found in the Hebrew text they were translating.[27]

The conclusion is clear: Gehman's hypothesis cannot stand. It is impossible to explain how a type of Greek like that found in the LXX, a Hebraic Greek, could have arisen as a spoken language when Aramaic, not Hebrew, was the Semitic language that had lately been in use among Egyptian Jews.

It is no answer to refer to the 'Semitic mind' or 'Semitic

---

21. Büchsel, *op.cit.* 138f., makes the interesting point that if Aram. speakers who learnt Gk. showed peculiarities in their use of the new language (as is quite probable), this would be so of non-Jews as well as Jews. Aram. had been the language of many non-Jews. The 'Aramaic Greek' spoken by Jews is unlikely to have differed much from that spoken by others.

22. Cf. Moule, *Idiom Book* 172.

23. Thackeray, *Gramm.* 47ff.

24. Gehman, *VT* I (1951)84, includes it among his examples of 'Jewish-Greek' usage.

25. Bl. DF §§198.6, 422, Moule, *Idiom Book* 178, Bauer p.xx for an example in Polyaenus.

26. Moulton-Howard, *Gramm.* II 443, Moule, *Idiom Book* 177.

27. Another example of a Hb. idiom imitated in the LXX but not usual in Aram. is אם in emphatic denials: Moulton-Howard, *Gramm.* II 468f. Cf. also εἰς c.acc. in place of predicative nom. or acc. = Hb. ל predicative, probably not in Aram., *ib.* 462.

mode of thought' of the Jew.[28] It is quite unsatisfactory to
suppose that speakers of Hebrew and Aramaic had the same
'Semitic mind', to which any feature of either language can be
attributed. (This 'Semitic mind' would also have to be shared
by speakers of all the other Semitic languages.) I am not
suggesting that one cannot speak of a 'Semitic mind', or that
there is no relationship of any kind between thought and
linguistic structures. But such matters are irrelevant to the
linguistic question we are dealing with. Any given feature of
LXX Greek must be accounted for first of all on the linguistic
level, not by reference to the 'Semitic mind' of the Jew.

In addition to the above objections to the hypothesis of
a 'Jewish-Greek', we must notice that there are serious weak-
nesses in Gehman's line of argument. He argues that 'if the
LXX made sense to Hellenistic Jews, we may infer that there was
a Jewish Greek which was understood apart from the Hebrew
language'.[29] There are two difficulties here. To begin with,
the basic assumption is precarious. It is unlikely that all
the oddities of LXX Greek were intelligible to the Egyptian
Jews. The translators often had difficulty both in understanding their original and in turning it into Greek. They frequently produced neologisms and unnatural usages in their efforts
to express what they took to be the sense of the original. In
some passages, as is generally agreed, they resorted to mechanical, word-for-word representation of the Hebrew, with little
concern for the over-all result. It is doubtful that the
meaning of what they wrote was always clear to others.

We cannot, then, make the bald assumption that 'the LXX
made sense to Hellenistic Jews'. It may however be agreed that
the LXX was intelligible to its audience in the sense that a
person hearing or reading it could make out, in the majority of

---

28. Cf. Bl. DF §4 (quoted above p.13 n.9), and Gehman's
reference to 'a familiar *Denkart*' (above p.13).

29. *VT* I (1951) 90.

instances, the meaning intended.[30] But — and this is the second
difficulty in Gehman's argument — it does not follow even from
this that the peculiarities of LXX Greek were current in the
spoken language of Egyptian Jews. The fact that one can
understand a certain locution does not prove that one uses it in
one's own speech. Take for example the LXX renderings of the
Hebrew 'infinitive absolute'. φευγῇ φεύγω, φεύγων φεύγω, and
the like were no doubt intelligible, or if you will, 'made
sense', to Egyptian Jews, but it does not follow that such expressions were normal in their own speech. These expressions
would also have been intelligible to non-Jewish speakers of
Greek, but one would scarcely maintain that they must therefore
have been normal Koine Greek. Similarly, no one would suppose
that because we can understand the English of the AV its idioms
must be a normal feature of the English we speak.

The whole subject of the LXX translators' techniques of
translation is clearly involved here. What methods and principles did they apply to their task? Why did they produce the
kind of Greek they did? Did they in fact expect that the Greek
of their version would seem normal to their audience? These are
questions that Gehman has not properly faced. Yet it is essential to take them into account in considering the nature of
LXX Greek.

It is not possible to go into this subject at any length
here, but attention may be drawn to certain points.[31]

---

30. This itself is a simplification. The meaning discerned by
the readers of the LXX must often have differed from that intended by the translators; in numerous instances the translators'
rendering has one meaning when read simply as Greek and another
when the original is taken into account (See e.g. ἐκδέχομαι,
p.59.) Also, in some passages the translators themselves do not
seem to have had a clear idea of the meaning they intended.

31. There is an extensive literature on LXX methods of translation generally and on the techniques of individual translators.
Especially relevant here are S.P. Brock, 'The Phenomenon of
Biblical Translation in Antiquity', Alta (The Univ. of Birmingham
Review) II. 8 (1969) 96-102; E.J. Bickerman, PAAJR XXVIII (1959)
esp. 13ff.; J. Merle Rife, 'The Mechanics of Translation Greek',
JBL LII (1933) 244-52. A particularly valuable discussion is that
by Chaim Rabin, 'The Translation Process and the Character of
the Septuagint', Textus VI (1968) 1-26. See also Swete, Introd.
315ff., Jellicoe, SMS 314ff.

Writers on the LXX have frequently pointed out, but it is worth repeating, that translation is an extremely difficult art. The problems involved have by no means been solved even today, when they are so much better understood.[32] The question of the general principles to be applied has long been and still is controversial. Moreover, in the translation of a religious document the difficulties are especially acute.

The task the LXX translators undertook was, then, a difficult one in any case, but, in addition, it was entirely without precedent.[33] They had no theories to guide them, or any of the aids which a modern translator takes for granted. They did the best they could, but the techniques they employed were inadequate. It is clear that they failed to overcome many of the problems of translation. Although some conventions were developed,[34] we find that different translators (or groups of translators) used widely differing methods: the LXX exhibits a variety of styles of translation, from the free and paraphrastic to the painfully literal. In cases of difficulty the translators from time to time resorted to a mechanical, and practically meaningless, rendering, leaving the reader to make what he could of it.[35]

All this goes to show that the supposition underlying Gehman's argument is unfounded: that is, the assumption that the translators always used the kind of Greek that would seem normal

32. See on the whole subject E.A. Nida, *Toward a Science of Translating, with special reference to principles and procedures involved in Bible translating*, Leiden, 1964, esp. 2ff.; cf. Rabin, *op.cit.* 4f., where the fundamental reasons for the difficulty of translation are brought out very clearly.

33. See especially Brock, *op.cit.*, Rabin, *op.cit.* 19ff., Swete, *Introd.* 318f.
   Rabin suggests (21) that the translators found a model for their task in the 'day-to-day oral translation activity of the commercial and court dragoman'. A similar suggestion was made by Bickerman, *op.cit.* 16.

34. Some of these are examined by P. Katz, 'Zur Übersetzungstechnik der Septuaginta', *Die Welt des Orients* II.3 (1956) 267-73. It has often been noted that the Pentateuch seems to have been used as a guide by later translators, see e.g. I.L. Seeligman, *The Septuagint Version of Isaiah*, Leiden, 1948,45; cf. Rabin, *op.cit.*22.

35. Cf. Rabin, *op.cit.* 23f. Flashar, Rabin notes, coined for such renderings the term 'Verlegenheitsübersetzung', 'a mechanical translation of embarrassment'.

to their audience. Not only were they unable to do so, given
the methods with which they worked, but what is more, it is
probable that they often did not even try.[36] In many of the
books it seems that the translators deliberately chose to produce a version that preserved the flavour of the original.
Certainly it is generally agreed that in most books fidelity to
the original was their primary aim. We ought not to assume that
the peculiar Greek which resulted was felt to be normal either
by the translators or by their audience. In sum, as Barr has
said, '"to make sense" in an ancient biblical translation meant
something different from making sense in daily language'.[37]

It is relevant to notice that other, more recent translators of the *OT* also did not succeed in avoiding Hebraic uses and
constructions. In the AV, as is well known, there are numerous
instances of Hebrew influence.[38] Similarly, attention has been
drawn to the Hebraisms in the German Bible,[39] and in a Modern
Greek translation of the Pentateuch made in 1547.[40] These
parallels show that it is at least unnecessary to posit the
existence of a living Hebraic Greek in order to account for the
Hebraisms of the LXX version.

So far I have spoken mostly of Gehman's argument for a
'Jewish-Greek', but mention must also be made of Turner. As was
noticed earlier, he has supported Gehman's view.[41] He is apparently in full agreement with Gehman's main argument, and offers

---

36. Cf. Moulton's remark, *Gramm.* II 17, that 'the Hebraisms of
the LXX were very often conscious sins against Greek idiom, due
to a theory that words believed to be divinely inspired must be
rendered so that every detail had its equivalent'. Similarly
Bickerman, *op.cit.* 26.

37. J. Barr, 'Common Sense and Biblical Language', *Biblica* XLIX
(1968) 379 (criticizing Hill's acceptance of Gehman's argument).
Rabin, *op.cit.* 13, points out that 'by continued translation
from the same source language, a sub-language adapted to this
translation is bound to develop in the reception language'.

38. See e.g. J. Isaacs, 'The Authorized Version and After', in
The Bible in its Ancient and English Versions, ed. H.W. Robinson,
Oxford, 1940, 210f., Moulton, *Proleg.* 98, Moule, *Idiom Book* 172.

39. Deissmann, *BS* 177.

40. Psichari, *Essai* 194.

41. Above p.13 and n.6.

in addition a variety of subsidiary arguments. These, in my
opinion, are quite unconvincing, and in no way provide an answer
to the objections we have been considering. We cannot go into
all of Turner's points in detail, but one or two call for
special mention.

One of Turner's arguments is as follows.[42] Having stated
his opinion that the language of the *OT* translators and the *NT*
writers was 'a living dialect of Jewish Greek' (p.45), he goes
on to observe some of the distinctive features of Biblical Greek.
He notes the specialized Christian meanings of words like 'brother', 'fellowship', 'worship', 'truth', etc. The change in use
in many words is due (he remarks) to the Greek *OT*. 'Thus,
Christians and Jews made "opinion" mean *splendour*, "to bind"
mean *to forbid*, "languages" mean *nations*, "to confess" mean *to
praise*, ... "to regret" mean *to repent* (religiously)' (p.47).
He then goes on: 'All such words are important. By contrast,
the light shed by the papyrus finds is negligible, almost restricted to words such as *milk* and ideas such as accountancy,
wills, receipts, deposits, and beggars' collecting-bags.'

Now no one would dispute that there are many Biblical terms
upon which the papyri shed little light, and that these are in
many instances terms which one would call 'important'. It is
quite true that the papyri are concerned with everyday matters
such as accountancy and with comparatively humble objects like
beggars' collecting-bags. But to conclude from this that the
language of the Biblical writings is a separate dialect is false
logic, depending on the deceptive use of the word 'important'.
Of course 'worship', 'truth', 'splendour', and the like are
important words, but in what way? Clearly, they are important
from the religious and ethical point of view. But for the linguistic question we are dealing with their importance in that
respect is irrelevant. For determining the relationship between
the 'secular' Koine and the Greek of the LXX and *NT* no word is
intrinsically more important than any other. It is as if one
were to say that for the purpose of establishing the affinities
between British and American English it is useless to point to

42. *ET* LXXVI (1964-5) 44-8.

the fact that 'milk' occurs in both, because 'milk' is not an 'important' word. And it is to be remembered that the greater part of any language is made up of words for rather insignificant ideas and objects. No language, not even that spoken by the Jews, consists solely of theologically important terms. The Jews, too, had occasion to speak of milk, wills, receipts, and deposits.

On another occasion Turner supports his contention that 'there was a distinguishable dialect of spoken and written Jewish Greek' with this statement: 'Certainly it was not artificial. Biblical Greek is so powerful and fluent, it is difficult to believe that those who used it did not have at hand a language all ready for use.[43] It is plainly useless to enter into discussion about this. One can only express the opinion that a subjective argument of this sort is of no value whatever for our question.

Finally, a point to which Turner keeps returning: the hypothesis that the Koine had itself been extensively influenced by Semitic idiom and that this explains why so many 'Semitisms' can be paralleled in the papyri.[44] Turner clearly favours this idea, even though he admits the force of Moulton's objections to it. In Turner's opinion 'the question of Jewish influence on the Koine ... has not yet been met'.[45] To my mind, however, Moulton has long since convincingly refuted this extraordinary theory.[46] It is of course not to be denied that some words, and perhaps uses and expressions, were borrowed into Hellenistic Greek from one or other of the Semitic languages. But there is not the slightest evidence that the Koine as a whole had been subject to extensive Semitic influence. Turner's approval of this theory seems to be based on the wish that it might be so,

---

43. *Grammatical Insights* 183.

44. *NTS* I (1954-5) 222f., *ET* LXXVI (1964-5) 47, *Grammatical Insights* 184.

45. *Grammatical Insights* 184.

46. *Proleg.* xvi ff., *Cambridge Biblical Essays*, ed. H.B. Swete, London, 1909, 468ff. See also G. Milligan, *The New Testament Documents*, London, 1913, 54f., and the discussion in Moulton-Howard, *Gramm.* II 415. Cf. Moule's cautious reference to this question, *Idiom Book* 171.

not on any satisfactory evidence for it. The only argument he can offer in its support is the improbable assertion that 'the Greek Bible and the synagogues of the Dispersion had a great influence on the world of Hellenism, not solely in Egypt and not on Jews and proselytes exclusively'.[47]

That the LXX translators frequently reproduce Hebrew idiom by literal rendering of their original is, as we have seen, well known. It is natural that such Hebraisms should have been emphasized, since they are the most noticeable characteristics of LXX Greek. But this is in fact only one side of the picture. The other is that the translators also fail to reproduce the idiom of the original in many places. I am not referring to instances in which this is due to misunderstanding, interpretation, or free paraphrase, in all of which the sense as well as the idiom of the original is altered. The examples I mean are those in which the translators avoid rendering a Hebrew use or expression by the obvious literal equivalent, rendering instead, but without changing the sense, into idiomatic Greek; in other words, examples in which they avoid using a Hebraism where one might have been expected. The extent of this avoidance of Hebrew idiom and its significance for our question have not, I believe, been fully appreciated.[48]

---

47. *Grammatical Insights* 184; similarly *NTS* I (1954-5) 223, where T. adds the extravagant claim that 'the Bible has always and everywhere exerted the greatest influence, not on thought only, but also on language'.

48. The argument presented here has been anticipated to some extent by Deissmann. He noted, *BS* 164f., that the translators do not always imitate Hb. idioms with ‏כן‎, and saw that this was a strong argument against supposing that they had a Semitic 'genius of language' lying behind their use of Greek. He did not, however, observe the wide extent of the phenomenon. Deissmann's remarks here seem to have been generally overlooked.
It has of course often been noticed that the translators render the same Hb. word in a great variety of ways (see e.g. Swete, *Introd.* 328f., Gooding, *The Account of the Tabernacle* 8f., 20), and that there is much variation between free and literal rendering (see e.g. Gehman himself, *Textus* V [1966] 125), but the relevance of these features to the question of 'Jewish-Greek' has not been brought out.
Moule, *Idiom Book* 187f., interestingly notes some 'obvious "Semitisms"' that are not represented in the *NT*, but draws no conclusion.

A good example to begin with is

Ge. 43.27 ἠρώτησεν δὲ αὐτούς Πῶς ἔχετε;

וישאל להם לשלום

'The expression found in MT is of course a common Hebrew idiom.
It could easily have been rendered literally.[49] Yet the translators turn it into idiomatic Greek. I find it difficult to see
how anyone who spoke a Hebraic Greek, in which this Hebrew idiom
would surely have been current, could have refrained from a
literal rendering here.

Other examples of this phenomenon are to be found throughout the Pentateuch. Indeed, they are so numerous that we can
notice only a small selection here.

A literal rendering of שלום is also avoided in

Ge. 43.23 εἶπεν δὲ αὐτοῖς ῞Ιλεως ὑμῖν, μὴ φοβεῖσθε

ויאמר שלום לכם אל-תיראו

43.27 καὶ εἶπεν αὐτοῖς Εἰ ὑγιαίνει ὁ πατὴρ ὑμῶν ...;

ויאמר השלום אביכם

Ex. 4.18 Βάδιζε ὑγιαίνων

לך לשלום

18.7 καὶ ἠσπάσαντο ἀλλήλους

וישאלו איש-לרעהו לשלום

In this last example we see that the translators also
avoid the Hebrew idiom used for describing reciprocal action.
There are other instances of this:

Ex. 14.20 καὶ οὐ συνέμιξαν ἀλλήλοις

ולא-קרב זה אל-זה

Ge. 42.28 καὶ ἐταράχθησαν πρὸς ἀλλήλους λέγοντες

ויחרדו איש אל – אחיו לאמר

Similarly *Ge.* 15.10, *Ex.* 25.20, 26.3,5.

---

49. As it is e.g. in 1 *Ki.* 25.5 καὶ ἐρωτήσατε αὐτὸν ... εἰς
εἰρήνην (but note that even here the translator has refrained
from a literal rendering of לו). Other examples of literal
rendering of this idiom: Thackeray, *Gramm.* 40.

Nu. 14.4 καὶ εἶπαν ἕτερος τῷ ἑτέρῳ

ויאמרו איש אל-אחיו

Ex. 26.3 ἑτέρα τῇ ἑτέρᾳ

אשה אל – אחתה

Similarly *Ex.* 16.15, 26.17.[50]

Hebrew expressions involving עין are, we know, often rendered literally, but not always. Consider for example

Ge. 19.8 χρήσασθε αὐταῖς, καθὰ ἂν ἀρέσκῃ ὑμῖν

עשו להן כטוב בעיניכם

Similarly *Ge.* 16.6.

De. 4.19 καὶ μὴ ἀναβλέψας εἰς τὸν οὐρανόν

ופן-תשא עיניך השמימה

Similarly *Ge.* 33.5.

Ge. 48.17 βαρὺ αὐτῷ κατεφάνη

וירע בעיניו

45.5 μηδὲ σκληρὸν ὑμῖν φανήτω

ואל-יחר בעיניכם

In the same way בן in expressions of age is often not translated literally. בן-שנה is rendered some 25 times by ἐνιαύσιος, as e.g. in *Nu.* 6.12 ἀμνὸν ἐνιαύσιον ~ כבש בן-שנתו . בן-חדש is rendered ten times by μηνιαῖος (*Le.* 27.6, *Nu.* 3.15, etc.). In other instances the translators use a compound of a numeral and -ετής,[51] as e.g. in

Le. 27.3 ἀπὸ εἰκοσαετοῦς ἕως ἑξηκονταετοῦς

מבן עשרים שנה ועד בן-ששים שנה

Other similar examples are found in *Le.* 27.5,6,7, *Ex.* 30.14, *Nu.* 1.3, 14.29, *Ge.* 17.17.[52]

---

50. For full details of LXX renderings of Hb. reciprocal expressions see Johannessohn, *Präpositionen* 374ff.
51. Such formations are normal Gk., attested since Class. times.
52. Cf. Deissmann, *BS* 164f.

Out of the many other examples of non-literal rendering of a Hebrew phrase or expression I mention only the following:

Nu. 24.1 κατὰ τὸ εἰωθός

כפעם-בפעם

Ex. 5.13 Συντελεῖτε τὰ ἔργα τὰ καθήκοντα καθ᾽ ἡμέραν

כלו מעשיכם דבר-יום ביומו

Ge. 19.14 ἔδοξεν δὲ γελοιάζειν

ויהי כמצחק

Le. 13.23 ἐὰν δὲ κατὰ χώραν μείνῃ τὸ τηλαύγημα[53]

ואם-תחתיה תעמד הבהרת

De. 29.10 ἀπὸ ξυλοκόπου ὑμῶν καὶ ἕως ὑδροφόρου ὑμῶν

מחטב עציך עד שאב מימיך

The renderings of individual words are equally significant. Take, for example, the way ראש is translated in the following:

Nu. 14.40 ἀνέβησαν εἰς τὴν κορυφὴν τοῦ ὄρους

ויעלו אל-ראש-ההר

Here, and in about 15 other instances where the context requires it, the translators render ראש by the normal Greek word for 'summit'.

Le. 5.24 καὶ ἀποτείσει αὐτὸ τὸ κεφάλαιον

ושלם אתו בראשו

Similarly *Nu.* 4.2, 5.7, 31.26,49.

Nu. 1.16 χιλίαρχοι Ισραηλ

ראשי אלפי ישראל

Ex. 30.23 τὸ ἄνθος σμύρνης ἐκλεκτῆς

ראש מר-דרור

Nu. 10.10, 28.11 ἐν ταῖς νουμηνίαις (ὑμῶν)

ובראשי חדשכם

---

53. An established Gk. idiom for 'remain in place', see below p.35.

Other examples, selected at random, are:

Ge. 28.11 ἔδυ γὰρ ὁ ἥλιος

כי-בא השמש

Similarly *Le.* 22.7, *De.* 23.12.

De. 25.13 οὐκ ἔσται ἐν τῷ μαρσίππῳ σου στάθμιον καὶ
στάθμιον, μέγα ἢ μικρόν

לא-יהיה לך בכיסך אבן ואבן גדולה וקטנה

Ex. 21.18 [ἐὰν] πατάξῃ τις τὸν πλησίον ..., καὶ μὴ ἀποθάνῃ,
κατακλιθῇ δὲ ἐπὶ τὴν κοίτην

....ולא ימות ונפל למשכב

κατακλίνω pass. is idiomatic Greek for 'take to one's bed' (see
LSJ s.v.I).

I would draw attention finally to a type of rendering that
is slightly different from those we have noticed, but no less
significant. Let us take as an example

Ge. 19.20 ἰδοὺ ἡ πόλις αὕτη ἐγγὺς τοῦ καταφυγεῖν με ἐκεῖ[54]

הנה-נא העיר הזאת קרבה לנוס שמה

Why have the translators used καταφεύγω, instead of the more
literal equivalent φεύγω? The latter could easily have been
used (נוס is of course often rendered by φεύγω); no Hebraism
would have resulted. The explanation is found in the fact that
καταφεύγω, rather than φεύγω, is the idiomatic Greek word for
'flee for refuge'. The translators, instead of rendering
mechanically, have used exactly the 'right word' for this context. This clearly suggests that the idiom they were accustomed
to was that of normal Greek.

Some other examples of the same kind are as follows:

Ge. 22.3 παρέλαβεν δὲ μεθ᾿ἑαυτοῦ δύο παῖδας

ויקח את-שני נעריו אתו

παραλαμβάνω, not λαμβάνω, is idiomatic Greek for 'take (someone)

---

54. Similarly *Nu.* 35.25,26, *De.* 4.42, 19.5.

along'.[55]   לקח is rendered in the same way in eight other
instances.

Ge. 29.33 καὶ προσέδωκέν μοι καὶ τοῦτον

ויתן-לי גם-את-זה

Ex. 34.9 συμπορευθήτω ὁ κύριός μου μεθ'ἡμῶν

ילך-נא אדני בקרבנו

Similarly elsewhere (*Ge.* 13.5, *De.* 31.8, etc.).

De. 24.15 καὶ οὐ καταβοήσεται κατὰ σοῦ πρὸς κύριον

ולא-יקרא עליך אל-יהוה

καταβοάω is idiomatic Greek for 'complain' (against a person),
'appeal for help'.

Ge. 43.25 ἤκουσαν γὰρ ὅτι ἐκεῖ μέλλει ἀριστᾶν

כי שמעו כי-שם יאכלו לחם

Ex. 4.12 καὶ συμβιβάσω σε ὃ μέλλεις λαλῆσαι

והוריתיך אשר תדבר

The last two examples are particularly instructive. μέλλω
would scarcely have been used here, where it is not required by
the Hebrew, by anyone not at home in normal Greek.

It is clear from these examples[56] that the translators do
not consistently reproduce the idiom of their original. They
are in fact often at pains to avoid it. To me this is strong
evidence against the theory that they spoke a dialect of Semitized Greek. The theory takes account of the (undoubtedly numerous) instances in which they reproduce Hebrew idiom but not
of those in which they avoid doing so. It is difficult to see
why, if the translators spoke a Hebraic Greek, the idiom of this
Hebraic Greek is not used at every opportunity.

It is not as if renderings into idiomatic Greek are rare.
If they were it might conceivably be argued that the translators

---

55. See e.g. Hdt. 6.73, 9.5, and Bauer.
56. A number of others, but by no means a complete list, are
collected in Appendix I, p.150.

accidently, as it were, fell into normal Greek in those places. But there can be no doubt that idiomatic renderings are much too common to be explained in this way.

My examples have been taken only from the Pentateuch. But the argument cannot be seriously affected by this limitation. It is very likely that similar examples are to be found elsewhere in the LXX. But even if this should not be so, the fact that there are such examples in the Pentateuch is a serious obstacle to the hypothesis of a 'Jewish-Greek' dialect. If it is admitted that the translators of the Pentateuch did not speak such a dialect it becomes difficult to maintain its existence at all.

It is clear from the arguments we have considered that a satisfactory case for regarding the LXX as a specimen of 'Jewish-Greek' has not been made out. To answer the question as put at the beginning of this chapter: in order to account for the peculiarities of LXX Greek it is sufficient to refer to the fact that the work is a translation, and unnecessary to posit the existence of a living 'Jewish-Greek' dialect.

I would emphasize, however, one final point. That there were *some* features peculiar to the Greek of Hellenistic Jews is not to be denied. Without doubt their Greek included a number of terms for specifically Jewish ideas and objects. Loan-words like σάββατα and πάσχα are obvious examples, and others of various kinds could easily be added. Moreover, it is probable that the 'translation language' which resulted from translation of the *OT* into Greek exerted an influence on the spoken language of Jews, particularly in regard to religious terminology.[57] The special uses of words like διαθήκη and δόξα, and terms like ἱλαστήριον and κιβωτός are likely to have become current in their speech. They may also have used certain Semitizing expressions or idioms found in the LXX. What I would deny is that such features were anything like extensive enough to justify regarding the language of the Jews as a dialect separate from ordinary Greek.

---

57. Cf. Rabin, *op.cit.* 10f.: 'In the receptor language, the translated text is a piece of literature like any other ... and its particular usages ... have the average chance of becoming part of the language'. Cf. Moulton, *Proleg* . 13 , Deissmann, *BS* 69f.

CHAPTER III

THE VOCABULARY OF THE PENTATEUCH:

A GENERAL SURVEY

There are, we have seen, good reasons for not accepting
the view that the Greek of the LXX was a living 'Jewish-Greek'
dialect. We can now turn to the consideration of evidence on
the positive side; that is, the evidence for regarding the Greek
of the Pentateuch as essentially the Greek of its time. To
assemble this evidence in full would require a detailed study of
the entire vocabulary (and ideally morphology and syntax would
be examined as well). It is clearly not possible to undertake
such a complete examination here. Nor indeed is it necessary.
A study of selected examples of various kinds provides as strong
an indication of the affinities of the Pentateuch vocabulary as
an exhaustive study. The parts of the vocabulary to be examined
will be explained as we proceed.

In this chapter, however, I propose to make a brief survey
of the whole vocabulary. The words and uses will be grouped on
the basis of their attestation, and examples representative of
each group will be discussed. A general picture of the Pentateuch vocabulary will thus be given, before we proceed to the
detailed study of particular parts of it.

Our knowledge of the affinities of the Pentateuch vocabulary is governed primarily by attestation. We are dependent on
whatever remains of the Greek vocabulary happen to have survived
from widely differing periods and places. This evidence necessarily gives an incomplete picture. We do not have what, ideally,
would be needed for a full understanding of the Pentateuch
vocabulary: that is, a large body of evidence of the language
from the same time and place as the Pentateuch.

It is best, then, to begin by grouping the words and uses
of the vocabulary on the basis of their present attestation. We
can then go on to consider what inferences need to be made about
their currency in Egyptian Greek of the third century B.C.

For many words, of course, to discover what attestation is available is not an easy matter, since we are largely dependent on the often incomplete material assembled by the dictionaries. More will be said of this later. Here I have necessarily had to rely on Bauer, MM, and above all LSJ. Though the limitation must be borne in mind it is not likely to vitiate the main results of this survey.

The words and uses comprising the vocabulary of the Pentateuch fall naturally into two major groups, depending on whether or not they are attested outside Biblical and related literature. Among 'related literature' I include not only the apocryphal books, the Apostolic Fathers, and the like, but also the writings of Aristeas, Philo, and Josephus. In fact an occurrence of a word or use in any of these last three authors may be as good attestation as any, depending on the circumstances in which it is used. For this brief survey, however, it is best to include them with the Biblical literature, since it is always possible to argue that they have adopted the word or use from the Greek Bible. In some cases they have obviously done so.

The two main groups will in turn be divided, so that the whole scheme is as follows:

I.   Words and uses attested outside Biblical and related
     literature
     (a) attested first in Classical Greek, with or without
         later attestation
     (b) attested only in Hellenistic Greek

II. Words and uses attested only in Biblical and related
     literature
     (a) likely to be normal Greek
     (b) likely to be peculiar to Biblical Greek

I.(a) A considerable part of the Pentateuch vocabulary consists of words and uses that go back to Classical Greek. Obviously, many of these will be everyday words that occur frequently in all periods and whose history is easy to trace. Words such as ἔχω, ὄνομα, μέγας, οὗτος, and ὅτι remained part of the ordinary post-Classical vocabulary and are naturally common in both the Pentateuch and documents contemporary with it. It

would be superfluous to illustrate this well-known, basic
element at any length.

There are also a large number of less common words and uses
that are attested first in Classical Greek. The later attestation of these varies greatly from word to word. Frequently the
only post-Classical examples so far recorded are in Koine writers,
sometimes two or three centuries later than the Pentateuch. This
is the case for example with ἄγροικος, Ar., Pl., et al., then
D.H. (i B.C.);[1] δασύπους, Cratin. and other comic poets, Arist.,
then Babr. (ii A.D.), Plin. (i A.D.), Eutecnius (?); λιμαγχονέω,
Hp., Antisth., then Gal. (ii A.D.); μετάφρενον, Hom., Pl.,
Arist., then Luc., Ruf. (both ii A.D.), Hld. (iii A.D.).

In other instances there is evidence from authors closer
in time to the Pentateuch, but as yet nothing from papyri or
inscriptions. So for example with θεραπεία in the sense of
'retinue', Hdt., X., then Plb. (ii B.C.) (also NT, Ph., J.);
σποδιά, Hom., etc., then Call. (iii B.C.), and later writers.

It is common also to find that what evidence there is from
papyri and inscriptions comes from much later than iii B.C.
Examples are ἀναιδής, Hom., Ar., etc. in Classical Greek, Diph.
(iv/iii B.C.), then in an inscription of i A.D. and a papyrus of
ii A.D.; θαυμάσιος, Hom., Hes., etc., papyri and inscriptions of
i A.D. and later (also Aristeas, Ph.); κῦμα, Hom., etc., Thphr.,
Luc. and other Koine writers, papyri of ii A.D. and later (also
Aristeas, Ph., J.).

There are also some instances of a word or use apparently
not attested elsewhere at all in post-Classical Greek, though
such examples are uncommon. Thus e.g. ληνός in the sense of
'trough' (for watering cattle) has been found apart from the
Pentateuch only in h. Merc.; οἰκέτις in the sense of 'household
slave' only in Hp., S., E.; τερατοσκόπος only in Pl., Arist.

Unless there is a special reason for thinking otherwise,
examples of this kind ought to be assumed to have formed part of
the vocabulary of third century Greek. Though they may not have
been in everyday use (some certainly were not), there is every
likelihood that they were part of the Greek vocabulary of that

1. The exact references are to be found in LSJ and Bauer.

time and could just as well be used by the Pentateuch translators as by anyone else.[2] Many of them are words for uncommon
ideas and it need cause no surprise that their attestation is
somewhat meagre. Certainly it is not surprising that many old
words do not appear in our iii B.C. documents, whose range of
subject-matter is limited.

However, many of the somewhat less common words and uses
found in the Pentateuch and attested first in Classical Greek
are in fact attested in iii B.C. papyri. The number of examples
in this category is considerable and it is worth while noticing
them at some length. In Appendix II (p.152) I have collected as
many as possible, though the list is not meant to be exhaustive.
It is quite certain that a full investigation, such as might be
undertaken by a lexicon, would bring to light many other examples. There is also much scope for illustrating from contemporary documents the various Classical phrases and constructions
used in the Pentateuch. I mention only γάμον ποιέω, διαβαίνω
εἰς, διατελέω + participle, ἐν γαστρὶ ἔχω, ἵλεως γίνομαι,
καταχέω + gen., ὁδὸς βασιλική, παύομαι + participle, στερεὰ
πέτρα, συμβαίνω + acc. and inf. and other constructions, ὑπακούω
+ gen., + dat., all of which are attested in iii B.C. documents.[3]

Examples of this kind are clearly important evidence for
the close connexion between the Pentateuch vocabulary and that
of contemporary Greek.

Of special interest in that part of the vocabulary which
goes back to Classical Greek are the many *idiomatic* expressions
and uses with which the translators show familiarity. These
have not received much notice in discussions of the nature of
LXX Greek. Yet they give, I suggest, an important indication of

---

2. The question of poetic words is rather difficult, and it is
wise to be very cautious in labelling any word as 'poetic'.
Many words that were apparently poetic in Attic appear in ordinary usage in the Koine and it seems clear that they came into
the Koine from other dialects, esp. Ionic. One must, above all,
not assume that the use by a Koine writer of a 'poetic' word is
a reminiscence of a Classical author. Cf. in general Thumb,
Hellenismus 216 ff.

3. These examples are taken from LSJ and MM, in which the
exact references may be seen.

the translators' intimacy with Greek idiom, an intimacy that
accords badly with the view that they spoke and wrote a distinguishable dialect of Semitized Greek.

In *Le*. 13.23, for example, the translators write ἐὰν δὲ
κατὰ χώραν μείνῃ τὸ τηλαύγημα καὶ μὴ διαχέηται, rendering MT
ואם-תחתיה תעמד הבהרת לא פשתה . κατὰ χώραν μένω, 'remain in
place', is an established Greek idiom, attested for example in
Hdt. 1.169, 8.108, Th. 4.26, Ar. *Eq*. 1354. As can be seen, it
is far from a word-for-word rendering of the Hebrew, though it
reproduces the meaning of the Hebrew perfectly. The translators
can have used such an expression only because it was familiar to
them in the language that they were accustomed to speak. Similar remarks apply to *Ge*. 31.35 μὴ βαρέως φέρε, κύριε, MT
אל-יחר בעיני אדני . The expression βαρέως φέρω, 'take (something)
ill', 'become annoyed', is idiomatic Greek, found also e.g. in
Hdt. 3.155, Plb. 15.1.1.

Many of the examples are adverbial phrases, such as διὰ
κενῆς, 'to no purpose', *Le*. 26.16 (MT לריק), often in Classical
Greek, e.g. Ar. *V*. 929, and also iii B.C. papyri, e.g. *PHib*.
66.5 (228 B.C.); κατὰ μόνας, 'alone', *Ge*. 32.17 (MT לבדו), e.g.
Th. 1.32, Is. 7.38, Men. *Fr*. 722.1; ἴσον ἴσῳ, 'in equal propor-
tions', *Ex*. 30.34 (MT בד בבד), e.g. Ar. *Pl*. 1132, Hp. *Epid*. 2.5.1.

Among idiomatic uses of words, the following may be mentioned: ἁλίσκομαι in the technical legal sense of 'be convicted',
D., Pl., etc., found in *Ex*. 22.8 καὶ ὁ ἁλοὺς διὰ τοῦ θεοῦ
ἀποτείσει διπλοῦν τῷ πλησίον (MT אשר ירשיען אלהים); ἡ ἵππος
collective, 'cavalry', Hdt., Th., etc., *Ex*. 14.7 καὶ πᾶσαν τὴν
ἵππον τῶν Αἰγυπτίων (MT רכב), al.; τελέω pass., 'be initiated',
'have oneself initiated' (into the mysteries of a god, dat.),
Ar., Pl., Hdt., etc., *Nu*. 25.3 καὶ ἐτελέσθη Ισραηλ τῷ Βεελφεγωρ
(MT ויצמד), similarly 25.5.

The translators' handling of verbs compounded with prepositions, whose senses tend to be varied and idiomatic, is
similarly indicative of their familiarity with Greek usage. A
good example is ἀφίστημι. This is used in the Pentateuch in a
variety of senses, all of which are established in Classical
Greek. I. trans.: 'cause to revolt', e.g. *De*. 7.4 ἀποστήσει
γὰρ τὸν υἱόν σου ἀπ᾽ἐμοῦ, καὶ λατρεύσει θεοῖς ἑτέροις. II.

36

intrans.: (i) 'stand back, aloof' (from), Nu. 16.27 ἀπέστησαν
ἀπὸ τῆς σκηνῆς Κορε κύκλῳ (ii) 'withdraw', 'depart' (from a
place), e.g. Ge. 12.8 καὶ ἀπέστη ἐκεῖθεν εἰς τὸ ὄρος (iii)
'withdraw' (from an activity), Nu. 8.25 καὶ ἀπὸ πεντηκονταετοῦς
ἀποστήσεται ἀπὸ τῆς λειτουργίας (iv) 'rebel', 'revolt', e.g.
Ge. 14.4 δώδεκα ἔτη ἐδούλευον τῷ Χοδολλογομορ, τῷ δὲ τρισκαι-
δεκάτῳ ἔτει ἀπέστησαν (v) 'shrink, abstain' (from), Ex. 23.7
ἀπὸ παντὸς ῥήματος ἀδίκου ἀποστήσῃ. Classical examples of these
uses can be seen in LSJ. It is to be noted that the translators'
use of this word has nothing to do with systematic representation of any Hebrew word or words: in each of the examples quoted
here ἀφίστημι renders a different Hebrew word.[4]

A particularly good illustration of the translators'
familiarity with idiomatic Greek is afforded by verbs for washing. As is well known, Greek has three words for the idea,
λούω, νίπτω (earlier νίζω), and πλύνω, each being used in a
different way. It is generally said that λούω is used of washing the whole body, νίπτω of parts of the body, especially the
hands and feet, πλύνω of clothes.[5] This description, though
not incorrect as far as it goes, is inadequate, as we shall see.
Before turning to the Pentateuch it will be worth while to try
to describe their usage more accurately.

λούω presents no difficulty. It is used of washing the
whole body, especially in the middle voice: 'wash oneself',
'bathe'.

νίπτω mostly describes washing of parts of the body, but
it is also used of things:[6] a table (with sponges) Hom. Od. 1.112
οἱ δ'αὖτε σπόγγοισι ... τραπέζας νίζον καὶ πρότιθεν, a brick
Theoc. 16.62 ὕδατι νίζειν θολερὰν διαειδέι πλίνθον, a wooden

---

4. Viz. סור hi., עלה ni., עתק hi., שוב qal, מרד qal, רחק qal,
respectively.

5. See e.g. LSJ under all three words; TWNT IV 295 (Oepke).
The description goes back to the ancient lexicographers:
see e.g. Ammon. Diff. 274. Cf. Stephanus, Thes. Gr. Ling.
s.v. πλύνω.

6. Noted by LSJ, s.v. fin., 'νίζω is sts. used of things',
quoting Od. 1.112, Il. 16.229, and Theoc. 16.62.

statue E. *IT* 1041 κἀκεῖνο [τὸ βρέτας] νῖψαι, σοῦ θιγόντος ὥς,
ἐρῶ, a cup Hom. *Il.* 16.229 [δέπας] ἔνιψ᾽ ὕδατος καλῇσι ῥοῇσι
(compounds of νίπτω are also used of washing cups: Eub. 56.5 ἐκ -,
Pherecr. 41 ἀπο-). In addition there is an instance in which
this verb describes the washing of cattle in the sea: E. *IT* 255
βοῦς ἤλθομεν νίψοντες ἐναλίᾳ δρόσῳ. Finally, it is worth noting
that νίπτω is the word used for washing something (blood, salt,
etc.) off one's body, e.g. Hom. *Il.* 11.830 ἀπ᾽ αὐτοῦ δ᾽ αἷμα
κελαινὸν νίζ᾽ ὕδατι λιαρῷ.

In the same way I find that πλύνω is by no means confined
to the washing of clothes. It is in fact applied to a wide
variety of objects, as follows: entrails Ar. *Eq.* 160 τί μ᾽,
ὦγάθ᾽, οὐ πλύνειν ἐᾷς τὰς κοιλίας πωλεῖν τε τοὺς ἀλλᾶντας; *Pl.*
1168 καὶ πλῦνέ γε αὐτὸς προσελθὼν πρὸς τὸ φρέαρ τὰς κοιλίας, the
tail and mane of a horse X. *Eq.* 5.7 καὶ οὐρὰν δὲ καὶ χαίτην
πλύνειν χρή (cf. 5.6 ὕδατι δὲ καταπλύνειν τὴν κεφαλὴν χρή), sand
Arist. *Mir. Ausc.* 833 b.25 ταύτην [τὴν ἄμμον] δ᾽ οἱ μὲν ἁπλῶς
φασὶ πλύναντας καμινεύειν, 26, Thphr. *Lap.* 58, sesame *PCair. Zen.*
562.19 (253 B.C.), flax *PSI* 599.7 (iii B.C.), wool *PEnt.* 2.5
(218 B.C.), nets *Ev. Luc.* 5.2, squill (the plant) Porph. *VP* 34
(iii A.D.)[7]

It is clear both that the traditional description is incomplete and misleading, and that it is unsatisfactory to try to
distinguish νίπτω and πλύνω in terms of the objects washed.[8]
The distinction between them is to be sought rather in the *type*
of washing each describes. I suggest that the above examples
are adequately accounted for if we define the words as follows:
νίπτω is 'to cleanse, rinse, by pouring, splashing, or wiping
water upon', πλύνω 'to cleanse by agitating or rubbing in water'.
The actions involved are different. νίπτω suggests merely the

---

7. The application of the verb to objects other than clothes is
also implied by the use of πλυτός in Hp. *Art.* 36 τῷ ἀλήτῳ ...
τῷ πλυτῷ, 'washed meal', Gal. 6.494 πλυτὸς ἄρτος, and πλύμα e.g.
in Arist. *HA* 534[a]27 τὸ πλύμα τῶν ἰχθύων, 'water in which fish
have been washed' (other examples in LSJ).

8. Hauck's more comprehensive description in the same terms,
TWNT IV 946, is still not satisfactory: 'Gk. πλύνειν applies to
the washing of inanimate objects, νίπτειν to the partial washing
of living persons, and λούειν or λούεσθαι to full washing or
bathing'.

38

application of water to the object washed; we think of cloths,
bowls, and pouring from jugs. With πλύνω, on the other hand, a
thorough scrub is implied. The action required to wash entrails,
sand, grain, and so on is essentially the same as that employed
in washing clothes. The instance of νίπτω of the washing of
cattle in the sea does not seem to me to be an exception. The
cattle, I imagine, would be washed down by having the sea-water
splashed, or perhaps poured, over them. When, however, one
wants to describe the washing of a horse's tail and mane, πλύνω
is the appropriate word, because they require the same sort of
rubbing or kneading action as would be applied to clothes.

All three words occur in the Pentateuch, and are used for
the most part in accordance with the traditional description.[9]
A convenient illustration is found in *Le.* 15.11 καὶ ὅσων ἐὰν
ἅψηται ὁ γονορρυὴς καὶ τὰς χεῖρας οὐ νένιπται, πλυνεῖ τὰ ἱμάτια
καὶ λούσεται τὸ σῶμα ὕδατι.[10] This fact by itself is a valuable
indication of the translators' adherence to Greek usage. But
there are also certain examples that are not accounted for by
the usual description:

Le. 15.12 καὶ σκεῦος ὀστράκινον, οὗ ἂν ἅψηται ὁ γονορρυής,
συντριβήσεται· καὶ σκεῦος ξύλινον νιφήσεται ὕδατι καὶ
καθαρὸν ἔσται[11]

Ex. 29.17 καὶ τὸν κριὸν διχοτομήσεις κατὰ μέλη καὶ πλυνεῖς

---

9. This has of course been noticed before, e.g. by Hauck, *TWNT*
IV 946.

10. For other examples see *Ex.* 2.5, *Nu.* 19.7, *De.* 23.12
(λούομαι); *Ge.* 18.4, *Ex.* 30.18,19ff. (νίπτω); *Ex.* 19.10, *Le.*
14.8, *Nu.* 8.7 (πλύνω).

11. νιφησεται BAFioa₂] πλυθησεται ek[a]prt: πληθησεται d: νιφθη-
σεται Mk*rell. (Brooke-McLean). It is difficult to know what
value to attach to the reading of ek[a]prt (and d, since πληθησεται
can only be a mistaken spelling of πλυθησεται). I have assumed
for the purpose of discussion that the majority reading νιφ(θ)η-
σεται is the correct one. A.V. Billen, *JTS* XXVI (1924-5) 276,
evaluated the groups dpt and ejsvz as 'of all the MSS least
likely to give us the LXX in its earlier forms'. It is hard to
explain how πλυθησεται might have arisen. Perhaps changes in the
usage of νίπτω and πλύνω in the later Koine are behind it. In
Mod. Gk. the latter has invaded the other's territory considerably (e.g. πλένω τὰ χέρια μου), see Swanson and *AELex.*, s.v.
wash.

τὰ ἐνδόσθια καὶ τοὺς πόδας ὕδατι καὶ ἐπιθήσεις ἐπὶ τὰ
διχοτομήματα σὺν τῇ κεφαλῇ

Le. 1.9 τὰ δὲ ἐγκοίλια καὶ τοὺς πόδας πλυνοῦσιν ὕδατι, καὶ
ἐπιθήσουσιν οἱ ἱερεῖς τὰ πάντα ἐπὶ τὸ θυσιαστήριον. Similarly 1.13.

Le. 8.21 καὶ τὴν κοιλίαν καὶ τοὺς πόδας ἔπλυνεν ὕδατι καὶ
ἀνήνεγκεν ... ἐπὶ τὸ θυσιαστήριον. Similarly 9.14.

Our re-examination of νίπτω and πλύνω shows, however, that
there is no reason to regard these examples as in any way con-
trary to Greek usage. They are clearly in accordance with the
definitions I have proposed, but even if my definitions are not
accepted, the examples noticed earlier provide satisfactory
parallels to the Pentateuch examples. The use of νίπτω of the
washing of a σκεῦος ξύλινον (probably 'wooden vessel'[12]) may be
compared with its use of washing a cup; and the examples of
πλύνω, which are all alike, are closely paralleled by the two
examples of πλύνω τὰς κοιλίας in Aristophanes.

The translators, then, express the idea of 'wash' in strict
accordance with idiomatic Greek. But we have still to consider
how Greek usage compares with that of Hebrew in the expression
of this idea. Greek divides up the field into three parts; does
this division correspond to a similar division in Hebrew? If
so, there would clearly be the possibility that the translators'
careful observance of Greek idiom was encouraged, perhaps even
brought about, by the similar structure of the Hebrew vocabulary.
In fact, however, Hebrew and Greek usage do not coincide here,
as is clear from a consideration of the Hebrew words and their
renderings. Hebrew כבס *Pi.*, usually of washing garments, is,
as would be expected, uniformly rendered by πλύνω (c. 40 times).
But the more general term רחץ , used of washing parts of the
body, parts of sacrificial victims, and of bathing, is rendered
at different times by all three Greek words: by λούω, λούομαι c.
29 times, by νίπτω c. 12 times, and by πλύνω 5 times (*Ex.* 29.17,

---

12. σκεῦος is of course a vague word, like Hb. כלי, which it
here translates; it can be 'implement', 'utensil', or just
'thing', but the parallelism with σκεῦος ὀστράκινον suggests
that we should take it here as 'vessel'.

Le. 1.9,13, 8.21, 9.14, quoted above). In addition νίπτω twice renders שטף , 'rinse', 'wash off' (*Le.* 15.11,12).[13] Although there are three Hebrew words involved, there is no exact correspondence between each of the Hebrew words and each of the Greek. Even the correspondence between πλύνω and כבס is not exact: πλύνω covers part of the area of רחץ as well as that of כבס . It is therefore apparent that systematic representation plays no part in the way the translators use the three Greek words. They employ the word that is 'correct' according to Greek idiom independently of the underlying Hebrew.

The above is only a sample of the established idiomatic expressions and uses that appear in the translators' Greek. Others could certainly be added.

What gives added point to these examples is the fact that they are independent of Hebrew idiom. In none of them is there any possibility that the usage is due to literal rendering. It is of course possible to mention instances in which that is the case. For example, κάθημαι in *Ex.* 18.14, in the Classical sense (e.g. Pl. *Ap.* 35c) of 'sit as judge', renders Hebrew ישב . In cases of this kind literal representation of the Hebrew may be suspected, although in my view it is likely that the translators were quite familiar with the Greek use.

Old words and uses, then, formed an important element in the vocabulary of the Pentateuch translators. They were familiar with a wide range of words and uses that had been current since Classical times, including idiomatic uses and expressions. Although the attestation of such words and uses in post-Classical Greek varies greatly and it is often necessary to assume their currency in the translators' time, evidence in documents of the third century B.C. is in fact available for a substantial number of them, and these give a definite indication of the affinities between the translators' vocabulary and that of contemporary Greek.

(b) As is well known, in the transition from Classical

---

13. Note too that this Hb. word is not rendered consistently by one Gk. word: in its one other occurrence in the Penataeuch, *Le.* 6.21, שטף is translated by ἐκκλύζω, 'wash out' (only here in Pent.).

to Hellenistic Greek a large number of changes occurred in the
language. Not the least of these changes were in vocabulary.
Innovations in this respect were of two main types. Old words
frequently developed new senses (not necessarily to the exclusion of earlier senses), and many new words, in the shape of new
formations on existing stems and borrowings from outside Greek,
came into use. Developments of the same kinds had of course
taken place from time to time in the language throughout its
history, but in the early Koine period they were especially
numerous. Since these were the changes that had occurred in the
Greek vocabulary of the translators' time, it is natural to find
in their vocabulary a large number of words and uses attested
only in Hellenistic Greek. Words and uses so attested do in
fact form as important an element in the Pentateuch vocabulary
as those going back to Classical Greek.

It must be remembered, of course, that attestation only in
post-Classical Greek does not automatically establish that the
word or use concerned is a new development in the Koine. The
random nature of our evidence, especially for words we know
would not be frequently used, makes it likely that a fair number
of words and uses attested only late are in fact old; it is
quite possible for an old word for an uncommon idea to have been
preserved by chance only in a late author or document. In a
number of cases it is not difficult to deduce that this must be
so. στοιβάζω, for example, has been found, apart from the LXX,
only in Lucian (ii A.D.) and a papyrus of ii/iii A.D.; yet
διαστοιβάζω is found in Herodotus.

For the most part, however, words and uses so attested are
undoubtedly new developments. We can often see some other indication, apart from the attestation, to this effect. Thus for
example it may be observed that a particular sense is a natural
semantic development from earlier senses, or that a certain
formation is a more regular equivalent of an earlier form with
an irregular, or for some other reason 'difficult', conjugation
or declension. Similarly, where a given word is synonymous with
an old one which shows signs of dropping out of use, it is likely
that the former is a newcomer. There remain, of course, many
doubtful cases. It is at times quite impossible to decide
definitely whether a word or use is new in the Koine.

To distinguish new words and uses from old is not essential. After all, the distinction would have been felt in few cases by the ordinary speakers of the language. But it is a useful practical one for us. It is the neologisms of the Hellenistic period that are often most in need of analysis and illustration, whether one's main interest is the LXX vocabulary alone or the wider subject of the development of the Greek language as a whole.

The type of attestation outside Biblical and related literature of words and uses in this category varies greatly from one instance to another. As would be expected, in many cases we do not have the extensive evidence from the contemporary vernacular that is desirable.

Frequently the only parallels recorded are separated from the time of the Pentateuch by some centuries. Thus e.g. ἴχνος in the sense of 'route' has so far been recorded elsewhere only in a papyrus of ii A.D.; the formation ἀγαθοποιέω, apart from Aristeas, only in S.E. (ii A.D.), Plot. (iii A.D.), and other late writers; βηρύλλιον only in D.S. (i B.C.); ὀλεθρεύω only in Vett. Val. (ii A.D.).

Other words appear once or twice in literature about the time of the Pentateuch or a little earlier and then not again until much later: e.g. γελοιάζω, Aristarch. (iii/ii B.C.), then Plu. (i/ii A.D.) and later writers; βροῦχος, Thphr. (iv/iii B.C.), Herod. (iii B.C.), then writers of iv A.D. and later; ἔκτρωμα, Arist. (iv B.C.), then Phryn. (ii A.D.) (also Ph. and NT).

Some words are at present attested only once in a rather out-of-the-way text of uncertain date: e.g. κερατίζω once in Schol. Theocr. (LSJ Suppl.), καταπενθέω once in the Greek Anthology (AP 7.618).

Moreover, as these examples illustrate, documentary evidence is often lacking. This makes it difficult to judge the currency of the word or use in the vernacular language. γελοιάζω, for example, is possibly a literary rather than vernacular word, if we are to judge by the examples so far known. When, on the other hand, documentary evidence is available it is often of later date than the Pentateuch. This is so for example with ἴχνος noted above, and κτηνοτρόφος, subst., recorded in

papyri of i B.C. and ii A.D., ἐχθρία in a papyrus of iii A.D.
(LSJ Suppl.).

Clearly, each example raises its own questions and will
need individual attention for a final assessment of the relation
of the Pentateuch vocabulary to the language of its time. Much
will always remain uncertain. In some cases it may be that the
translators were the originators of a certain word or use, which
then found its way into the common vocabulary; or that they
adopted and used frequently, because it was convenient for rendering a particular idea, a term that was not in fact as frequently used in contemporary Greek; or that the translators and
some other writer independently created a certain formation, or
put a word to a new use. These and perhaps other possibilities
will sometimes have to be considered. But, on the whole, any
attestation, even if rather remote, is likely to be an indication that the word or use concerned was a normal part of the
Greek vocabulary of the translators' time. Usually no other
interpretation is possible. The fact that a word or use was
also employed by some other writer strongly suggests that both
he and the translators knew of it from its currency in the
language.

There are, however, in addition to examples like those we
have just considered, a good many new Koine words and uses found
in the Pentateuch that are well attested in contemporary documents. These examples are valuable for my purpose and it is
upon them that attention will be concentrated in the next three
chapters. There as many as possible will be examined in detail,
with such contemporary evidence as I have been able to discover.

This selection has been made first of all for practical
reasons: clearly the field of study has had to be limited in
some way. This being so, there are two reasons for choosing
this section of the vocabulary. First, that it illustrates
better than almost all other sections the place of the Pentateuch vocabulary in the Greek language of its time. The words
and uses concerned are recent innovations whose currency in the
vernacular of the same time and locality as the Pentateuch can
be demonstrated beyond doubt. The papyri, from which the main
evidence comes, are almost all of Egyptian origin and can

mostly be accurately dated. Some are perhaps contemporary even
to the year, since the bulk of our iii B.C. papyrus evidence
dates from around the middle of the century. Although, as I
have suggested, any attestation outside Biblical and related
literature is useful, this evidence is clearly the best that
could be hoped for, and makes the first claim on our attention.

Secondly, words and uses that are recent innovations of
the Koine are for the most part more in need of eludication than
those whose usage is familiar from Classical Greek. The study
of the former is therefore likely to be a more useful contribution to LXX lexicography, at least at its present early stage.

To limit the field of detailed study in this way does not
mean that other parts of the vocabulary have been ignored. The
purpose of this chapter is to give due weight to all parts of
the vocabulary, including the evidence that might point in the
opposite direction to my general thesis. It is this evidence
that we have now to consider.

II. The second major group of words and uses in the
Pentateuch consists of those that are not attested outside
Biblical and related literature. The question naturally arises
whether these were in fact peculiar to the Biblical vocabulary.
As we shall see, there are reasons for thinking that many were
not. But first it would be useful to consider certain limita-
tions that affect any study of the Greek vocabulary, and are
particularly important for this question.

The material collected by the standard dictionaries is
incomplete. This is mostly well recognized, but needs empha-
sizing. LSJ's material, in particular, must be used with
caution in any study of LXX vocabulary.[14] It often happens that
an occurrence that is important for the LXX has gone unnoted.
Thus for example I have myself noted ἐτασμός, recorded by LSJ

---

14. These remarks are not intended as criticism of LSJ (though
there is much in it that is open to criticism). A dictionary of
its kind obviously cannot make an exhaustive collection of
examples, or treat all the material that would appear in a
dictionary specializing in the LXX. I wish only to make the point
that it is essential for students of the LXX not to regard LSJ's
collection as final.

only in the LXX, in *Antiatt.* 96 ἐτασμόν : τὸν ἐξετασμόν. μέρος
in the sense of 'side', again noted by LSJ only in the LXX, is
to be found not only in documents of iii B.C. and later but even
in Herodotus (see pp. 74 f.). Similar examples are provided by
the recent Supplement to LSJ, which now records other attestation for a number of words hitherto known only in Biblical and
related literature: for example ἀτεκνόω, formerly only LXX and
later versions, περιχαλκόω *Ex.* 27.6, σανιδωτός *Ex.* 27.8, all now
attested in inscriptions. Cf. ἀφόρισμα, διάλευκος.

Again, my own investigations have brought to light a
number of previously unrecorded occurrences of words in iii B.C.
papyri. See for example γόμος (p.62), καταφυτεύω (p.57),
σάγμα (p. 84), σιτομετρέω (p. 98). Often such examples are not
recorded even in Preisigke or Kiessling, and can be found only
by systematic checking of the indexes to various papyrological
publications.

Similarly, I find that ληνός in the sense of 'wine-press',
which to judge by the examples mentioned by LSJ and Bauer is
post-Classical, is in fact attested for Classical times by Is.
Fr. 24 (ap. Poll. 7.151).

Of course some of the examples I have mentioned were not
available for inclusion in the latest (9th) edition of LSJ,
completed in 1940. But this does not affect the point that we
must always allow for the possibility that information important
for the LXX vocabulary is not recorded in LSJ. This applies to
a lesser extent to Bauer's dictionary, which aims at completeness and is more recent (1957). However, its usefulness for the
LXX is limited because many LXX words and uses (perhaps more
than is generally realized) do not appear in the *NT*.

There is, then, always the possibility of finding parallels that have been previously overlooked. But in addition to
this, we must bear in mind the possibility that texts as yet
unpublished, and indeed undiscovered, may yield information of
importance for a number of words. Professor E.G. Turner has
pointed out that 'at least as many papyrus texts still await an
editor as have been published', and, furthermore, that 'papyri
are still being discovered in Egypt faster than scholars can

transcribe and edit them'.[15] We cannot expect any startling
discoveries affecting the LXX vocabulary in these documents, but
there are likely to be at least some examples that will extend
our knowledge of it.

Clearly we must be wary of placing too much confidence in
what the dictionaries at present record. Nor is this all. Even
when all the available evidence has been found, we have still to
remember that chance has played an important part in the sur-
vival of evidence of the Greek language. As Bauer has put it
(p.xvii), 'due allowance must be made for the chance which has
preserved one word while allowing another to disappear', and he
goes on to mention the case of προσευχή 'prayer', which is
common in the Biblical literature but by 'pure accident' has
come to light in only one pagan papyrus. 'If this had not
turned up, we would have had another "vox biblica".'

Another instructive example is ὀρθρίζω. This word is used
a number of times in the LXX and later versions, and once in the
NT, but has not been found anywhere else except in the grammarians Moeris (p.272) and Thomas Magister (p.256). But the way in
which they refer to it shows that its present attestation gives
a quite inaccurate indication of its currency. Thus Moeris'
remark is: ὀρθρεύει 'Αττικῶς. ὀρθρίζει 'Ελληνικῶς. It must be
entirely due to chance that we have no other non-Biblical
examples of the word, since Moeris would scarcely describe it in
this way if it were confined to Biblical Greek.[16]

The point is well illustrated also by the many words that
we know must have been in continuous use but yet are attested
seldom and only at intervals. Take for example ζύμη, the word
for 'yeast'. This is attested first in Aristotle, then apart
from LXX and *NT*, only in papyri and writers (Plu., Ph., J.) of
i and ii A.D. Clearly the word must have been more widely used
in the Koine period than this attestation would suggest. But
not only that: it is likely that it was established in Greek
well before the time of Aristotle; it is probably fortuitous
that there are no examples in any earlier remains of Greek.

---

15. *Greek Papyri. An Introduction,* Oxford, 1968, pp.vii and 40.
16. Cf. Thumb, *Hellenismus* 123.

These, then, are basic points to keep in mind in dealing with the part of the LXX vocabulary that is not at present attested outside Biblical and related literature. Before deciding that any word or use is peculiar to the Biblical vocabulary we must make allowance for the gaps in our knowledge of the Greek of the translators' time.

(a) Let us now look at some examples of words and uses that are likely to have been part of the normal Greek vocabulary, despite their present lack of attestation outside the Biblical writings. Although clearly each example is different and requires individual attention, a few examples of each of the main types will give a general idea of the words and uses that fall into this category.

A very common type is that in which the word concerned is a normal formation belonging to a well-attested group. Consider for example the noun πλινθεία, 'brickmaking', found so far only in the Pentateuch and Josephus.[17] This belongs to a very large group of derivatives of πλίνθος, itself attested since Alcaeus (vii/vi B.C.). πλινθεύω and πλινθεῖον are both old words and are well attested also in iii B.C. There is therefore no reason to doubt that πλινθεία was normal Greek. Similarly διασάφησις (only LXX) is a normal formation from the verb, which is well attested in iii B.C. papyri.

It is probably accidental that these two words, and others like them, have not turned up elsewhere. But even if we had all the evidence and could see that διασάφησις, for example, had not been used anywhere else in Greek, it must be borne in mind that the form could have been used by any Greek speaker without his being conscious of coining a new term. Nor would his hearers have felt it as such. Any Greek speaker who needed a noun from διασαφέω would be likely to have employed διασάφησις.[18] The

---

17. Apart from an occurrence in Suidas in a different sense.

18. Cf. MM's comment on βδέλυγμα, which they were unable to parallel outside Biblical literature: 'The verb having appealed to the LXX translators as an excellent rendering of תעב and other Hebrew verbs, it was inevitable that when a derived noun was wanted the regular formation should have been adopted or coined. Probably any Greek writer who wanted to express the idea of τὸ ἐβδελυγμένον would have done the same without hesitation.' How right they were is shown by the fact that the word has since been found by Bauer in *Vit. Aesopi*.

same applies to examples like καταδυναστεία, ἀσφαλτόω, λαξεύω, all of which are regular formations belonging to established groups. There is no reason to think that any of them gives an indication that the Pentateuch translators spoke an isolated form of Greek.

Naturally this argument must be used with caution. It is not applicable if there is any reason to think the translators (or the Alexandrian Jewish community) created the formation in order to describe a specifically Jewish idea or object; in other words, if the form appears to have been coined as a technical term. We shall presently see instances in which there can be no doubt that that is the case.

Somewhat similar considerations apply to words formed by composition. If a word so formed belongs to a common type, and there is nothing to suggest that it was created by the translators as a technical term, then it ought, in my view, to be accepted as normal Greek. A number of preposition compounds are obviously in this category. ἐκκαθαρίζω, for example, found only in the LXX, is the sort of compound that any Greek speaker might have used. καθαρίζω, equivalent to earlier καθαίρω, is well established in the Koine (see Bauer, MM), and compounds with ἐκ- are of course readily formed in Greek. In addition, ἐκκαθαρίζω is analogous to ἐκκαθαίρω, which is as old as Homer. Similar remarks apply for example to διανήθω, ἐπικαταράομαι, and καταπρονομεύω.

In the same way a number of compounds of other types show signs of being normal Greek. Compounds with ἀρχι-, of which there are several found as yet only in the LXX, are a clear case: e.g. ἀρχιδεσμοφύλαξ, found only in *Genesis*. Considering the readiness with which compounds of this type were formed in Hellenistic Greek,[19] and the fact that δεσμοφύλαξ is well attested from iii B.C. onwards, we can hardly regard the word as the property of the *Genesis* translator alone. Any writer wishing to express the idea of 'chief gaoler' would be likely to have used it. Indeed, it is probable in my opinion that this word was often used in the Greek of the translators' time, but has by

---

19. See MM s.v. ἀρχι-, Mayser, *Gramm*. I.iii 160f.

accident not been preserved outside the Pentateuch.[20]

Sometimes it happens that the word for which we have no
outside attestation is presupposed by a related formation that
is so attested. For example the word λῶμα, 'hem', 'fringe' (of
uncertain origin) is not known apart from some half dozen
occurrences in *Ex*. Yet the diminutive λωμάτιον is found in *AP*
11.210 (Lucill., i A.D.), implying a wider currency for λῶμα
than its present attestation suggests.

A number of uses as yet unattested outside Biblical and
related literature are also likely, for one reason or another,
to have been part of the normal Greek vocabulary.

One type is that in which the semantic development concerned is paralleled, and well attested, in another formation
of the group. For example ὀλιγοψυχία, originally 'swooning'
(Hp.), is found only in the LXX in the sense of 'faint-hearted-
ness'. But the semantic development from 'be faint' to 'be
dispirited' is amply attested in the verb (see p.76). It is
therefore quite improbable that this use of the noun was
peculiar to the translators' Greek. Similarly the use of
παροίκησις in the sense of 'sojourning', 'temporary residence',
unattested outside the LXX, is parallel to the Koine usage of
πάροικος with the meaning 'temporary resident', and παροικέω
'inhabit (a place), dwell, as a πάροικος' (see p.61).

The intransitive use in the active of certain verbs
normally transitive is another, fairly common, type. For
example, φλογίζω has so far been found (S. +) only with a transitive function in the active ('set on fire'); in *Ex*. 9.24 it is
used intransitively ('burn', 'blaze') τὸ πῦρ φλόγιζον
(MT אש מתלקחת). Clearly this use of φλογίζω is not brought
about by literal representation of Hebrew idiom; but more important, it is in accordance with a fairly widespread tendency
in Greek for verbs originally used only transitively in the
active to appropriate an intransitive function from the middle-
passive voice.[21] In the case of φλογίζω, moreover, the

---

20. Other ἀρχι- formations found in the Pentateuch but not
attested outside Biblical literature are ἀρχι-δεσμώτης, -οινοχοία,
-σιτοποιός, -στράτηγος (also J.), -φυλος.

21. Bl. DF §309.2.

development is analogous to that in the older word φλέγω, the intransitive use of which is found as early as Pindar.[22] It would be incorrect, therefore, in my opinion, to regard this use of φλογίζω as peculiar to the translators' Greek. The same is true of a number of other words used in this way in the Pentateuch, such as καταψύχω, σκιάζω, σπερματίζω, and ὑγιάζω.

Some unattested uses are natural semantic developments unconnected with Hebrew idiom that could have occurred almost at any time in Greek. For example, σκεπάζω is apparently used in the sense of 'conceal' in Ex. 2.2 (see p.77), a sense not attested outside the LXX. Yet the development from 'cover' to 'conceal' is a natural one and is paralleled in καλύπτω. Another example is the use of ἄλογος in the sense of 'not counted' in Nu. 6.12 αἱ ἡμέραι αἱ πρότεραι ἄλογοι ἔσονται (MT יפלו).[23] This use is not known elsewhere, but the etymology would lead us to expect such a sense in this word; and compare the sense 'unexpected' (i.e. 'not reckoned upon') in Th. 6.46 (LSJ s.v. III.1).

It is clear, then, that a number of the words and uses not attested outside Biblical and related literature are likely to have been part of the normal Greek vocabulary. The examples considered above are of necessity only a selection, representing the main types; many more could certainly be added. The total number of such examples forms a significant proportion of all the words and uses that would seem to be peculiar to Biblical Greek if we judged by their present attestation alone.

(b) Nevertheless, when all the examples like the above have been allowed for, there remain many words and uses that are undoubtedly peculiar to Biblical Greek. Although there is difficulty in deciding in some instances, those that are likely to be of this kind are for the most part easily recognized, and no one would wish to argue that they could be anything other than neologisms created by the Alexandrian Jewish community or the translators themselves in the course of their work.[24]

---

22. Cf. the fluctuation in Eng. 'burn'.

23. Note the idiomatic rendering of the Hebrew.

24. These have not been systematically studied, but many examples have been noted before: see the works referred to above p. 11, n.1.

Such neologisms mostly take the form of new uses. The most familiar type is that due to 'literalism'. Examples such as the Hebraistic use of ὀφθαλμός, στόμα, χείρ, πρόσωπον are well known. Others are ὁδόν as preposition 'towards' (~ דרך), οἰκοδομέω 'fashion', 'form' (~ בנה), εὑρίσκω 'befall' (~ מצא), ἀρχή 'sum', 'total' (~ ראש), ποιέω 'prepare' food (~ עשה), σκέπτομαι 'select' (~ ראה , חזה); and literal renderings of Hebrew expressions, such as πληρόω τὰς χεῖρας 'dedicate', 'consecrate', ἐπαίρω πρόσωπον 'show favour', ζητέω τὴν ψυχήν τινος 'seek to kill'.

Some new uses result from 'etymologizing' rendering of a Hebrew word, as e.g. κλητή subst. 'assembly' (~ מקרא), πᾶν τὸ ἀνάστημα 'everything that had grown' (Ge. 7.23, ~ יקום), ἀλήθεια (~ תמים), δήλωσις (~ אורים).

Certain words undergo an extension or alteration of meaning through application to specifically Jewish objects: e.g. ἐπωμίς 'ephod', κιβωτός 'ark', μίτρα head-dress of the high priest, κράσπεδον 'tassel'. Similarly there are a number of theological terms that have acquired special 'Biblical' significations, as e.g. πίστις, δόξα, δικαιόω and derivatives, πονηρός and related words.[25]

The overdoing of a possible Greek use is another type that belongs here.[26] A well-known case is ἰδού (~ הנה); similarly (ἐγ-)κάθημαι in the sense of 'dwell' (~ ישב), and apodotic καί.

In a few instances the new use seems to be due to rendering by means of a word with a phonetic resemblance to the Hebrew word: e.g. μῶμος in the sense of 'defect' in a sacrificial victim, translating מום .[27]

The number of new formations that are likely to be peculiar to Biblical Greek is much smaller. Most formations unattested outside the Biblical literature are like the examples we have considered in the preceding section; i.e. they belong to well-attested groups or common types and do not seem to have

25. Cf. Jellicoe, SMS 331.
26. Moulton, Proleg. 11, Thackeray, Gramm. 29
27. Cf. Thackeray, Gramm. 37f.

been created as technical terms.

There are however some clear cases of formations that are
likely to have been confined to the Biblical vocabulary.
θυσιαστήριον 'altar',[28] and ἱλαστήριον subst., of the lid on the
ark of the covenant, were clearly coined as technical terms.
Other possible examples of the same kind are ὁλοκάρπωσις,
ὁλοκάρπωμα, θηριάλωτος, παράθεμα, ἁγιαστήριον.

In a number of instances it seems fairly clear that the
formation has been created on the spot by the translators to
meet a particular need. So e.g. ἀποκιδαρόω 'take the κίδαρις
off' Le. 10.6, 21.10, σκληροκαρδία 'hardness of heart' De. 10.16.
Some words of this type are plainly 'nonce-formations' unlikely
to occur again: e.g. περάτης translating עברי Ge. 14.13,
πρωτοτοκεύω 'grant rights of first-born' (to) De. 21.16.

Finally there are a number of loan-words from Hebrew or
Aramaic: the familiar σάββατα and πάσχα, and a few others such
as γειώρας, γομορ, and χερουβ.

In this survey I have tried to bring into perspective all
parts of the Pentateuch vocabulary. It has been possible only
to consider a selection of examples, but these do give a fair
indication of the various elements in it. It is clear that a
very considerable part of the vocabulary is made up of well-
attested words and uses, whether new in the Koine or surviving
from Classical Greek. Although there are undoubtedly numerous
words and uses peculiar to Biblical Greek, they must be considered in relation to the vocabulary as a whole. They in fact
form only a small proportion of the total vocabulary.[29]

---

28. On this word see esp. Daniel, *Recherches* 367f.

29. For what it may be worth, an estimate of their extent may
be given. I have counted roughly 450 words and uses unattested
outside Biblical and related literature. Of these not more than
half could be considered peculiar to the Biblical vocabulary.
(The total number of words and uses in the vocabulary must be
well over 6,000.)

CHAPTER IV

NEW SEMANTIC DEVELOPMENTS
IN OLD WORDS

The use of many old words in new senses is a well-known
characteristic of the Koine. It is the purpose of this chapter
to show that the vocabulary of the Pentateuch is in close
agreement with many of the developments of this kind that had
taken place by the third century B.C. The examples selected are
those for which adequate evidence exists from the translators'
own time.

Some words are examined in detail, others more briefly,
with a note merely of the new sense, its occurrences in the
Pentateuch, and one or two examples close in time and place to
the Pentateuch. This briefer treatment has been given especially to the more straightforward examples and to those that
are well known or have been considered fully by others. It has
however been necessary to notice in this way some examples of
which a more detailed treatment would be useful.

The words have been grouped as far as possible according
to subject-matter. We begin with a number of agricultural
terms. Such terms are often required in the Pentateuch, and
are also of course very common in documents of the time.

παράδεισος[1]

Originally a borrowing of a Persian word[2] π. appears
first in Greek in Xenophon, who uses it specifically of the
parks or pleasure-grounds of the Persian kings and nobles. The
two features of a παράδεισος mentioned by X. are trees of all
kinds, An. 2.4.14 ἐγγὺς παραδείσου μεγάλου καὶ καλοῦ καὶ δασέος
παντοίων δένδρων, cf. Oec. 4.14, and wild animals for hunting,

---

1. Cf. Deissmann, BS 148, MM, Grenfell in PRev. Laws, pp.
94ff., Petropoulos in PSA Athen., pp.101-3.

2. "aw. [Avestan] pairi-daēza- m. 'Umwallung, Ummauerung' (= gr.
*περι-τοιχος) entsprechenden mitteliran. *pardēz, np. palēz
'Garten'", Frisk.

53

An. 1.2.7 ἐνταῦθα Κύρῳ βασίλεια ἦν καὶ παράδεισος μέγας ἀγρίων θηρίων πλήρης, ἃ ἐκεῖνος ἐθήρευεν ἀπὸ ἵππου, cf. e.g. *HG* 4.1.15. Presumably it also had, as the etymology suggests, a surrounding wall, though X. never mentions one.

The word is used in a similar way in Thphr. *HP* 4.4.1.

In the third century B.C. it had become an ordinary agricultural term like κῆπος, ἀμπελών, etc., having lost its earlier restricted application. From the papyri of this time, in which it is very common, its usage appears somewhat as follows.

It is clear first of all that a παράδεισος was composed chiefly of fruit-trees of various kinds, though it might, as the following example shows, also contain vines. In *PCair.zen.* 33 (257 B.C.) the writer explains to Apollonius, who had sent men to obtain fruit-trees, that he showed the men around the παράδεισοι, (1.3) ... περιαγαγὼν πάντας τοὺς παραδείσους ἔδειξα, and they took away with them a selection of fruit-trees and vines. A detailed list of what they took is added. This names fig-trees of six kinds, pomegranate, apricot, apple, and eleven varieties of vine. Elsewhere olives also are frequently mentioned in connexion with παράδεισοι, e.g. *PCair.zen.* 184.2 (255 B.C.) τὰ φυτὰ τῶν ἐλαῶν λαβὲ ἔκ τε τοῦ παραδείσου τοῦ ἡμετέρου καὶ ἐκ τῶν κήπων τῶν ἐμ Μέμφει, cf. 125.2 (256 B.C.).

In addition trees other than fruit-trees might be planted in a παράδεισος: in *PCair.zen.* 157.2 (256 B.C.) Apollonius gives orders that firs are to be planted in the παράδεισος (and elsewhere) on his estate: τῶν στροβίλων φύτευσον δι'ὅλου τοῦ παραδείσου καὶ περὶ τὸν ἀμπελῶνα καὶ τοὺς ἐλαιῶνας, and in 125.2 (256 B.C.) he commends Zenon's action in planting bay-trees there. It is clear however that παράδεισοι were culti-vated primarily for their produce rather than for decoration. Cf. e.g. *PPetr.* 1.16.2.7 (230 B.C.) τὰ γενήματα τῶν ὑπαρχόντων μοι παραδείσων, and *OGI* 90.15 (196 B.C.), *PTeb.* 5.53 (118 B.C.), both quoted in MM.

παράδεισοι are mentioned frequently in the papyri and were clearly a common feature of agriculture in Ptolemaic Egypt.[3]

---

3. They were however not confined to Egypt: see *PDura* 15.1 (ii B.C.).

Thus the word no longer describes something owned only by the
few. From the *PPetr.* example above we see that one person might
own, or at least have under his control, more than one παράδεισος.

As to the possibility of a wall surrounding the παράδεισος
the papyri give no clear information and it is impossible to say
whether or not a wall was an essential feature.[4] It is reasonable to suppose, however, that the valuable crop contained in a
παράδεισος would often have been protected in this way. That
παράδεισοι needed protection is clear from the mention of
παραδεισοφύλακες in *PCair.Zen.* 690.22 (iii B.C.).[5]

A παράδεισος, then, may be defined as 'an area of culti-
vated ground containing chiefly fruit-trees, at times also
other types of tree, vines, and possibly other plants, and perhaps protected by a wall'. There is no exact equivalent to
this term in English. 'Orchard' is probably the nearest to it.[6]
'Garden' is unsatisfactory, suggesting an area planted mainly
or only with vegetables or flowers, and a παράδεισος was
clearly not a 'garden' in that sense. The usual word in iii
B.C. for that type of garden seems to have been κῆπος, from
which παράδεισος is distinguished e.g. in *PPetr.* 3.26.6 (iii
B.C.) ἐὰν ἔμβηι βοῦς ἢ ὑποζύγιον ... εἰς ἀλλότριον κλῆρον ἢ
παράδεισον ἢ κῆπον ἢ ἀμπελῶνα .... Cf. also *PCair.Zen.*184
quoted above.

It is this word that the translators used (13 times altogether) to render גן in the story of the Garden of Eden in
Ge. 2 and 3, and the reason for their choice is clear. The
Garden of Eden is exactly what would have been called in iii
B.C. Egypt a παράδεισος. The description shows that its main
feature was fruit-trees, with possibly a number of trees of
other types as well.[7]

---

4. In *PCair.Zen.* 825.13f. (252 B.C.) a quantity of bricks is
referred to as coming, so it seems, from a παράδεισος.
Perhaps they were taken from the wall surrounding it.

5. There is definite evidence for walls surrounding vineyards,
Schnebel, *Landwirtschaft* 242ff.

6. So MM. π. is always an 'orchard' also for Rostovtzeff, *A
Large Estate in Egypt in the Third Century B.C.*, Madison, 1922,
e.g. 42.

7. There is no mention of a wall anywhere in the Genesis
account.

Ge. 2.8-9 καὶ ἐφύτευσεν κύριος ὁ θεὸς παράδεισον ἐν Εδεμ ...(9)
καὶ ἐξανέτειλεν ὁ θεὸς ἔτι ἐκ τῆς γῆς πᾶν ξύλον ὡραῖον εἰς ὅρασιν
καὶ καλὸν εἰς βρῶσιν καὶ τὸ ξύλον τῆς ζωῆς ἐν μέσῳ τῷ παραδείσῳ
καὶ τὸ ξύλον τοῦ εἰδέναι γνωστὸν καλοῦ καὶ πονηροῦ.

Compare

2.16 ᾿Απὸ παντὸς ξυλοῦ τοῦ ἐν τῷ παραδείσῳ βρώσει φάγῃ, (17) ἀπὸ
δὲ τοῦ ξύλου τοῦ γινώσκειν καλὸν καὶ πονηρόν, οὐ φάγεσθε ἀπ᾿αὐτοῦ.

The word is similarly used twice elsewhere in the Pentateuch, again translating גן :

Ge. 13.10 εἶδεν πᾶσαν τὴν περίχωρον τοῦ Ιορδάνου ὅτι πᾶσα ἦν
ποτιζομένη ... ὡς ὁ παράδεισος τοῦ θεοῦ.

Nu. 24.5-6 ὡς καλοί σου οἱ οἶκοι, Ιακωβ, αἱ σκηναί σου, Ισραηλ·
(6) ὡσεὶ νάπαι σκιάζουσαι καὶ ὡσεὶ παράδεισοι ἐπὶ ποταμῶν.[8]

παρίστημι

In addition to its numerous other uses, this word had
developed in iii B.C. a specialized sense as an agricultural
term, viz. 'be ripe', 'be fully grown' (intrans.), of crops.[9]

---

8 J. Jeremias, *TWNT* V 766, considers that the LXX use of the
word of God's garden involves a change of meaning: 'In Jewish-
Gk., from the LXX on, it is used esp. for the garden of God in
the creation story ... More exactly God's garden as distinct
from secular parks is ὁ παράδεισος τοῦ θεοῦ ... or ὁ παράδεισος
τῆς τρυφῆς ... This involves a notable shift in meaning; the
LXX has moved the term from the profane sphere to the religious.'
This seems to me quite mistaken. The mere fact of using a word
in a religious context - and that is all the Pentateuch translators have done with παράδεισος - does not change its meaning.
Is there a shift in meaning in the word 'garden' when used in
the phrase 'God's garden'? There is no change in the meaning of
π. until it is used as the technical term for a particular
religious idea, and J. himself notes that this step came later:
'Test.L.18.10 was then the first to give the simple word the
technical sense of "Paradise".' Cf. Barr's remarks on the
supposed semantic change in ἀλήθεια and the like in *NT* Gk.,
Semantics 249.
      LSJ similarly classify the *Ge.* use as a separate sense, s.v.
3, giving the meaning as *the garden of Eden*, a manifest
impossibility.

9. Its connexion with the other senses of the word is not
obvious. Perhaps it derives from the sense of 'to be here', 'to
have come' (LSJ s.v.II), the expression 'the crop has come'
being practically equivalent to 'the crop is ripe'. Similarly
Conybeare-Stock, *ad loc*.

So clearly in *OGI* 56.68 (Egypt, iii B.C.) ὅταν ὁ πρώϊμος σπόρος παραστῆι, ἀναφέρειν τὰς ἱερὰς παρθένους στάχυς τοὺς παρατεθησομένους τῶι ἀγάλματι τῆς θεοῦ. *PPetr.* 3.43(3).14 (241 B.C.) οὐκ ἀγνοεῖς ὧς σοι διελέγην περὶ τοῦ σησάμου καὶ κρότωνος ὅτι παρέστηκεν.

This must be what is meant also in *PLille* 8.5 (iii B.C.) γεωργῶ γῆν βασιλικὴν (ἀρουρῶν) ρξ, καὶ ἡ γῆ παρέστηκεν. (ἡ γῆ = the crop on it, by a common figure of speech, cf. Eng. 'mow a field'.) The writer of this letter asks for certain draught animals to be returned to him, so that, he explains, he can pay the assessment on the produce of his land (paid in kind): ll. 13f. ὅπως δύνωμαι ἀναπληροῦν τὰ ἐκφόρια τῆς γῆς. In other words, so that he can begin harvesting his crop.

No other examples outside the LXX are recorded except 1 *Ep.Cl.* 23.4 = 2 *Ep.Cl.* 11.3 σταφυλὴ παρεστηκυῖα, in a quotation of unknown origin (Bauer). There is however a very similar use in Thphr. *CP* 6.14.10 ὁ οἶνος τότε μάλιστα παρίσταται 'improves, becomes fit for drinking', LSJ (s.v., B.V.3.a); perhaps 'is mature'.

The Pentateuch provides a clear example of this use:

Ex. 9.31 τὸ δὲ λίνον καὶ ἡ κριθὴ ἐπλήγη· ἡ γὰρ κριθὴ παρεστη-κυῖα, τὸ δὲ λίνον σπερματίζον. (32) ὁ δὲ πυρὸς καὶ ἡ ὀλύρα οὐκ ἐπλήγη· ὄψιμα γὰρ ἦν.

MT   השעה אביב , 'the barley was in the ear', RSV.

The translation is an accurate yet fully idiomatic rendering of the Hebrew original.[10]

καταφυτεύω

This compound is attested first in a letter of Darius of the early fifth century B.C., *SIG* 22.13, with the meaning 'transplant', τὴν ἐμὴν ἐκπονεῖς γῆν, τοὺς πέραν Εὐφράτου καρποὺς ἐπὶ τὰ κάτω τῆς Ἀσίας μέρη καταφυτεύων. So probably also in Posidon. 58 M (ii/i B.C.), Str. 15.3.11.

---

10. It may be noted in passing that the use of πλήσσω of the devastation of crops, although of course here a literal render-ing of the Hb. (נכה), was not unfamiliar in the translators' time, cf. *PPetr.* 2.23(1).2 (iii B.C.) καὶ ἡ ζέη ἡ δὲ κριθὴ ἐπλήγη. It is not recorded otherwise outside LXX.

In the Pentateuch, however, it is found in the sense of
'plant', being synonymous with the older word φυτεύω (itself
used seven times). *Le*. 19.23 καταφυτεύσετε πᾶν ξύλον βρώσιμον,
De. 6.11 ἀμπελῶνας καὶ ἐλαιῶνας, οὓς οὐ κατεφύτευσας, *Ex*. 15.17.
Cf. φυτεύω e.g. in *De*. 28.30,39 ἀμπελῶνα φυτεύσεις. Both words
render MT נטע in all their occurrences.

This use of καταφυτεύω, previously noted elsewhere only in
Pl.*Cim*.13, Luc.*VH* 2.42, can now be quoted from papyri contemporary with the Pentateuch. E.g. *PCair.Zen*. 157.1-3 (256 B.C.),
where it is interchanged with φυτεύω:

τῶν στροβίλων φύτευσον δι'ὅλου τοῦ παραδείσου ..., καὶ ὅπως
πλείονα μάλιστα μὲν φυτά, εἰ δὲ μή, μὴ ἐλάσσω τῶν τ
καταφυτεύσεις.

Also *PCol.Zen*. 42.2 (254 B.C.), 75.38 (c.248-6 B.C.).

Other words of the group are attested only in post-Classical Greek: καταφυτεία ii B.C. pap.+, καταφύτευσις LXX,
κατάφυτος Plb. +.[11]

κουρά, 'fleece', *De*. 18.4 τὴν ἀπαρχὴν τῶν κουρῶν τῶν προβάτων
σου δώσεις αὐτῷ, *PCair.Zen*. 433.26 (iii B.C.) ἔχουσιν τά τε
πρόβατα καὶ τὰς κουράς.

πεδίον, 'land or piece of land appropriated to pasture or
tillage', 'field', *Ge*. 37.7 ᾤμην ἡμᾶς δεσμεύειν δράγματα ἐν μέσῳ
τῷ πεδίῳ, *Le*. 25.12 ἀπὸ τῶν πεδίων φάγεσθε τὰ γενήματα αὐτῆς.
Ex. 9.3, al., *PHib*. 63.10 (265 B.C.) ἔφη καθέξειν τὸν χόρτον
μου τὸν ἐν τῶι πεδίωι, *PCair.Zen*. 362.23 (242 B.C.) ἡ δὲ τοιαύτη
ἐστὶν διὰ πάντων τῶν πεδίων, others in Preisigke. (This sense is
not noted by LSJ).

χλωρόν, τό, subst., 'plant', a general term covering all types
of green plant; esp. in pl. 'green-stuffs', 'green fodder',
Nu. 22.4 ... ὡς ἐκλείξαι ὁ μόσχος τὰ χλωρὰ ἐκ τοῦ πεδίου, *Ge*.
2.5, *De*. 29.22 (both sing.), often papyri, e.g. *PSI* 400.14

---

11. The example illustrates the well-known fondness of the
Koine 'for composite verbs where the classical language was
content with the simple forms', Bl. DF §116.1.

(iii B.C.) ὄσα δ'ἂν χλωρὰ τὰ κτήνη ἐξανηλώσηι σου ἀνυπόλογόν σοι οἴσω, *PHib.* 112.9,117.4 (both iii B.C.).[12]

In the next group are a number of legal and other technical terms.

ἐκδέχομαι

The use of this word in iii B.C. in the non-Classical sense of 'stand surety for', or more precisely 'make oneself responsible for, guarantee, the due appearance or payment of' (a person, sum of money), is definitely established.[13] Thus e.g. in *PCair.Zen.* 36.26 (257 B.C.) a sum of 3000 drachmae comprising a στέφανος is advanced on the guarantee of Apollonius to Epikydes: ... ὁ στέφανος τῶι βασιλεῖ, ὃν ἐξεδέξατο ᾽Απολλώνιος ᾽Επικύδει. Similarly in 636.4 (iii B.C.) the writer, interceding on behalf of an arrested person, guarantees his not absconding if released: ἐάν σοι δόξηι ἀφεῖναι αὐτόν, ἐγδέχομαι αὐτὸν μονῆς.[14] Cf. 323.4 (250-249 B.C.), *PPetr.* 3.64.b.6 (iii B.C.).

In the papyrus example cited by LSJ (s.v. I.7) the construction is slightly different: *PSI* 349.1 (254/3 B.C.) καλῶς ἂν ποιήσαις ἐγδεξάμενος ἡμᾶς πρὸς τὸν τελώνην Ζήνωνα τοῦ κίκιος. Here the acc. after ἐκδέχομαι is not the object guaranteed (the castor-oil), but the person on whose *behalf* the guarantee is given. Similarly *PCol.Zen.*121.3 (181 B.C.) ... σὺν οἷς ἐξεδέξατο ὑμᾶς ῞Αρπαλος, (τάλαντα) ιγ, 'along with the amounts for which H. has become surety on your behalf, 13 talents'.

The existence of this sense is demonstrated also by ἐκδοχή 'giving of security', ἔκδοχος 'surety', cited by LSJ (and Suppl.) from iii B.C. papyri.

---

12. Cf. Schnebel, *Landwirtschaft* 213ff.; D.B. Bagiakakos, ᾽Αθηνᾶ LVIII (1954) 100ff., with details of this use and others like it in Mod. Gk. dialects.
13. Cf. Mayser, *Gramm.* II.ii 191f.
   The same use is found with ἀναδέχομαι in Class. and later Gk.
14. For ἐγ = ἐκ see Mayser, *Gramm.* I.i 226.

60

The usual Classical word for the idea was ἐγγυάω, found
also in later Greek (but not in the Pentateuch or *NT*).

In *Ge*. 43.9 ἐκδέχομαι is found in exactly this sense.[15]
Judas makes himself responsible for bringing Benjamin back safe
and sound from Egypt:

ἐγὼ δὲ ἐκδέχομαι αὐτόν, ἐκ χειρός μου ζήτησον αὐτόν· ἐὰν
μὴ ἀγάγω αὐτὸν πρὸς σὲ καὶ στήσω αὐτὸν ἐναντίον σου,
ἡμαρτηκὼς ἔσομαι ...

ἐκδέχομαι renders Hebrew ערב , 'go surety for' the safety of, BDB.

The other occurrence in the Pentateuch, *Ge*. 44.32 raises a
typical problem of LXX lexicography.

ὁ γὰρ παῖς σου ἐκδέδεκται τὸ παιδίον παρὰ τοῦ πατρὸς λέγων
'Εὰν μὴ ἀγάγω αὐτὸν .. (as in 43.9).

If the Greek is considered alone, it seems necessary, with παρὰ
τοῦ πατρός following, to take ἐκδέδεκται as 'received', a possible sense of the word. A comparison of the original, however,
shows that the construction is due to mechanical rendering of
the Hebrew and that ἐκδέχομαι represents Hebrew ערב as before:
MT ערב את-נער מעם אבי . Therefore it would seem that the translators did intend ἐκδέδεκται in the sense of 'stand surety for'
despite the indications of the immediate context, and that we
must translate in some such way as 'your servant became surety
for the boy to my father'. Whether the sentence would have been
understood in this way by those who read it without knowledge of
the original is another matter.

διακούω, 'conduct a hearing', 'hear a case', *De*. 1.16 καὶ
ἐνετειλάμην τοῖς κριταῖς ὑμῶν ... λέγων Διακούετε ἀνὰ μέσον τῶν
ἀδελφῶν ὑμῶν καὶ κρίνατε δικαίως ἀνὰ μέσον ἀνδρὸς καὶ ...,
papyri, inscriptions, e.g. *PYale* 42.31 (229 B.C.) ὁ γὰρ βασιλεὺς
αὐτὸς καθήμενος διακούει, *OGI* 335.30 (ii/i B.C.), cf. Kiessling,
MM, s.v.

πάροικος, ο, 'stranger', 'temporary resident', 'resident alien',

---

15. Noted by LSJ. Cf. Conybeare-Stock *ad loc.*, 'perhaps "I
undertake him"'; Anz, *Subsidia* 377, 381.

Ge. 23.4, *Ex.* 2.22, etc., often inscriptions from iii B.C.
onwards, e.g. *OGI* 55.29, *SIG* 398.37 (both iii B.C.). Deissmann,
BS 227f., MM.

παροικέω, 'inhabit (a place, acc.) as a πάροικος', 'dwell as a
πάροικος', *Ge.* 12.10, 17.8, etc., *PSI* 677.2 (iii B.C.), *SIG*
709.9 (ii B.C.).

πρεσβύτερος as the designation of an official, or person in
authority, 'elder', *Ge.* 50.7, *Ex.* 17.5, 18.12, etc., often
papyri, inscriptions, see LSJ, MM, Deissmann, *BS* 154ff.

The translators likewise show their familiarity with a
number of new commercial terms that were current in the Greek of
their time.

ἀπέχω
The very common Hellenistic use of this word with the
meaning 'to have received', especially as a technical term in
receipts, has been often noted and discussed.[16] Typical examples are *PHib.* 209.6 (263/2 B.C.) ὁμολογεῖ Λυσικράτης ...
ἀπέχειμ παρὰ Δημητρίου ... τὰ ἐκφόρια, Wilcken *Ostr.* 1027.3
(Ptol.) ἀπέχω παρὰ σοῦ τὸ ἐπιβάλλον μοι ἐκφόριον.

An early, non-technical, instance of it is found in
Aeschin. 2.50 ἀπέχετε, ἔφη, τὴν ἀπόκρισιν, καὶ λοιπὸν ὑμῖν ἐστι
βουλεύσασθαι, 'you have your answer ...', but this appears to be
isolated. Normally in Classical Greek the uses of ἀπέχω are
quite different, the most usual words for 'receive' (a sum of
money) being ἐκλαμβάνω and ἀπολαμβάνω (the latter also in later
Greek). Note also that ἀποχή, 'receipt', is only late (iii B.C.
papyri +).

The Pentateuch has two examples of this use; both are
present tense (not past), in full accordance with contemporary
usage. In *Ge.* 43.23 Joseph's steward replies as follows to
Joseph's brothers, who, on their second visit to Egypt, have

16. Deissmann, *BS* 229, *LAE* 110ff.; Mayser, *Gramm.* I.i 487, with
references to other discussions there. Examples especially in
MM, Kiessling.

offered to return the money they found in their sacks after the first visit:

῞Ιλεως ὑμῖν, μὴ φοβεῖσθε· ὁ θεὸς ὑμῶν ... ἔδωκεν ὑμῖν θησαυροὺς ἐν τοῖς μαρσίπποις ὑμῶν, τὸ δὲ ἀργύριον ὑμῶν εὐδοκιμοῦν ἀπέχω.

'I have received your money, which was quite genuine', that is to say, I have received payment for the grain purchased on the first visit; there is no need to return the money found in the sacks.

Nu. 32.19 οὐκέτι κληρονομήσωμεν ἐν αὐτοῖς ἀπὸ τοῦ πέραν τοῦ Ιορδάνου καὶ ἐπέκεινα, ὅτι ἀπέχομεν τοὺς κλήρους ἡμῶν ἐν τῷ πέραν τοῦ Ι. ἐν ἀνατολαῖς.

In both cases the LXX rendering neatly paraphrases the idiomatic Hebrew of the original: כספכם בא אלי in the former, באה נחלתנו אלינו in the latter.

γόμος

Originally γόμος was used specifically of a ship's load, 'cargo' (Hdt. 1.194, D. 32.4), only in later Greek of any load. The development runs parallel to that in γεμίζω, at first used of loading ships, only later of animals, etc.

The later use appears in the one example of the word in the Pentateuch:

Ex. 23.5 ἐὰν δὲ ἴδῃς τὸ ὑποζύγιον τοῦ ἐχθροῦ σου πεπτωκὸς ὑπὸ τὸν γόμον αὐτοῦ ... (MT משאו)

A contemporary example of this use, which was previously not known before i A.D. apart from the LXX (examples in MM, LSJ), is now available:

PCol.Zen. 2.8 (259 B.C., an account of earnings of a camel caravan) ἀπὸ τῶν Σκηνῶν εἰς Αἴγυπτον γόμων δ̄ φοινίκων καμήλων δ̄ μισθὸς (δραχμαὶ) ρδ.

'From the Tents to Egypt, 4 loads of dates, 4 camels, pay, 104 dr.' (ed.).

ὁλκή

In Classical Greek the main meanings were 'drawing',

'dragging'; 'inhalation'; 'attraction' (LSJ). The new use, in the sense of 'weight', is attested first in Arist., *Mir.* 833^b 10 λέγουσι δ'ἐν τῇ Παιονίᾳ οὕτω χρυσίζειν τὴν γῆν ὥστε πολλοὺς εὑρηκέναι καὶ ὑπὲρ μνᾶν χρυσίου ὁλκήν. Then Men. 325 (Körte), Thphr. *HP* 9.16.8. For this idea the usual Classical word was σταθμός.

To the examples in inscriptions noted by LSJ can be added numerous instances in Egyptian papyri of iii B.C., e.g. *PCair. Zen.* 327.102 φιάλη οὗ ὁλκὴ σξ, 774.4 ἔχει Νικάνωρ πόνους λα ὧν ὁλκὴ τά(λαντον) α. Similarly 851.9,16, *PMich.Zen.* 120.6,7.

The word is used in the same way in the Pentateuch:

Ge. 24.22 ἔλαβεν ὁ ἄνθρωπος ἐνώτια χρυσᾶ ἀνὰ δραχμὴν ὁλκῆς καὶ δύο ψέλια ἐπὶ τὰς χεῖρας αὐτῆς, δέκα χρυσῶν ὁλκὴ αὐτῶν.

'... golden ear-rings each a drachma in weight and two braclets [he put] on her hands, their weight ten χρυσοῖ.'[17]

Nu. 7.13-79 *passim* τρυβλίον ἀργυροῦν ἕν, τριάκοντα καὶ ἑκατὸν ὁλκὴ αὐτοῦ.

In all instances ὁλκή renders משקל 'weight'.

χρυσοῦς

The ordinary adjectival use of χρυσοῦς is of course common in later Greek and occurs frequently in the Pentateuch. The use that concerns us here is that of ὁ χρυσοῦς as the name of a measure of value and weight,[18] attested from iii B.C. onwards, both in Egypt and elsewhere. A χρυσοῦς was equivalent to 20 silver drachmae, though it appears that, at least in Ptolemaic Egypt, there was no actual gold coin of that value and weight minted. The term derives from earlier στατὴρ χρυσοῦς (a stater = 20 drachmae), e.g. Ar. *Pl.* 816, cf. στατὴρ χρυσοῦ Pl. *Euthd.* 299e, Hdt. 1.54, but in iii B.C. it had become simply ὁ χρυσοῦς,

---

17. The idiomatic use of ἀνά (Class. and later Gk., LSJ s.v. C.III, MM) is noteworthy (ἀνὰ δρ. ὁλκ. ~ בקע משקלו). For the χρυσοῦς see below.
18. See e.g. C.C. Edgar, *Aegyptus* IV (1923) 79; *PLille* I p.270; A. Segrè, *Metrologia e circolazione monetaria degli antichi,* Bologna, 1928, 261, 267.

and στατήρ is not to be thought of as always 'understood'.

Examples of the χρυσοῦς as a sum of money are *PMich.Zen.* 28.11 (256 B.C.) εἰς ζ τοῦ χρυσοῦ ἀρ(τάβας), 'at the rate of seven artabs to the χρυσοῦς'; *PCair.Zen.* 194.10 (255 B.C.) [ἔστιν δὲ ἡ τιμὴ τῶν υι] εἰς ιβ τοῦ χρυσοῦ ⊢χπγ = 'the value of the 410 (jars), at 12 (jars) to the χρυσοῦς, is 683 drachmae 2 obols'. It is attested also in inscriptions (see LSJ, and index to *SIG*), Plb., and later papyri (Preisigke, MM). In reference to weight it is found in *PLille* 6.13 (iii B.C.) ἀφείλοντό μου κρόκης καὶ στήμονος ὁλκὴν μνᾶς τρεῖς χρυσῶι ἐλάσσω, 'they took from me wool (literally woof and warp) in weight three minae less one χρυσοῦς'.

It is interesting to find that the translators have made use of this term a number of times in the Pentateuch. As a sum of money it occurs in

Ge. 37.28 καὶ ἀπέδοντο τὸν Ιωσηφ τοῖς Ισμαηλίταις εἴκοσι χρυσῶν   MT   בעשרים כסף

Ge. 45.22 καὶ πᾶσιν ἔδωκεν [Ιωσηφ]δισσὰς στολάς, τῷ δὲ Βενιαμιν ἔδωκεν τριακοσίους χρυσοῦς
MT   שלש מאות כסף

The use of χρυσοῦς as a rendering of כסף is unexpected, but in the case of *Ge.* 37.28 it is possible to suggest a particular reason for it. If כסף were rendered as the ordinary silver coin, δραχμή, the sum paid for Joseph would seem abnormally low. Prices of slaves in iii B.C. Egypt of course vary considerably, but a price less than 100 drachmae for a male slave would be unusual, and figures between 100 and 300 drachmae are more often mentioned.[19] In *PSI* 406 (iii B.C.) 300 drachmae are paid for a girl slave. The same difficulty would be felt with δίδραχμον, which was also available and is used by the translators elsewhere (though usually as a rendering of שקל), and with ἀργύριον, which in any case was not normally used as the name of a specific coin or sum of money in the translators' time. These were, as far as I know, the only terms available to the

---

19. Cf. W.L. Westermann, *Upon Slavery in Ptolemaic Egypt*, New York, 1929, 60f.

translators if they wished to render כסף literally. It would seem therefore that they avoided a literal rendering in order to make the sum for which Joseph was sold a more realistic one, viz. 400 drachmae.

No such reason can be offered for the rendering in *Ge*. 45.22. We can only suppose that the translators felt justified in interpreting כסף freely in order to enhance the value of the gift to Benjamin.

In the remaining examples, fourteen in all, χρυσοῦς is used as a measure of weight, rendering Hebrew זהב.

Ge. 24.22 καὶ δύο ψέλια ἐπὶ τὰς χεῖρας αὐτῆς, δέκα χρυσῶν ὁλκὴ αὐτῶν.[20]

MT עשרה זהב משקלם

Nu. 7.13-14 καὶ προσήνεγκεν τὸ δῶρον αὐτοῦ τρυβλίον ἀργυροῦν ἕν, τριάκοντα καὶ ἑκατὸν ὁλκὴ αὐτοῦ, φιάλην μίαν ἀργυρᾶν ἑβδομήκοντα σίκλων ...· (14) θυίσκην μίαν δέκα χρυσῶν πλήρη θυμιάματος.

The same words are repeated eleven times in vss. 20-80. Then in 7.86 the total weight of the twelve censers is given:

θυίσκαι χρυσαῖ δώδεκα πλήρεις θυμιάματος· πᾶν τὸ χρυσίον τῶν θυισκῶν εἴκοσι καὶ ἑκατὸν χρυσοῖ

The translators' use of this term illustrates very well their familiarity with the business terminology and practice of their time. It shows also their concern for producing an up-to-date version of the Hebrew text. They have taken care here to use a term with which their audience would be familiar. It seems also that they have tried to render realistically according to current monetary values, even though this has meant departing from the literal meaning of the original.

The next examples are two words used idiomatically in

---

20. Ten χρυσοῖ = approx. 25 oz (1 drachma being equivalent to 3.63 grams: David and van Groningen, *Papyrological Primer* 33*). Presumably this is the weight of both bracelets together, so each weighs 12½ oz. They are thus fairly heavy, but certainly not impossible.

the sense of 'be ill'.

ἐνοχλέω

The Classical senses were 'trouble', 'annoy', 'be a
bother', and these continue in the Koine. But we find in addition an interesting semantic development in the passive.
ἐνοχλοῦμαι, 'be bothered', comes also to mean 'be unwell, ill'.
For this sense MM cited PPetr. 2.25(a).12 (iii B.C.) εἰς ἵππον
ἐνοχλούμενον.[21] To this can be added a clear example of the use
applied to persons, PCair.Zen. 812.5 (257 B.C.) Μένης περὶ τοῦ
ἀγοραζομένου μέλιτος τοῖς ἐνοχλουμένοις (note on the verso of a
letter), and this is almost certainly the meaning in numerous
other places where the word could be, and has usually been,
taken as 'be busy, occupied': e.g. 816.7 (257 B.C.) ἐπεὶ [οὖν]
αὐτὸς οὐ δεδύνημαι παραγενέσθαι διὰ τὸ ἐνωχλῆσθαι, 396.2, 516.8,
PCol.Zen. 6.1 (all iii B.C.).[22]

The word quite clearly has this sense in its one occurrence in the Pentateuch:

Ge. 48.1 ἀπηγγέλη τῷ Ιωσηφ ὅτι ᾽Ο πατήρ σου ἐνοχλεῖται.

MT   חלה

The context shows that Joseph's father is ill and about to die
(his death is described in 49.33); moreover, the translators
could not have failed to know the meaning of חלה .[23]

μαλακίζομαι also develops the sense of 'be ill' in the Koine
(though from a quite different starting-point, 'be soft, weak'):
Ge. 42.38, Arist. HA 605a 25, PSI 420.16 (iii B.C.), Sammelb.

---

21. Similarly also 2.25(b).12,17, PMich.Zen. 21.8 (both iii B.C.).

22. Cf. Edgar's note on PCair.Zen. 812: 'perhaps the latter
meaning ["to be indisposed"] is more common than has been recognized'.
    This use is no doubt due to euphemism, which is common in
words for illness. Eng. disease shows exactly the same semantic
development as the Gk. word: orig. 'lack of ease', 'uneasiness',
'trouble'(cf. Ullmann, Semantics 187).

23. The same use is found elsewhere in LXX, e.g. 1 Ki. 19.14,
but not in NT, and has not survived into Mod. Gk. It probably
fell out of use in the later Koine. No pap. examples later than
iii B.C. are known to me, and Pollux, Onom. 3.104, listing words
for the idea, does not mention it.

158.2. Anz, *subsidia* 347f. (μαλακία and μαλακός show parallel
developments.)

Two words connected with imprisonment are also conveniently grouped together.

ἐξάγω

In iii B.C. this was the word commonly used for 'release'
from prison. More precisely, two uses may be distinguished:
(a) 'lead out', 'release', of the action e.g. of a gaoler; (b)
'cause to be released', of the action of any person instrumental
in getting a prisoner released. The former, though not actually
attested before iii B.C., is merely a particular application of
the basic sense of the verb and could be old. The latter, also
not found before iii B.C., may reasonably be regarded as a new
development. ἐξάγω in this sense forms a pair with its opposite
ἀπάγω, the usual word in Classical and later Greek for 'arrest',
'put in prison'.

The literal sense of ἐξάγω is felt e.g. in *PHib*. 73.11
(243-2 B.C.) ὁ φυλακίτης παραγενόμενος εἰς τὸ δεσμωτήριον τὸ ἐν
Σινάρυ ἐξήγαγεν τὸν Καλλίδρομον [ἐκ τοῦ δεσμωτηρίου], cf. *PCol.
zen*. 155(f).2 (250 B.C.). But in *PCair.zen*. 619.5 (iii B.C.)
the more developed sense is found. The writer explains that he
had been imprisoned, and continues: Ζήνων δὲ ἀκούσας ἐξήγα[γεν
– δέομαι οὖν] σοῦ, βασιλεῦ .... ἐξήγαγεν is not 'led me out',
but 'got me released', since Zenon was an important official,
not the gaoler. Cf. *PPetr*. 2.4(7).5 (c. 255 B.C.).

The examples in the Pentateuch are:

Ge. 40.14 μνησθήσῃ περὶ ἐμοῦ Φαραω καὶ ἐξάξεις με ἐκ
τοῦ ὀχυρώματος τούτου. MT והוצאתני

The use of ἐξάγω here is closely paralleled by the example in
PCair.zen. 619 above. 'Make mention of me to Pharaoh and secure
my release from this prison'.

Ge. 41.14 Φαραω ἐκάλεσεν τὸν Ιωσηφ, καὶ ἐξήγαγον αὐτὸν
ἐκ τοῦ ὀχυρώματος καὶ ἐξύρησαν αὐτόν ...
MT ויריצהו
ἐξήγαγον Rahlfs, with DEM etc.; ἐξήγαγεν A.

ὀχύρωμα

Attested first in Xenophon, *HG* 3.2.3. οἱ δ' ἐπεὶ ἐτιτρώσκοντο
μὲν καὶ ἀπέθνησκον, ἐποίουν δ' οὐδὲν κατειργμένοι ἐν τῷ σταυρώ-
ματι ὡς ἀνδρομήκει ὄντι, διασπάσαντες τὸ αὐτῶν ὀχύρωμα ἐφέροντο
εἰς αὐτούς. Here the meaning of the word is as the etymology
would lead us to expect, namely 'fortification', the reference
in this context being to a palisade. It is not recorded again
until iii B.C., when it is found in the sense of 'prison' (as
well as 'fortification', 'fortress'), the line of development to
this meaning being quite straightforward: a fortress would
naturally have been often used as a prison.

Thus e.g. *PPetr.* 2.13(3).2 (258-3 B.C.) τὸ πρὸς νότον τοῦ
ὀχυρώματος τεῖχος μέρος μέν τι αὐτοῦ πεπτωκός ἐστιν. The
remainder of the document shows clearly that a prison is meant;
δεσμῶται are mentioned in 1.9. Cf. also *PPetr.* 2.13(4).3,5,10
(same date).

In the Pentateuch ὀχύρωμα occurs four times, always in
the sense of 'prison':

Ge. 39.20 καὶ λαβὼν ὁ κύριος Ιωσηφ ἐνέβαλεν αὐτὸν εἰς τὸ
ὀχύρωμα, εἰς τὸν τόπον, ἐν ᾧ οἱ δεσμῶται τοῦ βασιλέως
κατέχονται ἐκεῖ ἐν τῷ ὀχυρώματι. MT בית הסהר *bis*

Similarly 40.14 (MT הבית), 41.14 (MT הבור).

The near synonymity of ὀχύρωμα with the usual older word
δεσμωτήριον (also in papyri) is clear from the alternation of
the two words in this passage: the latter occurs in 39.22 *bis*
23; 40.3,5, rendering MT בית הַסֹּהַר in all.

The remaining examples cover a wide variety of subjects.
Most are the words for everyday activities such as 'ask',
'decide', 'speak', and common ideas such as 'side', 'here',
'owner'.

ἀξιόω

From iii B.C. onwards the most common use of this word is
in the sense of 'request', 'ask', a natural development from
the Classical senses of 'consider fitting', 'expect, require,

insist that'. Examples verging on the later use may be found
in Classical Greek, especially in Xenophon, e.g. *HG* 3.4.7
ἅτε γιγνώσκοντες πάντες τὸν Λύσανδρον, προσέκειντο αὐτῷ
ἀξιοῦντες διαπράττεσθαι αὐτὸν παρ᾽ Ἀγησιλάου ὧν ἐδέοντο, cf.
1.6.8, *An.* 5.6.2; Pl. *Phdr.* 255e.

This use may be illustrated from the translators' time by:

PCol.zen. 41.2 (c. 254 B.C.) προσῆλθόν τινες ἡμῖν τῶν
γνωρίμων ὑπὲρ Μητροδώρου ... ἀξιοῦντες γράψαι πρὸς σέ.

PTeb. 772.11 (236 B.C.) ἀξιῶ οὖν σε, εἴ σοι φαίνεται, γράψαι...

Cf. the numerous examples in Preisigke and especially Kiessling.

ἀξιόω occurs twice in the Pentateuch, once clearly as in
the papyri, viz.

Nu. 22.16 καὶ ἦλθον πρὸς Βαλααμ καὶ λέγουσιν αὐτῷ·Τάδε λέγει
Βαλακ ὁ τοῦ Σεπφωρ Ἀξιῶ σε, μὴ ὀκνήσῃς ἐλθεῖν πρός με.
MT   אל־נא תמנע

The other example is quite different, but will be examined
here for its own interest. It is found in the words spoken by
Laban, Jacob's father-in-law. Jacob, having departed in secret
with his family, has been pursued and overtaken by Laban, who
now reproaches him:

Ge. 31.27-8 καὶ εἰ ἀνήγγειλάς μοι, ἐξαπέστειλα ἄν σε μετ᾽
εὐφροσύνης καὶ μετὰ μουσικῶν, τυμπάνων καὶ κιθάρας. (28) οὐκ
ἠξιώθην καταφιλῆσαι τὰ παιδία μου καὶ τὰς θυγατέρας μου.
νῦν δὲ ἀφρόνως ἔπραξας.

It is difficult to decide precisely what is meant by ἀξιόω here.
'I was not considered worthy to kiss my children ...' may at
first sight seem correct,[24] and although this old sense of the
word is rare in the vernacular in iii B.C. compared with the
new one, it is possible to cite at least two examples, *PTeb.*
703.277, *Sammelb.* 5942.13 (both iii B.C.). There seem to me,
however, to be two difficulties with this. The first is that

---

24. So Bauer (s.v. 1.a), Brenton, Thomson-Muses. Schleusner
does not commit himself: ' נטש, *permitto*. Gen. 31.28. Libere
verterunt'.

of explaining the rendering in relation to the Hebrew. οὐκ
ἠξιώθην renders ולא נתשטו׳ , 'and you did not allow me'.
Although נטש is found only here in the sense of 'allow', its
usual senses being 'leave', 'let alone'; 'forsake', 'abandon',
this is unlikely to have caused the translators difficulty. The
context shows how נטש is to be taken, and they were clearly
familiar with the normal uses of the word, since they render it
accurately in its three other occurrences in the Pentateuch, *Ex*.
23.11 ἀνίημι, *Nu*. 11.31 ἐπιβάλλω, *De*. 32.15 ἐγκαταλείπω. It is
hard to see, therefore, why they would have taken the Hebrew as
'you did not think me worthy'.

Secondly, the meaning 'I was not considered worthy' (in
its literal sense) seems to me unsatisfactory in the context.
How does worthiness come into it at all? What is required is,
I suggest, 'I was not permitted, I was not given the opportunity',
and this would of course be almost the same as the meaning of
the Hebrew. There is as yet no evidence of such a sense for
ἀξιόω in the translators' time, but later Greek provides a
number of examples which seem close to it. *POxy*. 1837.16 (vi
A.D.) ὁ θεὸς ἀξιώσι ἡμᾶς προσκ(υνεῖν) ἐν οἰγίᾳ, 'God grant that
we may make our salutations to you in health', edd., similarly
1857.3, *PSI* 238.11 (both vi-vii A.D.); *Ep.I.Mag*. 2 ἐπεὶ οὖν
ἠξιώθην ἰδεῖν ὑμᾶς διὰ Δαμᾶ, similarly 14. In both these,
though it is possible to translate ἀξιόω as 'find worthy', it
is very close to just 'permit', 'give an opportunity to'. The
same use is found also in Modern Greek, e.g. in δὲν ἀξιώθηκε νὰ
ἰδῆ τὰ παιδιά του μεγάλα, 'he was not permitted to see his
children grow up'.[25] It is not impossible, therefore, that such
a use was current in iii B.C. Greek.

ἐνάρχομαι

In Classical Greek (E. +) a sacrificial technical term,
e.g. E. *IA* 1470 κανᾶ δ'ἐναρχέσθω τις. In the Koine from iii B.C.
onwards it is found in the sense of 'begin' generally, hardly
differing from ἄρχομαι. Thus e.g. *Sammelb*. 4369 b. 23 (iii B.C.)
μὴ οὖν ἄλλως ποιήσῃς, ὑπομένω γάρ σε ὥστε ἐνάρξασθαί σε, *PTeb*.

---

25. I am indebted to Mr. Papastavrou for this example.

24.36 (117 B.C.) ἐναρχομένου τ[οῦ Με]χείρ, and followed by inf.
Plb. 5.1.5 ἐνήρχοντο πολεμεῖν ἀλλήλοις.

    Similarly in the Pentateuch:

(a) abs.

    Ex. 12.18 ἐναρχομένου τῇ τεσσαρεσκαιδεκάτῃ ἡμέρᾳ τοῦ μηνὸς
τοῦ πρώτου ...
Similarly *Nu.* 9.5.

    Nu. 17.12 καὶ ἤδη ἐνήρκτο ἡ θραῦσις ἐν τῷ λαῷ.

(b) c. inf.

    De. 2.31 καὶ εἶπεν κύριος πρός με ᾽Ιδοὺ ἦργμαι παραδοῦναι
πρὸ προσώπου σου τὸν Σηων βασιλέα Εσεβων τὸν Αμορραῖον καὶ
τὴν γῆν αὐτοῦ· ἔναρξαι κληρονομῆσαι τὴν γῆν αὐτοῦ.
Similarly *De.* 2.24,25.

    In *De.* 2.31, where ἦργμαι and ἔναρξαι both render החל *hiph.*,
the latter appears to be merely a variation for the sake of
style. So also in *Nu.* 17.12 above: cf. the preceding verse
ἐξῆλθεν γὰρ ὀργὴ ἀπὸ προσώπου κυρίου, ἦρκται θραύειν τὸν λαόν.
Again both words render החל *hiph.*

κατατείνω

    In *Le.* 25.39ff. certain provisions are made regarding the
treatment of a fellow-Israelite (ὁ ἀδελφός σου) reduced to
servitude. These stress that whether he is sold into one's own
household (39-46) or into that of a stranger or sojourner (47-55)
he is not to be treated as if he were a slave, but a hired
servant: 39 οὐ δουλεύσει σοι δούλειαν οἰκέτου (40) ὡς μισθωτὸς
ἢ πάροικος ἔσται σοι. Provisions for his release in the year of
the ἄφεσις follow here, and then in 43 οὐ κατατενεῖς αὐτὸν ἐν τῷ
μόχθῳ καὶ φοβηθήσῃ κύριον τὸν θεόν σου. Similarly in the provisions regarding an Israelite sold to a stranger or sojourner:
53 ὡς μισθωτὸς ἐνιαυτὸν ἐξ ἐνιαυτοῦ ἔσται μετ᾽αὐτοῦ· οὐ
κατατενεῖς (1. κατατενεῖ? MT לא־ירדנו) αὐτὸν ἐν τῷ μόχθῳ
ἐνώπιόν σου. The verb occurs in the same expression once more
in this passage: vss. 44-46 explain that slaves are to be
purchased from among non-Israelite peoples, but, 46 goes on,

τῶν ἀδελφῶν ὑμῶν τῶν υἱῶν Ισραηλ ἕκαστος τὸν ἀδελφὸν αὐτοῦ οὐ κατατενεῖ αὐτὸν ἐν τοῖς μόχθοις.

The most suitable meaning for κατατείνω in this context seems to be 'overwork', 'strain'.[26] The implication of these regulations in the Greek then is that one must not exact from an Israelite in servitude the same amount of work as could be expected from an actual slave. To do so would be to overwork him. The Hebrew original is somewhat different, the word rendered by κατατείνω in these three instances being רדה 'rule', 'dominate' (so KB, BDB).

This is a new use of κατατείνω, though its development from earlier senses is easy. (In Classical Greek, Homer + , the main senses are 'stretch', 'stretch out'; 'rack', 'torture'; and intrans. 'extend'; 'strive'.[27]) A good parallel to it is provided by the following example from the second century B.C. (noted by LSJ).

> *PTeb.* 61[b] 197 (118-7 B.C.) = 72.115 (114-3 B.C.), both land surveys, with the same wording in both places: ... ὑπὲρ ὧν ἀπολογίζεται ὁ κωμογραμματεὺς εἶναι τὴν προσεξευρεθεῖσαν ὑπὸ ᾿Οσορ<ο>ήριος τοῦ γενομένου βασιλικοῦ γραμματέως ἐν τοῖς ἔμπροσθεν χρόνοις κατατείνειν τοὺς γεωργούς.

The editors translate '[the land] ... regarding which the komogrammateus reports that it is the land which was found by Osoroëris ... to have put in former times too heavy a tax upon the powers of the cultivators'. The piece of land concerned is thereby registered as unproductive.

The use is not as yet known elsewhere (not *NT* or elsewhere in LXX).

μέρος

In the Pentateuch, as also in other parts of the LXX, this

---

26. Cf. Schleusner, s.v.: 'non *conficies* illum labore'.
   I note as a curiosity the meaning given to it by N.H. Snaith, *Leviticus and Numbers* (Century Bible) 167: 'hold down tight' (due to confusion with Lat. *teneo*?).
27. LSJ's examples under I.7.a 'metaph. *strain, exert*' are not the same as the Pent. use.

word is frequently to be found in contexts where the only possible meaning for it is 'side'. E.g.

Ex. 32.15 πλάκες λίθιναι καταγεγραμμέναι ἐξ ἀμφοτέρων τῶν
μερῶν αὐτῶν, ἔνθεν καὶ ἔνθεν ἦσαν γεγραμμέναι

MT   לחת כתבים משני עבריהם מזה ומזה הם כתבים

Clearly 'part' will not do here. The meaning is 'written on
both their sides'. (ἔνθεν καὶ ἔνθεν is normal Greek for 'on
this side and on that', see LSJ s.v. I.1.)

Nu. 8.3 καὶ ἐποίησεν οὕτως Ααρων· ἐκ τοῦ ἑνὸς μέρους κατὰ
πρόσωπον τῆς λυχνίας ἐξῆψεν τοὺς λύχνους αὐτῆς

MT   ...אל-מול פני המנורה...

Ex. 26.22 καὶ ἐκ τῶν ὀπίσω τῆς σκηνῆς κατὰ τὸ μέρος τὸ πρὸς
θάλασσαν ποιήσεις ἓξ στύλους

MT   ...ולירכתי המשכן ימה...

Nu. 20.16 κύριος ... ἐξήγαγεν ἡμᾶς ἐξ Αἰγύπτου, καὶ νῦν ἐσμεν
ἐν Καδης, πόλει ἐκ μέρους τῶν ὁρίων σου.

MT   ...עיר קצה גבולך

The meaning of this phrase, found also in 22.36, is evidently
'on the edge of', 'beside'.[28]

It is clear that in none of the above examples can the
use of μέρος in the sense of 'side' be attributed to Hebraism.

This use receives meagre treatment in the dictionaries,
particularly LSJ, who fail even to classify it as a separate
sense. The only examples they record of it are three LXX
occurrences of ἐκ μέρους τινός, 'by the side of', noted with
other uses of μέρος with prepositions (IV.2.b). Bauer too
gives the impression that it is confined to Biblical and related

---

28. Cf. Johannessohn, *Präpositionen* 291 n.1: 'ἐκ μέρους c. gen.
Reg. I 6.8, 23.26 = מצד "von [der] Seite" (d.h. neben)'.
   This phrase has other meanings when used without gen.
following: see Bl. DF §212.
   The use of ἐκ in the examples quoted above is of course
normal Gk.: cf. Class. ἐκ δεξιᾶς, ἐξ ἀριστερᾶς, and the examples
below. See Bauer s.v. ἐκ 2, Mayser, *Gramm.* II.ii 384.

literature, though he does actually note a non-Biblical example, *PGM* 13.438, but under a different heading (l.c). MM's otherwise thorough collection of parallels throws no light on it at all.

Investigation shows, however, that μέρος in the sense of 'side' is not only attested in iii B.C. and later, but is even to be found in Herodotus, as follows:[29]

2.121a βουλόμενον δὲ αὐτὸν ἐν ἀσφαλείῃ τὰ χρήματα θησαυρίζειν οἰκοδομέεσθαι οἴκημα λίθινον, τοῦ τῶν τοίχων ἕνα ἐς τὸ ἔξω μέρος τῆς οἰκίης ἔχειν.

'... a stone chamber, one of its walls abutting on the outer side of the palace.'

4.101 ἔστι ὦν τῆς Σκυθικῆς ὡς ἐούσης τετραγώνου, τῶν δύο μερέων κατηκόντων ἐς θάλασσαν, πάντῃ ἴσον τό τε ἐς τὴν μεσόγαιαν φέρον καὶ τὸ παρὰ τὴν θάλασσαν.

'Scythia, then, being a four-sided country, whereof two sides are sea-board, the frontiers running inland and those that are by the sea make it a perfect square' (Godley, *Loeb*). Cf. 4.99.

In the following examples from iii B.C. and later the meaning 'side' for μέρος seems to me indisputable.

OGI 56.52 (Canopus, iii B.C.) καὶ ἡ ἀναγωγὴ τοῦ ἱεροῦ πλοίου τοῦ 'Οσείριος εἰς τοῦτο τὸ ἱερὸν κατ'ἐνιαυτὸν γίνεται ... τῶν ἐκ τῶν πρώτων ἱερῶν πάντων θυσίας συντελούντων ἐπὶ τῶν ἱδρυμένων ὑπ'αὐτῶν βωμῶν ὑπὲρ ἑκάστου ἱεροῦ τῶν πρώτων ἐξ ἀμφοτέρων τῶν μερῶν τοῦ δρόμου.

'... on both sides of the δρόμος', i.e. the avenue leading up to the temple ('ante introitum templi', Dittenberger, *ad loc.*).

PPetr. 3.43(2) *verso* IV.11 (247/6 B.C.) καὶ π[αρ]αφρυγανίσαι τὸ χῶμα τῆι μυρακινῆι κόμηι καὶ ἀπο[...]ονι[..]αι ἀνοῦχι ἐξ ἑκατέρου μέρους ἐπὶ πᾶν τὸ μῆκος εἰς ὕψος

Despite the fragmentary nature of this document (a contract for

---

29. Powell, *Lexicon*, s.v.

work to be done on bridges, dykes, etc.) it is difficult to see
how ἐξ ἑκατέρου μέρους can be anything but 'on each side', i.e.
of the χῶμα, 'dyke'. The phrase occurs again in *PPetr*. 3.42
F(b).1 = (c).5 (252 B.C.).[30]

PHib. 200.5 (iii B.C.) ...] πλατείας ἐκ τοῦ πρὸς λίβα μέρους
ἐχόμενον τυγχ[άν]ηι [...

'... a disturbance ... coming from the room which] happens to
be adjacent to the street on its south side', ed.

BGU 999.4ff. (99/8 B.C.) ἀπέδοτο Εὔνους ... ἀπὸ τῆς ὑπαρχούσης
αὐτῷ οἰκίαν (1. οἰκίας) ᾠκοδομημένης ... τῆς οὔσης ἐν τῷ ἀπὸ
νότου καὶ ἀπηλιώτου μέρει τῆς ἐν Παθύρει κρήνης τὸ ἐν τῷ ἀπὸ
λιβὸς μέρει ὑπερῶν α καὶ τὸ ...

I take this to be: 'Eunous has sold, of the house ... which is
on the south-eastern side of the spring in Pathyris, the upper
room [ὑπερῶν = ὑπερῷον] on the western side and the ...'

There are also many instances where the context will
permit μέρος to be taken both as 'side' and as 'region' or
'part'. Though these cannot be used as evidence here, we can
note that there is a possibility, since 'side' has been established as a possible sense of the word, that μέρος was in fact
intended thus in these instances also. E.g.

BGU 994.II.12 - III.2 (113 B.C.) ... ἀπὸ τοῦ ὑπάρχοντος αὐτῇ
ψιλοῦ τόπου τοῦ ὄντος ἐν τῷ ἀπὸ λι(βὸς) μέρει Παθύρεως
πήχεις στερεοῦ ε

Cf. *PGrenf*. 2.25.9 (103 B.C.), 2.35.7 (98 B.C.), *Archiv* I 63.12
(123 B.C.), *SIG* 495.98 (c. 230 B.C.).

μέρος in the sense of 'side' is also found in Modern
Greek, ad e.g. in the phrase ἀπὸ τὸ ἕνα μέρος, 'on one side'.[31]
Cf. also μεριά, one of the normal vernacular words for 'side'
(Swanson).

The semantic development from 'part' to 'side' is one

---

30. Mayser translates 'auf beiden Seiten', *Gramm*. II.ii 384.
31. I am indebted to Mr. Papastavrou for this example. Others
can be seen in *AELex*. s.v. 'side'.

which can be paralleled in other languages. Cf. e.g. Lat. *pars*,
Eng. *part* itself (*SOED* s.v. A.III.2), Ital. *parte*, Fr. *part*.

ὀλιγοψυχέω

Recorded first in Isoc. 19.39 in the sense of 'be faint':
τετρωμένον αὐτὸν καὶ βαδίζειν οὐ δυνάμενον ἀλλ᾽ ὀλιγοψυχοῦντα
ἀπεκόμισ᾽[α]. The noun ὀλιγοψυχία is similarly found early
only in the sense of 'fainting', 'swooning' (Hp.).

Later ὀλιγοψυχέω has the meaning 'be discouraged, dispirited', e.g. in *PPetr.* 2.40(a).12 (iii B.C.) μὴ οὖν
ὀλιγοψυχήσητε ἀλλ᾽ ἀνδρίζεσθε, ὀλίγος γὰρ χρόνος ὑμῖν ἐστιν
ἑτοιμάζεται γὰρ ἡ διαδοχή, *UPZ* 78.10 (ii B.C.) ὅρα μὴ
ὀλιοψυχῆσθαι, cf. 63.1 (ii B.C.).

It is so used in the Pentateuch in

Nu. 21.4 καὶ ὠλιγοψύχησεν ὁ λαὸς ἐν τῇ ὁδῷ· (5) καὶ κατελάλει
ὁ λαὸς πρὸς τὸν θεὸν καὶ κατὰ Μωυσῆ ...
MT ותקצר נפש-העם [32]

σκεπάζω

In Classical Greek (Hp., X., Arist.) in the sense of
'cover', but already on its way to the later use in many contexts, where the notion of protecting as well as covering is
clearly felt. E.g. X. *Eq.* 12.8 πάντων δὲ μάλιστα τοῦ ἵππου τὸν
κενεῶνα δεῖ σκεπάζειν, cf. *Cyr.* 8.8.17. This development is of
course a natural one, since the object that covers something
frequently also protects it (cf. e.g. L. *protegere*).

In iii B.C. we find the further development to 'protect',
'shelter', without any idea of covering in the literal sense.
Thus e.g.

PHib. 35.10 (c.250 B.C.) καὶ νῦν καὶ ἐν τοῖς ἔμπροσθε
χρόνοις ὑπὸ ὑμῶν σκεπάζομεθα.

PCair.zen. 491.30 (iii B.C.) Πᾶτις οὖν αὐτοὺς σκεπάζει διὰ
τὸ συνδιαιρεῖσθαι αὐτῶι τὰς λείας

---

32. Note that the rendering is an idiomatic translation of the
Hb. idiom but at the same time reproduces, in a fashion, the
word-for-word meaning of the Hb: ὀλιγο-: קצר ('be short'), ψυχ-:
נפש . The translators no doubt appreciated this.

'Patis is protecting them [certain robbers] because they have shared the stolen goods with him.' Cf. 451.14 (iii B.C.), *PSI* 440.14 (iii B.C.).

The word occurs as follows in the Pentateuch:

1. (a) 'cover', literally: *Nu*. 9.20 ... ὅταν σκεπάσῃ ἡ νεφέλη ἡμέρας ἀριθμῷ ἐπὶ τῆς σκηνῆς. Similarly *Ex*. 40.3,21.

    (b) 'cover' or 'protect' (by covering): *Ex*. 33.22 ἡνίκα δ' ἂν παρέλθῃ μου ἡ δόξα, καὶ θήσω σε εἰς ὀπὴν τῆς πέτρας καὶ σκεπάσω τῇ χειρί μου ἐπὶ σέ, ἕως ἂν παρέλθω, *De*. 32.11.

2. 'protect, 'shelter', without the idea of covering:

    Ex. 12.13 ὄψομαι τὸ αἷμα καὶ σκεπάσω ὑμᾶς, καὶ οὐκ ἔσται ἐν ὑμῖν πληγὴ τοῦ ἐκτριβῆναι, ὅταν παίω ἐν γῇ Αἰγύπτῳ. Cf. 12.27.

    De. 13.9 οὐ φείσεται ὁ ὀφθαλμός σου ἐπ' αὐτῷ, οὐκ ἐπιποθήσεις ἐπ' αὐτῷ οὐδ' οὐ μὴ σκεπάσῃς αὐτόν.

Here, as in the *PCair.Zen.* example above, σκεπάζω is used of protecting a guilty person.

3. 'conceal':

    Ex. 2.2-3 ... καὶ ἔτεκεν ἄρσεν· ἰδόντες δὲ αὐτὸ ἀστεῖον ἐσκέπασαν αὐτὸ μῆνας τρεῖς. (3) ἐπεὶ δὲ οὐκ ἠδύναντο αὐτὸ ἔτι κρύπτειν, ...

'Protect', as in sense 2., is possible here, but 'conceal' suits the context better. Moreover ἐσκέπασαν αὐτό renders MT ותצפנהו (צפן 'hide'); and the same Hebrew verb is rendered by κρύπτειν in the next sentence. Though there is as yet no contemporary evidence for this further development in meaning, it is a natural one and is paralleled e.g. in καλύπτω, 'cover'>'conceal'.[33]

---

33. Elsewhere in LXX there are a number of probable examples of σκεπάζω 'conceal', especially 1 *Ki*. 26.1 ἰδοὺ Δαυιδ σκεπάζεται μεθ' ἡμῶν ἐν τῷ βουνῷ τοῦ Εχελα (סתר *hithp*.).
    In Mod. Gk. 'cover' is the usual sense (Papastavrou), though in some expressions signs of a development from 'cover' to 'conceal' are apparent: cf. *Lex. Pr.* s.v.: 'συγκαλύπτω πρᾶξιν ἔνοχον, ἀποσιωπῶ, ἰδίᾳ ἐν τῇ φρ. << τὰ σκεπάζω >>', *AELex*. s.v. 'hide': σκεπάζω σκάνδαλον.

συγκρίνω

The earlier senses are 'bring together', 'combine', 'compare' (Hp., Pl., Arist., etc.). From iii B.C. onwards it is commonly found in the sense of 'decide', both of judicial decisions proper, and more generally of any decision, but especially one made by a person in authority. E.g. *PMagd*. 24.12 (iii B.C.)ὅπως ... τύχηι ζημίας, ἧς ἂν ὁ στρατηγὸς συγκρίνηι, *PCair.Zen*. 371.14 (239 B.C.) παραγενοῦ, ὅπως ὑποστῶμεν ('offer', 'bid') καθὰ ἂν συγκρίνηις, *PLille* 1 *verso*. 27 (259-8 B.C.) ὕστερον δὲ ἐπισκοπούμενος τὸ περίχωμα συνέκρινεν τὰ χώματα ποῆσαι [...].[34]

Cf. σύγκρισις, in the sense of 'decision' attested first in iii B.C. papyri (examples in LSJ s.v. III.2).

This use is found in the Pentateuch in

Nu. 15.33-34 καὶ προσήγαγον αὐτὸν [a man found gathering wood on the Sabbath] πρὸς Μωυσῆν καὶ Ααρων καὶ πρὸς πᾶσαν συναγωγὴν υἱῶν Ισραηλ. (34) καὶ ἀπέθεντο αὐτὸν εἰς φυλακήν· οὐ γὰρ συνέκριναν, τί ποιήσωσιν αὐτόν.

συγκρίνω is also used in the Pentateuch in the quite different sense of 'interpret', 'explain' (a dream), *Ge*. 40.8 Ἐνύπνιον εἴδομεν, καὶ ὁ συγκρίνων οὐκ ἔστιν αὐτό, similarly 16,22; 41.12,13,15 *bis* (in all ~ פתר). This use is not yet satisfactorily paralleled outside Biblical literature, the example in Plb. 14.3.7 cited by Bauer, LSJ, being rather uncertain: μετὰ δὲ ταῦτα τοὺς κατασκόπους ἀνακαλεσάμενος ... συνέκρινε καὶ διηρεύνα τὰ λεγόμενα ... 'Compare' is just as possible here as 'interpret'. There is however no reason to doubt that 'interpret' was normal Greek. κρίνω is old in this sense, e.g. Hdt. 1.120 ... τοὺς αὐτοὺς τῶν μάγων οἳ τὸ ἐνύπνιον οἱ ταύτῃ ἔκριναν, 7.19 *bis*, and the same semantic development is attested later in διακρίνω (cited by LSJ, s.v. V, from Ph., Junc.; cf. διάκρισις 'interpretation' in Ph., Paus., LSJ s.v. II).

συγκυρέω (-κύρω)

The older meanings (Homer +) were 'meet by chance';

---

34. Further examples in MM, LSJ.

'happen', 'occur'. From iii B.C. onwards we find it used in the sense of 'adjoin', 'be attached to', 'belong to', 'pertain to'. More than one sense could be distinguished here, but it is difficult to do this with accuracy. The differing uses shade into one another, and in some of the examples it is not possible to say whether one sense rather than another is intended.

The Koine usage of the word may be illustrated by the following:

PYale 46.11 (246-221 B.C.) ὁ δὲ ... πέπρακεν τὸ [τρίτο]ν ἀπὸ τοῦ συνκύροντος τῆι οἰκίαι [τόπου] Πετητει Πετήσιος οἰκοδομεῖν ...

'... one third of the land adjoining, belonging to, the house.'

Similarly

PLond. 604.2 (47 A.D.) παρὰ ... Σωτηρίχου κωμογραμμ(ατέως) Κροκοδείλων πόλεως καὶ τῶν συνκυρουσῶν κωμῶν.

Compare

PYale 46.5 ὑπαρχούσης γάρ μοι οἰκίας καὶ τῶν συνκυρόντων τῶν πατρικῶν ἐν τῆι προγεγραμμένηι κώμηι ...

PPetr. 3.57(a).12 (iii B.C.?) ... πρὸς ἃ ὑποτίθημι τὴν ὑπάρχουσάν μοι οἰκίαν καὶ αὐλὴν καὶ τὰ συνκύροντα ἐν Εὐεργέτιδι

In these two examples, though the value of συνκύρω itself is clear, it is not easy to tell whether τὰ συνκύροντα refers to the 'appurtenances', 'accessories' of the house (and courtyard), or the adjoining ground (sc. e.g. χωρία). OGI 52.1 (Ptolemais, iii B.C.) is similarly ambiguous.

The purely local sense, 'adjoin', is clear however e.g. in

Plb. 3.59.7 ... τὴν ἔξωθεν ταύταις ταῖς χώραις συγκυροῦσαν θάλατταν.

For the sense of 'pertain, relate, to' we may quote

PRev. 43.14 (iii B.C.) καὶ τὰ λοιπὰ φορτία τὰ συ[νκ]ύρ[ο]ντα εἰς τὴν ἐλαϊκήν.

'And the other kinds of produce pertaining to the oil-monopoly.'

PHib. 82.19 (239-8(238-7) B.C.) περὶ τῶν εἰς ταῦτα
συγκυρόντων.

The examples in the Pentateuch, which are fully in accordance with contemporary usage, are as follows:

Nu. 21.25 καὶ κατῴκησεν Ισραηλ ἐν πάσαις ταῖς πόλεσιν τῶν
Αμορραίων, ἐν Εσεβων καὶ ἐν πάσαις ταῖς συγκυρούσαις αὐτῇ
MT   ובכל-בנתיה...

Here the verb has the same rather vague sense as in *PYale* 46 and
PLond. 604 above. We could translate 'all the cities belonging
to it' (sc. πόλεσιν or κώμαις). The turning of the Hebrew
idiom into ordinary Greek is noteworthy.

Nu. 35.4 καὶ τὰ συγκυροῦντα τῶν πόλεων, ἃς δώσετε τοῖς
Λευίταις, ἀπὸ τείχους τῆς πόλεως καὶ ἔξω δισχιλίους πήχεις
κύκλῳ.

τὰ συγκυροῦντα, rendering Hebrew מגרשים 'common-land', BDB,
refers to the farm-land lying around and belonging to these
cities, and may be translated 'the adjoining ground', 'the
outskirts'. 'Suburbs',[35] now suggesting a residential area, is
less satisfactory. In vs. 3 it is clearly stated that this
land is for the pasturing of the Levites' cattle.

De. 2.37 πλὴν εἰς γῆν υἱῶν Αμμων οὐ προσήλθομεν, πάντα τὰ
συγκυροῦντα χειμάρρου [-ῳ A] Ιαβοκ καὶ τὰς πόλεις τὰς ἐν
τῇ ὀρεινῇ, καθότι ἐνετείλατο ἡμῖν κύριος ὁ θεὸς ἡμῶν.
MT   כל-יד נחל יבק

'All the parts bordering on wady Jabok.'[36]

As to the form, the word fluctuates between -έω and -ω
(cf. aor. -έκυρσα, Homer, dram., etc.) throughout its history,

---

35. MM, s.v. συγκυρία, Brenton, Thomson-Muses, cf. Thackeray,
Gramm. 4 n.4.
   As Thackeray notes, *ib.*, the translators use no less than
four different words to render מגרשים in 35.2-7, a good illustration of their conscious effort to make their version more
readable by the use of stylistic variation.

36. *De.* 3.4 πάντα τὰ περίχωρα Αργοβ B; πάντα τὰ]+ συγκυροῦντα
B*†: dl. Rahlfs ('ex 2.37').

as does κυρ-έω, -ω (and cf. προσκυρ-έω, -ω). However, συγκύρω
is usual in the Ptolemaic papyri.[37] The fact that our text of
the Pentateuch shows the other form has no particular significance. Original -κύρω could have been altered to -κυρέω in the
course of transmission,[38] or alternatively the -έω form may
have been more common in the translators' time than our present
evidence indicates. It was certainly used by Polybius (2.20.8,
6.6.5, and probably therefore 3.59.7 quoted above) and is
attested, though infrequently, in later papyri, e.g. POxy. 907.9,
13 (iii A.D.), PSI 698.6 (iv A.D.), 705.8 (iii A.D.).[39]

ὧδε

     In Classical usage the meanings of ὧδε were 'thus' (etc.),
and 'hither'. Its use in the sense of 'here' appears first in
iii B.C., Herod. 2.98, 3.96, in papyri e.g. PCair.Zen. 376.11
(iii B.C.) ὅτε ὁ γλαυκὸς ἵππος ἔμενεν ὧδε, ..., PHib. 46.15
(258/257 B.C.) ἔδει δὲ πάλαι τὰ ἐνέχυρα αὐτῶν ὧδε εἶναι καὶ
πεπρᾶσθαι.[40] It continues to be used also in the sense of
'hither', e.g. PSI 599.3 (iii B.C.), but 'thus' becomes very
rare.

     The translators of the Pentateuch frequently use the word
in the new sense. To classify the examples fully:

     1. 'hither', Ge. 15.14,16; 42.15; 45.5,8,13; Ex. 3.5. The
phrase ὧδε καὶ ὧδε, 'this way and that', found also in AP 5.128,
Call. Epigr. 30.2, occurs in Ex. 2.12 περιβλεψάμενος δὲ ὧδε καὶ
ὧδε οὐχ ὁρᾷ οὐδένα.

---

37. Mayser, Gramm. I.i 348.

38. There is however no sign of -κύρω in the MS tradition
(Brooke-McLean).

39. There is no case for treating συγκυρέω and συγκύρω as separate words, as LSJ's separate entries (with different senses)
suggest. (They further confuse the matter by proceeding to add,
at the end of the entry under συγκύρω,'also -κυρέω ...'.)
    On the fluctuation between -έω and -ω generally see Thack-
eray, Gramm. 243f., Schwyzer, Gramm. I 720f.

40. Cf. Mayser, Gramm. I.ii 66; II.i 74.
    The distinction between place where and place whither in
adverbs of place, not always maintained even in Class.Gk., tends
to disappear altogether in the Koine. Other examples are ποῦ for
both 'where?' and 'whither?', with ποῖ lost; ἐκεῖ 'there' and
'thither', ἐκεῖσε frequently 'there'. Cf. Bl. DF §103, Jannaris,
Gramm. §435. Mod.Eng. has also abandoned this distinction.

2. 'here', *Ge.* 19.12 Ἔστιν τίς σοι ὧδε, γαμβροὶ ἢ υἱοὶ ἢ θυγατέρες; 31.37; 38.22 (ἐνταῦθα A) 40.15; 42.33; *Nu.* 14.23 οὐκ ὄψονται τὴν γῆν ... ἀλλ᾽ ἢ τὰ τέκνα αὐτῶν, ἅ ἐστιν μετ᾽ ἐμοῦ ὧδε, 23.29 *bis*; 32.16; *De.* 5.3; 12.8; 29.14 *bis*; 31.21.

Ge. 22.4-5 Αβρααμ ... εἶδεν τὸν τόπον μακρόθεν. (5) καὶ εἶπεν Αβρααμ τοῖς παισὶν αὐτοῦ Καθίσατε αὐτοῦ μετὰ τῆς ὄνου, ἐγὼ δὲ καὶ τὸ παιδάριον διελευσόμεθα ἕως ὧδε καὶ προσκυνήσαντες ἀναστρέψωμεν πρὸς ὑμᾶς.

The Greek here is a literal rendering of נלכה עד-כה , literally 'we shall go as far as here', and is probably to be taken, like the Hebrew (see BDB), as accompanied by a gesture indicating the place in the distance.

ἀναστρέφω, 'return', 'come, go, back', *Ge.* 8.11 καὶ ἀνέστρεψεν πρὸς αὐτὸν ἡ περιστερά, 18.14, etc., *PMich.Zen.* 55.7 (240 B.C.) ... ἵνα ταχέως πρός με ἀναστρέφηι , *PCair.Zen.* 815.4 (257 B.C.); others in Kiessling. (Pass. in this sense already in Pl. *Plt.* 271 a.)

ἀντίκειμαι, 'resist', 'oppose', 'be an adversary', *Ex.* 23.22 ἐχθρεύσω τοῖς ἐχθροῖς σου καὶ ἀντικείσομαι τοῖς ἀντικειμένοις σοι, *UPZ* 69.6 (152 B.C.) ὁρῶ ἐν τῷ ὕπνῳ τὸν δραπέδην Μενέδημον ἀντικείμενον ἡμῖν.

διαφωνέω (a) 'be missing', 'be lost', 'go astray', often in papyri, e.g. *PSI* 527.15 (iii B.C., a list of items) διαπεφώνηκεν ἱδρῶια γ, 666.7,17, *PCair.Zen.*787.65, *PCol.Zen.* 81.7, 90.6 (all iii B.C.), Plb. 21.42.23. Hence euphemistically (as in English, e.g. '100 men were lost'): (b) 'perish', 'die', of plants *BGU* 530.31 (i B.C.), books D.S. 16.3, persons Agatharc. 84, *SIG* 611.10 (ii B.C.), and probably *PPetr.* 2.13.3.4 (iii B.C.) (quoted in MM). In the two Pentateuch examples, *Ex.* 24.11, *Nu.* 31.49 (see the whole context), either sense is possible, owing to the ambiguity of the word.[41]

δοχή, 'entertainment', 'feast', *Ge.* 26.30 καὶ ἐποίησεν αὐτοῖς

---

41. Cf. Anz, *Subsidia* 352f., Caird, *JTS* XIX (1968) 468.
   LSJ's entry under this word is a muddle, only made worse by the Supplement's alteration.

δοχήν, καὶ ἔφαγον καὶ ἔπιον, 21.8, *PSI* 858.10 (iii B.C.)
ἡμιταινίδια ... τὰ δοθέντα εἰς τὴν δοχὴν τὴν Κρίτωνος, *PCair.*
Zen. 87.7 (iii B.C.); others in Kiessling. (The same semantic
development is seen in Eng. 'reception'.)

ἐντρέπομαι, 'be ashamed', 'feel shame', *Le.* 26.41, *Nu.* 12.14,
UPZ 62.29 (161/160 B.C.).

ἡγεμονία, a military unit, 'regiment', 'company', *Nu.* 1.52 καὶ
παρεμβαλοῦσιν οἱ υἱοὶ Ισραηλ ἀνὴρ ἐν τῇ ἑαυτοῦ τάξει καὶ ἀνὴρ
κατὰ τὴν ἑαυτοῦ ἡγεμονίαν σὺν δυνάμει αὐτῶν, 2.17 B, *SIG* 374.23
(c. 287/6 B.C.) τοὺς μὲν βουλομένους στρατεύεσθαι διώίκησεν
ὅπως ἂν καταχωρισθῶσιν ἐν ἡγεμονίαις, *PRein* 9.13 (112 B.C.).

καιρός, generally 'time', 'period of time' (synonymous with
χρόνος), *Nu.* 22.4, *De.* 1.9,16,18, etc., Arist., papyri, inscriptions, Plb., evidence in J. Barr, *Biblical Words for Time*
(Studies in Biblical Theology 33), London, 1962, 32ff.

κατατρέχω, 'pursue', 'assail', *Le.* 26.37 ὑπερόψεται ὁ ἀδελφὸς
τὸν ἀδελφὸν ὡσεὶ ἐν πολέμῳ οὐθενὸς κατατρέχοντος, *UPZ* 68.6
(152 B.C.) ἐγὼ γὰρ ἐνύπνια ὁρῶ πονηρά, βλέπω Μενέδημον
κατατρέχοντά με.

κύριος, 'owner', *Ex.* 21.28 ὁ δὲ κύριος τοῦ ταύρου ἀθῷος ἔσται,
29,32,34, al., *PHib.* 34.3 (243-2 B.C.) ἐπαναγκάσαι ... τὸ
ὑποζύγιον ἀποδοῦναι τῶι κυρίωι, *PCol.Zen.*30.8 (256 B.C.).

λαλέω, 'speak', often in Pentateuch, Arist., Men., Herod.,
papyri e.g. *PSI* 412.1, *PPetr.* 2.13.6.9 (both iii B.C.); often
already in Ar. Anz, *Subsidia* 309f.

παρακαλέω (i) 'comfort', 'cheer up', *Ge.* 24.67 καὶ παρεκλήθη
Ισαακ περὶ Σαρρας τῆς μητρὸς αὐτοῦ, 37.35, 38.12, 50.21, now
PHaun. 10.28 (end iii B.C.) ἐγὼ γὰρ ὑπάρχων ὑμῖν οὐθὲν κακὸν
οὐ μὴ πάθητε. ὥστε παρακαλῶ ὑμᾶς. (ii) 'Beseech', 'entreat',
'request', *De.* 13.7 ἐὰν δὲ παρακαλέσῃ σε ὁ ἀδελφός σου ... λάθρᾳ
λέγων Βαδίσωμεν καὶ λατρεύσωμεν θεοῖς ἑτέροις, commonly papyri,
inscriptions, from ii B.C. onwards, see MM, Bauer. Add, s.v.l.,
PCol.Zen 11.6 (257 B.C.) π[αρακ]αλοῦμεν σὲ τήν τε ἐπιστολὴν ...
ἀποδοῦναι.

84

περίβλημα, 'garment', Nu. 31.20 πᾶν περίβλημα καὶ πᾶν σκεῦος δερμάτινον ... ἀφαγνιεῖτε, cf. PCair.Zen. 92.2 (iii B.C.) περίβλημα λινοῦν πεπλυμένον α.

περιδέξιον, τό, 'bracelet', Ex. 35.22, Nu. 31.50, PPetr. 2. p.22.24 (iii B.C.). Deissmann, BS 150.

πλεονάζω intrans., 'be more', 'be in excess', Ex. 16.23 πᾶν τὸ πλεονάζον καταλίπετε αὐτὸ εἰς ἀποθήκην εἰς τὸ πρωί, 26.12, al., PRev. 57.13 (iii B.C.) τὸ πλεονάζον τοῦ προκηρυχθέντος ἐξάγωμεν σήσαμον ἢ κρότωνα, ..., PLille 1 verso. 16 (iii B.C.).

προσνοέω, 'observe', 'perceive', Nu. 23.9 ἀπὸ κορυφῆς ὀρέων ὄψομαι αὐτὸν καὶ ἀπὸ βουνῶν προσνοήσω αὐτόν, PEnteux. 30.3 (iii B.C.) προσνοήσας ἱμάτιόν μου ... αὐτὸ ᾤχετο ἔχων.

σάγμα, 'saddle-bag', Ge. 31.34 ἔλαβεν τὰ εἴδωλα καὶ ἐνέβαλεν αὐτὰ εἰς τὰ σάγματα τῆς καμήλου, now PRyl. 562.30 (251 B.C.) ἔρσενος σὺν σάγμασι (δραχμαὶ) κη ('for a male donkey with saddle-bags 28 dr.').

συναντάω, 'befall', 'happen' (to a person, dat.), Ex. 5.3 ... μήποτε συναντήσῃ ἡμῖν θάνατος ἢ φόνος, De. 31.29 A, PSI 392.1 (242/1 B.C.) εἰ ἔρρωσαι καὶ τἆλλά σοι κατὰ τρόπον συναντᾶι, ... 10, Plu., Plb., al.

σῶμα, 'slave', Ge. 34.29, probably 36.6, very common in papyri, e.g. PCair.Zen. 698.3,7,23 (iii B.C.). Deissmann, BS 160.

CHAPTER V

NEW FORMATIONS

In addition to new semantic developments, such as those
just considered, we find in the Koine vocabulary a large number
of new formations; that is, words newly formed on existing
stems. These are the subject of the present chapter. Here too
it will be seen that the Pentateuch vocabulary is in close
agreement with many developments that had taken place by the
third century B.C. The formations examined are those that are
new in the Koine and are attested in documents of the translators' time. They are of a wide variety of types, including
not only formations by means of suffixes, but also compounds
formed with prepositions and in other ways.

As before, some examples are less fully treated than
others. In many cases it is necessary only to notice that the
word occurs in the Pentateuch and contemporary documents. If
it is not expressly stated it is to be assumed that the word
under discussion is or appears to be a new formation of the
Koine.

Compounds with prepositions

Among new compounds of verbs with prepositions an important group is that formed by compounds of πορεύομαι. Apart from
διαπορεύομαι (Th., Hdt. +), συμπορεύομαι (Th. +), and of
course ἐμπορεύομαι ('be a merchant', 'trade'), the compounds of
this verb are not usual in Classical Greek. In the Koine, as
will become clear from the examples dealt with below, they come
into use as the main replacements for the earlier compounds of
-έρχομαι, which tend to drop out.[1] The new compounds usually

1. Cf. *Antiatt.* 91 εἰσπορεύομαι καὶ ἐκπορεύομαι: ἀντὶ τοῦ ἐξέρχομαι
[read ἀντὶ τοῦ εἰσέρχομαι καὶ ἐξέρχομαι]. Cf. LSJ s.v. ἔρχομαι.
It is worth mentioning that ἔρχομαι becomes obsolete only in
compounds. The simplex continues in use in the Koine, but with a
restriction in meaning: it now has the sense of 'come' only, not
'come' and 'go' as in Class. Cf. Bl. DF §101 s.v.

supply the present and imperfect, the future and aorist being
supplied as before by compounds of -ελεύσομαι (Attic -ειμι),
and -ἦλθον.[2] In the perfect -πεπόρευμαι and the older sup-
pletive -ελήλυθα seem to be equally normal. This pattern,
though usual, is affected in some cases by compounds of other
verbs, notably -βαίνω,[3] which overlap with the main suppletives.[4]
In the case of words for 'go away', it is remarkable that, the
present tense being provided by ἀποτρέχω, the -πορεύομαι compound is uncommon (see pp. 125 ff.).

εἰσπορεύομαι

      Apart from an example of the active in the sense of 'lead
in' in E. *El.* 1285, the word appears in Classical times only in
Xenophon, who in this, as so often, foreshadows Koine usage:
Cyr. 2.3.21 οὕτω δ᾽ εἰσαγαγὼν κατέκλινεν ἐπὶ τὸ δεῖπνον ὥσπερ
εἰσεπορεύοντο.

      In the third century B.C. we have *PCair.Zen.* 15 *verso.* 18
(259 or 258 B.C.) ἡμῶν εἰς Αἴγυπτον εἰσπορευομένων, *OGI* 56.4
(Egypt, 239/8 B.C.) ... καὶ οἱ εἰς τὸ ἄδυτον εἰσπορευόμενοι
πρὸς τὸν στολισμὸν τῶν θεῶν, *PCol.Zen.* 6.10 (257 B.C.) ... τοῦ
Δύστρου μηνὸς οὗ εἰσπορεύεται ʽΗρόφ[ντος] πρὸς ὑμᾶς, 81.14.
Later examples are found e.g. in *POxy.* 717.7, 744.4 (both i B.C.,

---

2. G.D. Kilpatrick, *JTS* XLVIII (1947) 61-3, observed this feature
in the vocabulary of *Ev. Marc.,* but, since he made no comparison
with the Koine generally, thought it was peculiar to Mark, and
found it hard to explain. It is clear that Mark simply reflects
current usage. The fact that *Evv. Matt.* and *Luc.* do not conform
to the pattern, as K. notes (p.63), is almost certainly due to
their tendency towards more literary Greek.

3. Cf. Mod.Gk. vernac. βγαίνω (< ἐκβαίνω), μπαίνω (< ἐμβαίνω),
κατεβαίνω, ἀνεβαίνω, the usual words for 'go out, in, down, up',
respectively (Swanson).

4. An interesting detail is the way compounds of εἶμι, which are
in general lost in the Koine vernacular, as is the simplex (Bl.
DF §99.1), hang on in certain forms, notably the participle.
'The participle and the inf. of a few compounds seem to have
been the last to go', Thackeray, *Gramm.* 257. In the Pentateuch
ἄπ-, εἴσ-, ἔξ-, and ἔπ-ειμι all occur only in the participle:
Ex. 33.8; 28.29, 35; 28.35; *De.* 32.29. Likewise in iii B.C.
papyri almost all occurrences of compounds of εἶμι are participial in form (exceptions are *PPetr.* 2.16.6 εἰσιέναι, 2.38(b).12
εἰσίασι s.v.l.): see Preisigke, Kiessling and Suppl., Mayser,
Gramm. I. i 355, and cf. exx. quoted in MM s. vv.

and pres. tense), quoted in MM, and in the *NT* (c.18 times, always pres. or impf.).[5]

The word is very common in the Pentateuch, occurring over fifty times, usually as a rendering of Hebrew בוא . Its usage is straightforward: it has the same sense as Classical εἰσέρχομαι, 'go in, into', 'enter', in various constructions. E.g. with εἰς *Ex.* 28.30 ... ὅταν εἰσπορεύηται εἰς τὸ ἅγιον ἐναντίον κυρίου, 34.12 ... τῆς γῆς, εἰς ἣν εἰσπορεύῃ εἰς αὐτήν, abs. *De.* 28.6 εὐλογημένος σὺ ἐν τῷ εἰσπορεύεσθαί σε, *Nu.* 4.47 πᾶς ὁ εἰσπορευόμενος πρὸς τὸ ἔργον τῶν ἔργων.

Most of the examples in the Pentateuch are in the present tense, four in the impf. (*Ge.* 6.4 *Ex.* 33.8, 34.34, *Le.* 33.40). Conversely εἰσέρχομαι is not found in the pres., and in the impf. only once (*Ge.* 38.9,[6] without apparent justification). For the future εἰσελεύσομαι is usual (over 40 times), εἰσπορεύσομαι occurring only in *De.* 1.22 B (εἰσπορευόμεθα A, al.); similarly the aor. is normally εἰσῆλθον (very common), with εἰσεπορεύθην only in *De.* 1.8 B (εἰσελθόντες A, al.). In the pf. we find both εἰσελήλυθα, *De.* 26.3, and εἰσπεπόρευμαι, *Ex.* 1.1, 14.28.

The synonymity of εἰσπορεύομαι with the verbs supplying the other tenses is well illustrated by *Ge.* 7.16 καὶ τὰ εἰσπορευόμενα ἄρσεν καὶ θῆλυ ἀπὸ πάσης σαρκὸς εἰσῆλθεν, καθὰ ἐνετείλατο ὁ θεὸς τῷ Νωε.

The available evidence suggest that the above pattern is in accordance with contemporary usage. In papyri of the third century B.C. εἰσπορεύομαι is, as we have seen, usually present tense; εἰσέρχομαι occurs only in *PSI* 418.16 ὡς ἂν εἰσερχώμεθα. I do not, however, know of any example of εἰσπεπόρευμαι (εἰσελήλυθα is found in *PEleph.* 13.6). In the *NT* εἰσέρχομαι is confined to the more literary gospels and *Ep. Hebr.*, whereas Mark uses for the pres. and impf. only εἰσπορεύομαι.

---

5. See also Anz, *Subsidia* 332.
6. εἰσήρχετο A D̲ E and various cursives, εἰσῆλθεν abcfikmorvxc₂, εἰσεπορεύετο hl꞊. In view of the above evidence perhaps εἰσῆλθεν or εἰσεπορεύετο is to be preferred here. (Either aor. or impf. is possible in the context: see Bl. DF §367 on the construction.)

In each of the compounds of πορεύομαι discussed below we
find the same agreement between the pattern of suppletion in the
Pentateuch and that in contemporary Greek. I have not repeated
the details of the papyrus evidence each time: as far as I am
aware, in each case the πορεύομαι compound is usual in the
present and imperfect, while the ἔρχομαι compound is attested
rarely or not at all in those tenses.

ἐπιπορεύομαι

There are occasional examples of the word in Classical
times, but not as a synonym of ἐπέρχομαι.[7] From iii B.C. onwards it is common in the present tense in the same senses as
ἐπέρχομαι.[8] Thus e.g. 'visit', 'go the rounds of', *PLille* 3.78
(iii B.C.) συντετάχαμεν Μιύσει τῶι τοπ[ογρ(αμματεῖ) ἐπὶ]
τούτους ἐπιπορεύεσθαι τοὺς τόπους, *PHib*. 249.2 (iii B.C.) (=
ἐπέρχομαι III, LSJ); 'take legal action' (against) *PSorb*.
15.5-12 (c. 266 B.C.) ἀλλ᾽ ὅταν ὁποτεροσοῦν αὐτῶν ἐπιπορεύηται
..., ἥ τε ἔφοδος ἄκυρος ἔστω καὶ προσαποτεισάτω ὁ ἐπιπορευόμενος
ἐφ᾽ ὃν ἂν ἐπιπορεύηται δραχμὰς χιλίας, and often elsewhere
(= ἐπέρχομαι I.1.d).

The synonymity of the various suppletives is well illustrated by an example such as *PAdler* 2.10-14 (124 B.C.), where
we have first the future ἐπελευσομένους, then present
ἐπιπορεύεσθαι, and then aorist ἐπέλθηι, all in the sense of
'take legal action'. Similarly *PHib*. 96.10, *PHamb*. 190.7
(both iii B.C.).

The word occurs once in the Pentateuch:

Le. 26.33 καὶ διασπερῶ ὑμᾶς εἰς τὰ ἔθνη, καὶ ἐξαναλώσει ὑμᾶς

---

7. Those known to me are Heraclit. 45 (Diels) (vi/v B.C.) ψυχῆς
πείρατα ἰὼν οὐκ ἂν ἐξεύροιο, πᾶσαν ἐπιπορευόμενος ὁδόν. Clearly
this must be '... though you travelled over the whole road',
with πορεύομαι having its original sense (cf. MM s.v.). Ephor.
Fr. 5 (Jac., = 70 Müller) (iv B.C.) αἱ πάλαι γυναῖκες ἑστῶσαι
ὕφαινον καὶ ἐπιπορευόμεναι τὸν ἱστόν, 'plying the loom', =
ἐποίχομαι II.4, LSJ.

8. Cf. LSJ s.v. ἐπέρχομαι I.1.d: 'ἐπιπορεύομαι (q.v.) is more
common in the pres. in the Hellenistic period'. But this note
seems to refer to only one sense of ἐπέρχομαι, viz. 'take
legal proceedings'.

ἐπιπορευομένη ἡ μάχαιρα· καὶ ἔσται ἡ γῆ ὑμῶν ἔρημος, ...

MT   והריקתי אחריכם חרב

The translators evidently did not recognize ריק in the sense of 'draw' (a sword), and attempted to render its other sense 'empty out'. ἐπιπορευομένη is a paraphrastic addition rather than a literal rendering of any of the Hebrew words.

ἐπιπορεύομαι here has the sense of 'come upon', with the idea of surprise, hostility, or violence. Cf. *PPetr.* 2.10(1).11 (c. 240 B.C.) Ἰσχύριας ὁ οἰκονόμος ἐπιπορεύεται ἡμῖν συντάσσων διδόναι εἰς τὰ ξένια χῆνας ιβ ἡμῶν οὐ δυναμένων, 'I. descends on us and ...'; *PYale* 53.11 (mid ii B.C.) ἔτι δὲ καὶ ἐπιπορευόμενος ἐπὶ τὸν κεκομμένον ὑπ' ἐμοῦ χόρτον καὶ ἐκβιασάμενος τὸν φύλακα ἀπενήνεκται εἰς ∠. This is an old established use of ἐπ-έρχομαι -ελεύσομαι -ῆλθον: see LSJ s.v. I.1 and 2, Bauer s.v. 2. In the Pentateuch cf. e.g. *Ge.* 42.21 ἕνεκεν τούτου ἐπῆλθεν ἐφ' ἡμᾶς ἡ θλῖψις αὕτη.

There are no occurrences of ἐπέρχομαι present tense in the Pentateuch.

προσπορεύομαι

The earliest examples are in Arist., *HA* 625a 13, *Oec.* 1353 b1. Then from the third century B.C. onwards it is common: e.g. *PSI* 403.16 (iii B.C.) ἐὰν προσπορεύηται ἢ ἐνοχλῆι σε, ἔγδειρον αὐτόν, *SIG* 338.15 (Rhodes, iv/iii B.C.) θέμειν δὲ τὰς στάλας μίαμ μὲν ἐπὶ τὰς ἐσόδου τὰς ἐκ πόλιος ποτιπορευομένοις, μίαν δὲ ... For other examples see MM and below.

In the Pentateuch it is found about ten times, usually in the sense of 'go, come, to', 'draw near', 'approach' (in space), as in the examples just quoted. Thus *Ex.* 28.43 ὅταν προσπορεύωνται λειτουργεῖν πρὸς τὸ θυσιαστήριον, 30.20, *Le.* 10.9 etc.; *Nu.* 1.51 καὶ ἐν τῷ ἐξαίρειν τὴν σκηνὴν καθελοῦσιν αὐτὴν οἱ Λευῖται ...· καὶ ὁ ἀλλογενὴς ὁ προσπορευόμενος ἀποθανέτω,[9]

---

9. LSJ's classification of this example under 'II. *attach oneself to* ...; of proselytes' is simply wrong. *Ex.* 30.20 is also mistakenly classified here. (The whole entry under this word is in need of reorganization.)

similarly 18.7.

In two instances we find idiomatic uses that are paralleled in the papyri.

In *Ex.* 24.14 Moses and Joshua leave the camp, saying to
the elders

Ἡσυχάζετε αὐτοῦ, ἕως ἀναστρέψωμεν πρὸς ὑμᾶς· καὶ ἰδοὺ
Ααρων καὶ Ωρ μεθ' ὑμῶν· ἐάν τινι συμβῇ κρίσις,
προσπορευέσθωσαν αὐτοῖς   (MT וגי)

Compare *PMich.Zen.* 46.5 (251 B.C.): Pyron writes to Zenon that
although he has long wanted to ask him for money, διαισχυνόμενος
καὶ πλείους προσπορευομένους ἀπείρημαι, 'I have refrained until
now, being ashamed to see so many others applying to you' (ed.).
In both cases the sense of προσπορεύομαι is not simply 'draw
near' in space, but rather 'apply to', 'address oneself to' (a
person for a purpose).[10] *PMich.Zen.* 60.9 (248/7 B.C.) is I think
another example of this use: Pais recommends that Zenon's boat,
of which P. is captain, be repaired so that it may find work,
νυνὶ γὰρ ὄντος παλαιοῦ οὐθεὶς προσπορεύεται, 'no-one applies
(to hire it)'. Cf. *PCair.Zen.* 393.2 (iii B.C.) προσῆλθέν μοι
ὠνητὴς περὶ τοῦ ἵππου τοῦ μεγάλου.

In the other instance we find the word in the sense of
'apply oneself to', 'proceed with' (an activity):

Ex. 36.2 καὶ ἐκάλεσεν Μωυσῆς Βεσελεηλ καὶ Ελιαβ ... καὶ
πάντας τοὺς ἑκουσίως βουλομένους προσπορεύεσθαι πρὸς τὰ
ἔργα ὥστε συντελεῖν αὐτά   (MT לקרבה)

Compare *PCair.Zen.* 60.6 (257 B.C.) προσπορεύεται δὲ καὶ πρὸς
[ταῦτα] καὶ πρὸς τὰ λοιπὰ μαθήματα, 'he is proceeding with this
and his other studies; 132.4 (256 B.C.) οὐ προσπορευόμεθα πρὸς
τὰ γενήματα τὰ ἐκ ταύτης τῆς γῆς, ἀλλὰ συμβαίνει καταφθείρεσθαι,

---

10. Cf. Eng. 'go to' in the sense of 'have recourse, appeal
to', *SOED* s.v. *go* III.4 Lat. *adeo*, 'to go to for help, redress,
etc., appeal or apply to', *OLD* s.v. 7.

'we are not getting on with (the harvesting of) the crops...'[11]

In both the above instances προσπορεύομαι can also be
taken as a literal equivalent of the Hebrew, in the sense of
'draw near'. This raises a problem, often encountered elsewhere.
In which sense are we to understand the word? In my opinion we
are justified in taking it in the sense it would normally have
in these contexts. The translators must have been conscious of
the sense their rendering would have as Greek. Indeed, I think
it possible that they welcomed the opportunity of using a word
which, while a literal equivalent of the Hebrew, also gave a
sense more appropriate to the context. (A merely literal
rendering could have been achieved by the use of ἐγγίζω, which
often translates קרב and נגש in the Pentateuch.)

προσπορεύομαι is always present tense in the Pentateuch.
Conversely προσέρχομαι does not occur in the present (or imperfect), and προσελεύσομαι and -ῆλθον are common.

The remaining compounds of πορεύομαι I note more briefly,
giving only the essential points.

ἐκπορεύομαι

First in Critias (25.36, v B.C.), then Xenophon (An. 5.1.8,
5.6.33, 6.6.37, Ages. 2.26), but not common until the Koine.
There are as yet no examples in iii B.C. papyri, PRein. 109.13
(131 B.C.) being the earliest, but from the inscriptions we
have SIG 1219.15 (Gambrea, iii B.C.), and also 700.12,26 (117
B.C.). It occurs 19 times in Plb., then in later papyri (see
MM), and in NT. In the majority of these occurrences it is
used in the present tense.

---

11. Similarly 531.2 (iii B.C.) 'μὴ προσπορεύει πρὸς τὰ [ἔργα
...]', 16 ταῦτα δ[ὲ γέγραφά σοι]ἵνα εἰδῆις ὅτι [προσπορεύο] μαι
πρὸς τὰ ἔρ[γα. (The restorations may be regarded as certain.)
Note the similarity with the Ex. example. This is all the more
significant in that the pl. τὰ ἔργα in Ex. 36.2 is independent of
the original (as often elsewhere in the Pentateuch): MT לקרבה אל-
המלאכה לעשת אתה. The pl. can have been used here only because
it was the more idiomatic Gk.
    PAmh. 33.17 (ii B.C.), quoted in MM and LSJ, could also be
classified as an example of this use.
    See also the use of προσέρχομαι in this sense, LSJ s.v. I.6.
    Lat. adeo once again shows a parallel semantic development:
see OLD s.v. 10.

The word appears often in the Pentateuch (over 40 times), almost always in the present and imperfect. The perfect occurs in the B text of *Nu.* 31.28,36, *De.* 11.10, while A has the present in each case. ἐξέρχομαι, on the other hand, is used only in the future, aorist, and perfect.

παραπορεύομαι

Found first in Arist. *HA* 577b 32, then in Plb. and other Koine writers (see LSJ and Anz, *Subsidia* 348); in papyri *PPetr.* 2.13.5.3 and *PSI* 354.13 (quoted in MM), and now also *PSorb.* 33.3 (all iii B.C.). It is also found in the *NT*. In most instances it is present tense.

In the Pentateuch there are 10 occurrences (counting *Ge.* 32.22, where Rahlfs reads it with 911 against A etc.). The present and imperfect are usual, but we also find the future in *De.* 2.18 B (present A), and aorist in 2.14 (stylistic variation? παρῆλθον precedes and follows). παρέρχομαι is used only in the future and aorist.

Another group is formed by compounds in which the preposition adds little or nothing to the sense. The new compound is usually synonymous with the earlier uncompounded verb (which may continue in use). The Koine shows a distinct fondness for such formations.[12]

ἐκτοκίζω ('lend at interest')

The simplex is old in this sense (e.g. D. 45.70). The compound has so far been recorded only in the third century B.C.: *BGU* 1246.24 οὐχ οἷοί εἰσιν τὴν ἀσφάλεάν μοι δοῦναι τῶν κερμάτων ὧν ὁ πατὴρ λαβὼν παρ' ἐμοῦ ἐξετόκισεν τῶι Βιήγχει, 'they are not able to give me an assurance regarding the money my father took from me and lent on interest to Bienchis'. Similarly in

De. 23.20-1 οὐκ ἐκτοκιεῖς τῷ ἀδελφῷ σου τόκον ἀργυρίου καὶ τόκον βρωμάτων καὶ τόκον παντὸς πράγματος, οὗ ἂν ἐκδανείσῃς·

---

12.   Bl. DF §116.1
      Cf. ἐνάρχομαι and καταφυτεύω discussed above, pp. 70 and 57.

(21) τῷ ἀλλοτρίῳ ἐκτοκιεῖς, τῷ δὲ ἀδελφῷ σου οὐκ ἐκτοκιεῖς

MT נשך hi. in all three places.

The first example here is a little awkward, with the cogn. acc., but ought nevertheless to be taken in the same sense, rather than as 'exact interest'. We may translate: 'you shall not lend to your brother charging interest on money or ...'

ἐκδανείζω ('lend')

De. 23.20 (quoted above), Ex. 22.24, IG. 4.841.16 (Calauria, iii B.C.) οἵτινες τό τε ἀργύριον ἐκδανεισοῦντι κατὰ δραχμὰς τριάκοντα, and other inscriptions of the same date (LSJ). Equivalent to δανείζω.

ἐκτρυγάω ('gather' fruit, crop)

Le. 25.5 τὴν σταφυλὴν τοῦ ἀγιάσματός σου οὐκ ἐκτρυγήσεις· ἐνιαυτὸς ἀναπαύσεως ἔσται τῇ γῇ, PGurob 8.10 (210 B.C.) ἐξετρύγησαν ... ἀμπέλους ῑ, and now also Sammelb. 9209 Inv. E. 7154.2,5 (iii-ii B.C.).

Essentially the same phenomenon is seen in the following example of a verb compound with two propositions.

ἐξαποστέλλω

Except for an occurrence in Ep. Philipp. ap. D. 18.77, no doubt a late insertion, this compound is first found in the third century B.C. It has the same senses as Classical ἀποστέλλω, and is clearly just a more vigorous form of the older word. The latter continues in use alongside the new formation.

ἐξαποστέλλω is frequently found, both in papyri and Koine writers.[13] E.g. PYale 39.12 ἐξαπόστειλον αὐτὸν πρὸς ἡμᾶς, PCair.zen. 93.7, 578.2 (all iii B.C.). It occurs over 200 times in Plb. (Mauersberger).

The Pentateuch translators have used the word some 80 times, mostly as a rendering of שלח pi. It has several senses.

---

13. See Anz, Subsidia 356f., O. Glaser, De ratione quae intercedit inter sermonem Polybii et eum qui in titulis saeculi III, II, I apparet, Diss. Giessen, 1894, 33f., Mayser, Gramm. I.iii 243, and MM.

1. 'send away', 'dismiss', e.g. *Ge*. 45.1 Ἐξαποστείλατε
πάντας ἀπ᾽ ἐμοῦ, *Ex*. 18.27, *Nu*. 5.2,3,4.

2. 'send', 'dispatch' (to a destination, on a mission), e.g.
Ge.32.14 ἔλαβεν ὧν ἔφερεν δῶρα καὶ ἐξαπέστειλεν Ησαυ τῷ ἀδελφῷ
αὐτοῦ, 8.10, *Le*. 26.25.

3. 'allow to leave', 'release', e.g. *Ex*. 4.23 Ἐξαπόστειλον
τὸν λαόν μου, ἵνα μοι λατρεύσῃ, and so commonly elsewhere in
Ex.; cf. *Le*. 14.7, al., of releasing an animal. This use is
not found outside the LXX and must be due to literal rendering
of the Hebrew word. The extension is however a fairly natural
one (cf. the same development earlier in ἀφίημι).

4. 'give a send-off to', e.g. *Ge*. 31.27 εἰ ἀνήγγειλάς μοι
ἐξαπέστειλα ἄν σε μετ᾽ εὐφροσύνης, 26.31. This too is a
Hebraistic use.

ἀποστέλλω is also used in the Pentateuch, occurring, as in
the Koine generally, more often than the double compound.

The remaining examples in this section are of various
types. They are all straightforward and will be noticed only
briefly.

ἀνθυφαιρέω ('deduct in turn')

Le. 27.18. LSJ cite the word from *PLond. ined*. 2361[V]
(iii B.C.) (still unpublished). It is not attested again until
much later.

διοδεύω ('travel through')

Ge. 12.6 διώδευσεν τὴν γῆν εἰς τὸ μῆκος αὐτῆς, similarly
13.17. Arist. *Mir*. 832a 28, Plb. and other Koine writers, *NT*,
and *PAmh*. 36.13 (ii B.C.).[14] It can now be quoted also from
iii B.C. papyri: *BGU* 1273.56 (222/1 B.C.) διοδευόμενοι διὰ τῆς
προυπαρχούσης ἐκ τοῦ πύργου εἰς τὴν ῥύμην διόδου, *PCair.zen*.
367.33 (240 B.C.) διοδεύ[ειν. For the use with acc. as in *Ge*.
cf. Plb. 2.15.5.

14. LSJ, MM, Anz, *Subsidia* 344.
Helbing, *Kasussyntax* 82, notes 'dass die Komposita von ὁδεύω
erst in der Κοινή häufiger sind'.

ἐπαύριον

This word, synonymous with αὔριον, (the) 'next' (day), is found in the Koine from the third century B.C. onwards:[15] e.g. *PHamb.* 1.27.4 (250 B.C.) τῆι δὲ ἐφαύριον αὐτὸν ἐπεζήτουν, *PLille* 15.2 (242 B.C.). It also occurs in Plb. (3.53.6, etc.), and the *NT.* In the Pentateuch it is found a number of times: e.g. *Ge.* 19.34, *Ex.* 9.6 τῇ ἐπαύριον, *Le.* 23.11 τῇ ἐπαύριον τῆς πρώτης.

αὔριον nevertheless remains the usual word (for examples in iii B.C. papyri see Kiessling), and is the commoner of the two in the Pentateuch.

καταγίγνομαι ('dwell')

Ex. 10.23 πᾶσι δὲ τοῖς υἱοῖς Ισραηλ ἦν φῶς ἐν πᾶσιν, οἷς κατεγίνοντο, *Nu.* 5.3, *De.* 9.9. First in Test. ap. D. 21.22, Teles p. 19.3,5 (Hense). In papyri e.g. *PMagd.* 9.3 (iii B.C.) ὑπάρχει ἐμοὶ 'Ισιεῖον ..., ὃ συμβέβηκεν πεπονεκέναι καὶ διὰ τοῦτο μὴ δύνασθαι ἐν αὐτῶι καταγίνεσθαι, *PTeb.* 5.175 (118 B.C.). Cf. Anz, *Subsidia* 354.

περίζωμα

A type of garment, though its precise nature is uncertain. It presumably refers to an apron-like undergarment, fastened around the waist. *UPZ* 121.12 (ii B.C.) περὶ τὸ σῶμα χλαμύδα ('mantle', 'cloak') καὶ περίζωμα, *PRev.* 94.7 (iii B.C.) (broken context). It is used of a cook's apron in Hegesipp. Com. 1.7 (iii B.C.). Cf. also Plb. 6.25.3, where it describes a light undergarment contrasted with a cuirass. The word is found in the Pentateuch in *Ge.* 3.7 ἐποίησαν ἑαυτοῖς περιζώματα (~ חגרה). The translators probably based their rendering on the etymology of the Hebrew word.

συλλαλέω ('converse with')

The word is not found before the third century B.C., and was obviously formed after λαλέω had become established as the ordinary word for 'speak'. It is common in papyri of the

---

15. On the origin of it see Bl. DF §§12.3, 233.3.

translators' time: e.g. *PCair.Zen.* 315.2 (250 B.C.) ἐπίστηι δὲ ὅτι συνελάλησά σοι περὶ τῶν ..., 428.9, *PCol.Zen.* 11.3 (both iii B.C.). In the Pentateuch it is found in *Ex.* 34.35 περιέθηκεν Μωυσῆς κάλυμμα ἐπὶ τὸ πρόσωπον ἑαυτοῦ, ἕως ἂν εἰσέλθῃ συλλαλεῖν αὐτῷ.

συντίμησις ('valuation')

Le. 27.4 τῆς δὲ θηλείας ἔσται ἡ συντίμησις τριάκοντα δίδραχμα, 27.18, *Nu.* 18.16. Cf. *PCair.Zen.* 300.3 (250 B.C.) ἵνα ἐξ συντιμήσεως καθὰ καὶ πρότερον τὸ ἡμίσευμα τάξωνται, *PRev.* 24.11 (iii B.C.).

Other compounds

ἀρχιοινοχόος

Found in *Ge.* 40.1,2,5,9,20,21,23. LSJ record it elsewhere only in Plu. *Alex.* 74, but ἀρχοινοχόος found in the following is the same word: *PTeb.* 72.447 (114-3 B.C.) παρὰ Διονυσίου τοῦ γενομένου ἀρχοινοχ<ό>ου, *IG* 9(1).486.19 (ii or i B.C.) ἀρχοινόχους· Κάλλιππος.[16]

ἐργοδιώκτης

The word is used in the Pentateuch of the overseers of the children of Israel in Egypt: *Ex.* 5.6 συνέταξεν δὲ Φαραω τοῖς ἐργοδιώκταις τοῦ λαοῦ καὶ τοῖς γραμματεῦσιν λέγων ..., similarly 3.7, 5.10,13 (MT שׁגנ in all). Cf. *PPetr.* 2.4(1).2 (c. 255 B.C., a complaint from certain quarrymen) ἀδικούμεθα ὑπὸ ᾽Απολλωνίου τοῦ ἐργοδιώκτου ἐμβαλὼν ἡμᾶς εἰς τὴν στερεὰν πέτραν. To this can be added much later examples in papyri of v and vi A.D.,

---

16. See Mayser, *Gramm.* I.i 81, iii 160f., on ἀρχ-, ἀρχε-, ἀρχι- compounds in general. Mayser (I.i 81) seems to regard ἀρχ- as usual before vowels though he notes some exceptions, as ἀρχιιερεύς *PPetr.* 3. (p).2 (iii B.C.). Bl. DF §124 note that in the Koine hiatus in composition is often not avoided (as it is generally in Attic). Similarly Thackeray, *Gramm.* 130. Thackeray may be right in suggesting (131) that assimilation is usual in earlier exx., hiatus in the later (though the whole question needs re-examination). The form in our MSS in *Ge.* 40 need not be original. (Brooke-McLean note v.l. only in *Ge.* 40.5: <αρχοιονοχοου 76>.)

PHarris 100.11, *POxy*. 2195.128, 2197.176, et al. It is not known otherwise except in Philo (3 p.58.12, clearly Biblical language).

It is to be noticed that the word does not have an unfavourable connotation, but the neutral sense of 'foreman', 'overseer'. 'Taskmaster' (LSJ), which now has the suggestion of harshness, is unsuitable.

The example is an instructive one. Without the occurrences in papyri it would be easy to suppose that the word was created by the translators. (ἐργοδιωκτέω, the only other word of the group, is confined to the LXX.)

ἑτερόζυγος

Le. 19.19 τὰ κτήνη σου οὐ κατοχεύσεις ἑτεροζύγῳ (~ כלאים), 'you shall not make your cattle breed with one of a different kind'. A similar use is found in *PCair.Zen*. 38.12 (257 B.C.) Ἀντιπατρίδια (type of vase) ἑτερόζυγα δύο καὶ ψυκτήριον καὶ κύαθον ('not pairs', LSJ). The word is found elsewhere later in slightly different senses (see LSJ).

εὐδοκέω

A common Koine verb, found from the third century B.C. onwards.[17] It is used in a number of slightly differing senses, not easily distinguished, but all derived from the basic sense of 'be well pleased'.

In the Pentateuch we have: (a) abs. 'be pleased', 'be content', *Ge*. 24.26 εὐδοκήσας ὁ ἄνθρωπος προσεκύνησεν κυρίῳ, similarly 48; (b) c. acc. 'be pleased with' *Ge*. 33.10 εὐδοκήσεις με, 'enjoy' *Le*. 26.34 *bis* εὐδοκήσει ἡ γῆ τὰ σάββατα αὐτῆς, cf. 41.

With these examples may be compared *PRev*. 29.8 (iii B.C.) ἐὰν μὲν εὐδοκῆι ὁ τελώνης, συγγραφὴν προϊέσθωσαν αὐτῶι, *SIG* 672.27 (162/0 B.C.) καθιστάντων δὲ καὶ ἐγγύους ὁ δανειζόμενοι οὕς κα οἱ ἐπιμεληταὶ εὐδοκέωντι.

---

17. See Anz, *Subsidia* 358, LSJ, and the numerous papyrus examples in MM. It occurs 57 times in Plb. (Mauersberger).

νευροκοπέω ('hamstring')

De. 21.6 τῆς δαμάλεως τῆς νενευροκοπημένης, 21.4, *Ge*. 49.6.
Cf. *PCair.Zen*. 462.4 (iii B.C.) τήν τε ὗν νυκτὸς ἐκ τῆς αὐλῆς
ἐξέβαλλε... φάμενος νευροκοπήσειν. Also in Koine writers (see
Anz, *Subsidia* 359).

σιτομετρέω

The whole group of words formed on σιτομετρ- is new in the
Koine. The verb is condemned by Phrynichus (360). In addition
to the examples from inscriptions and authors noted by LSJ and
Anz (*Subsidia* 360), a papyrus example contemporary with the
translators can now be cited: *PCol.Zen*. 69.52 (c. 257-249 B.C.)
ἃς κατὰ μῆνα σιτομετροῦμεν[. It is used in the Pentateuch in
Ge. 47.12 ἐσιτομέτρει Ιωσηφ τῷ πατρὶ καὶ τοῖς ἀδελφοῖς αὐτοῦ
... σῖτον κατὰ σῶμα, 14.

τοπάρχης

In *Ge*. 41.34 Joseph advises Pharaoh about preparations for
the coming famine: καὶ ποιησάτω Φαραω καὶ καταστησάτω τοπάρχας
ἐπὶ τῆς γῆς. The word τοπάρχης, which is not found before the
third century B.C., was a technical term of the Ptolemaic
administration. It was the title of the official in charge of
a τόπος or τοπαρχία, a sub-division of the nome.[18] From among
the numerous examples we may cite *PRev.Laws* 41.7 (iii B.C.)
ὅ τε νομάρχης καὶ ὁ τοπάρχης καὶ ὁ οἰκονόμος ...

The translators have aptly used a term of their own time
in the Egyptian context of the story of Joseph. The choice of
such a word (more specific than פקיד of the original) shows
very clearly their familiarity with the affairs and terminology
of their time, and that they expected their audience to be
similarly familiar with them.

Noun formations

In -μα

---

18. See e.g. E.Bevan, *A History of Egypt under the Ptolemaic
Dynasty*, London, 1927, 143.
    For examples of the word see Preisigke vol.III, Abschnitt 8 s.v.

γένημα ('produce')

A new formation of the Koine, not attested before iii B.C. and not connected with Classical γέννημα, 'that which is produced or born' (of living creatures). γένημα is formed from γεν- of γίγνομαι, γέννημα from γεννάω (though the two are often confused in MSS).[19]

The word is common in the papyri from iii B.C. onwards, being the normal term for vegetable produce of all kinds: see e.g. PCair.Zen. 179.11,17, PCol.Zen. 16.7 (both iii B.C.), and examples quoted in Deissmann[20] and MM. It is used often throughout the Pentateuch: e.g. Le. 26.4 ἡ γῆ δώσει τὰ γενήματα αὐτῆς, καὶ τὰ ξύλα τῶν πεδίων ἀποδώσει τὸν καρπὸν αὐτῶν (MT יבולה), Ge. 47.24, De. 16.15. Note the use of the plural, as often in the papyri.

κατάλυμα

This word, whose meaning may be defined as 'accommodation for rest at night' ('lodging'), is the Koine equivalent of Attic καταγώγιον.[21] It appears first in the third century B.C. E.g. PSI 341.8 (256 B.C.) σύνταξον δὲ Νικίαι δοῦναι ἡμῖν κατάλυμα, PCair.Zen. 847.1 (iii B.C.) ἐν τῶι καταλύματι τοῦ βασιλέως, 830.16 (248 B.C.), UPZ 120.5,10 (ii B.C.). It is also found in Plb., NT, and elsewhere (see Bauer).

It occurs in the Pentateuch in Ex. 4.24 ἐν τῇ ὁδῷ ἐν τῷ καταλύματι (∼ מלון), 15.13 παρεκάλεσας [τὸν λαόν σου] τῇ ἰσχύι σου εἰς κατάλυμα ἅγιόν σου (∼ נוה).

πλεόνασμα ('excess', 'surplus')

Nu. 31.32 τὸ π. τῆς προνομῆς, cf PTeb. 78.7 (110-8 B.C.) τοῦ ... ἐκβεβηκότος πλεονάσματος, 81.27 (ii B.C.), Ostr. Bodl. 1.97.5 (134 B.C.).

---

19. Bauer s.v. γένημα, Bl. DF §11.2, Deissmann, BS 184, Thackeray, Gramm. 118, Mayser, Gramm. I.i 214. The use of γενήματα for καρποί is censured by the Atticists: Phryn. 251 (R), Th.Mag. 74.8.

20. BS 110

21. So Moeris 241.

χόρτασμα ('fodder'; usually pl.)

Ge. 24.32 ἔδωκεν ἄχυρα καὶ χορτάσματα ταῖς καμήλοις, 24.25
42.27, 43.24, De. 11.15 (all pl.). Similarly in iii B.C. papyri,
e.g. PSI 400.15 ὥστε καὶ τὰ κτήνη σου ἔχειν χορτάσματα δωρεάν,
354.5 (quoted in MM).

In -μα formations on primary verbal stems (e.g. ἀνάθημα)
the Koine normally has the short stem vowel where Classical
Greek had the long.[22] Thus εὕρεμα, κρίμα, χύμα, and the like
are the normal Koine forms. Hence the following formation:

δόμα ('gift')

Undoubtedly new in the Koine. The Classical words were
δόσις and δῶρον. *δῶμα 'gift' is not found, probably because
of its homonymity with δῶμα 'house'.[23]

To the example of δόμα in PPetr. noted by MM and LSJ can
be added PCair.Zen. 825.3 (252 B.C.) Πρωτομάχωι δόμα
ἀναπόδοτον ⊢ λ, UPZ 2.8 (ii B.C.). It is also found in [Pl.]
Def. 415b, Aristeas, Plu., NT.

In the Pentateuch it occurs some 14 times. E.g. Ge. 25.6
τοῖς υἱοῖς τῶν παλλακῶν αὐτοῦ ἔδωκεν Αβρααμ δόματα, Le. 23.38,
Nu. 3.9.

In -σμός

ἀγορασμός ('purchase')

Ge. 42.19 ἀπαγάγετε τὸν ἀγορασμὸν τῆς σιτοδοσίας ὑμῶν, 33.
The whole group is old (ἀγοράζω etc.), and this formation could
also be old. It is however not attested before PCol.Zen. 5.34
(c. 257 B.C.) Σώσωι εἰς ἀγορασμὸν σίτου. For examples of ii
B.C. and later see Kiessling.

ἐμπυρισμός ('burning')

Le. 10.6 κλαύσονται τὸν ἐμπυρισμόν, ὃν ἐνεπυρίσθησαν ὑπὸ
κυρίου, Nu. 11.3, De. 9.22. Commonly in papyri, e.g. PSI 560.7

---

22. See Thackeray, Gramm. 79, Mayser, Gramm. I.i 65, Bl. DF
§109.3.
23. Chantraine, Formation 179.

67762

σώματα κγ εἰς ξυλοκοπίαν καὶ ἐμπυρισμόν, 500.5, 338.15, 339.7
(all iii B.C.). Phrynichus, 313 (R), censures Hyperides' use
of the word, saying he ought to have used ἐμπρησμός.

ἱματισμός (collective, 'clothing')

   Ge. 24.53 ἱματισμὸν ἔδωκεν Ρεβεκκα (~ בגדים), similarly
Ex. 3.22, 11.2, 12.35, 21.10 (all sing.). Frequently in papyri
of iii B.C. and later: e.g. *PHib.* 54.16 (c. 245 B.C.), quoted in
MM, *PCair.Zen.* 28.1 (iii B.C.). Also found in inscriptions,
authors, and *NT* (see LSJ, Bauer).

In -ή

ἀναζυγή ('breaking camp', 'setting-off')

   Ex. 40.37-8 εἰ δὲ μὴ ἀνέβη ἡ νεφέλη, οὐκ ἀνεζεύγνυσαν ... (38)
νεφέλη γὰρ ἦν ἐπὶ τῆς σκηνῆς ἡμέρας ... ἐν πάσαις ταῖς ἀναζυγαῖς
αὐτῶν. Similarly Plb. 3.44.13, and I now find it also in *PHamb.*
91.8 (167 B.C.) τῆ[ς δὲ ἀν]αζυγῆς ἐνστάσης.

ἀποσκευή

   This word is, like the other examples we have been considering, a new formation attested first in the third century
B.C. It is chiefly of interest, however, for the remarkable
semantic development it undergoes. As we shall see, this example
illustrates very clearly the importance of investigating the
Pentateuch vocabulary in conjunction with the vocabulary of
its time.

   The word occurs frequently in Koine authors, and a number
of times in papyri. This evidence, which is rather complicated,
has been discussed at some length by others.[24] In what follows I
shall attempt to summarize what has been established.

---

24. M. Holleaux, *Études d'épigraphie et d'histoire grecques*, vol.
III, Paris, 1942, 15-26 (= *REG* 1926 355-66); E. Kiessling,'Die
Aposkeuai und die prozessrechtliche Stellung der Ehefrauen im
ptol. Ägypten', *Archiv* VIII (1927) 240-9; U. Wilcken, *ib.* 88f.
Cf. also Kiessling, *Wörterbuch* s.v., and the discussion by the
editors of *PHal.* 1 (pp. 85ff.).
   LXX usage is not dealt with in any of these discussions.

The primary sense is, as the etymology leads us to expect, 'movable property', 'baggage' (both sing. collective, and pl.). This is seen in Plb. 1.68.3 προέμενοι τὰ τέκνα καὶ τὰς γυναῖκας σὺν τούτοις τὰς ἀποσκευάς, and elsewhere in Plb. (e.g. 1.70.5, 2.3.8). It is probably the meaning also in PCair.Zen. 93.9 (257 B.C.)

The important step in meaning is that the word comes to include persons as well as inanimate objects. The context in which this development originally took place was, as Holleaux shows (18ff.), a military one. Each soldier had his ἀποσκευή, which included not only his baggage proper, but also his wife and children, and other persons attached to him. This is clearly seen for example in Plb. 1.66.7-9: the Carthaginians request their mercenary troops to leave Carthage and withdraw to another town until they can be paid off. The mercenaries agree, καὶ βουλομένων αὐτοῦ καταλιπεῖν τὰς ἀποσκευὰς καθάπερ καὶ τὸν πρῶτον χρόνον ὑπῆρχον. At this the Carthaginians demur, fearing μήποτε διὰ χρόνου παραγεγονότες, καὶ τινὲς μὲν τέκνων, ἔνιοι δὲ καὶ γυναικῶν ἱμείροντες, οἱ μὲν οὐκ ἐκπορευθῶσι τὸ παράπαν, οἱ δ' ἐκπορευθέντες αὖθις ἀνακάμπτωσι πρὸς ταῦτα ('lest, longing to be with their wives or children after their recent protracted absence, they might in many cases refuse to leave, or, if they did, would come back again to their families'[25]). Consequently the Carthaginians compel the mercenaries to take τὰς ἀποσκευάς with them.[26]

The word is also used in the singular of the baggage-train of an army, comprising all the persons attached to the army as well as the baggage. So e.g. in Polyaen. 4.6.13 Ἀντίγονος δὲ τῶν Εὐμενείων στρατιωτῶν εἰδὼς ἑπομένην τὴν ἀποσκευήν, ἐν ᾗ γυναῖκες ἦσαν αὐτῶν καὶ τέκνα καὶ παλλακαὶ καὶ οἰκέται καὶ χρυσὸς καὶ ἄργυρος καὶ ὅσα ἄλλα ἐκτήσαντο .... Similarly in D.S. 19.42.2, 43.7, and probably also in Plb. 2.3.7, 11.18.10.ʼ

---

25. Paton's translation, Loeb ed.
   On this passage cf. F.W. Walbank, A Historical Commentary on Polybius,Oxford, 1957 and 1967, ad loc.

26. A similar example is found by Wilcken, op.cit. 89, in D.S. 20.47.4. For further examples of the word in the pl. see Holleaux 19 n.3.

In a number of examples in Egyptian papyri we find a
further development, though a slight one: the word is used exclusively of persons, viz. the family (wife and children especially, but also other household members) left behind by a
soldier on active service. Most of the occurrences are in legal
contexts: in Ptolemaic Egypt the families of soldiers in the
field were accorded certain privileges in legal proceedings.[27]
Thus in *PHal*. 1.128-44 (iii B.C.) the word is found six times
in regulations concerning the treatment of cases involving
soldiers' families: e.g. 134-6

ἐὰν δέ τινες φάσκωσιν εἶναι τῆς ἀποσκευῆς, οἱ δικασταὶ περὶ
τούτου διαγινωσκέτωσαν καὶ ἐὰν γνωσθῶσιν ὄντες τῆς
ἀποσκευῆς καὶ ...

Compare *PBaden* 48.9 (126 B.C.), a letter from a wife to her
husband:

ἔλεγε γὰρ μήτε σε στρατεύεσθαι μήτ' ἐμὲ εἶναι ἀποσκευήν.

Other similar examples are found in *UPZ* 110.199 (164 B.C.)
πάλιν ἡμῖν ἐντετεύχασιν οἱ ἐν τῆι πόλει μάχιμοι προφερόμενοι
καὶ ταῖς ἀποσκευαῖς αὐτῶν ἐπιγεγράφθαι γῆν, 'the troops in the
city have again petitioned me claiming that land has been
registered also for their families', 90, 206, *Sammelb*. 8009.3
(i B.C.).

In these examples ἀποσκευή refers specifically to a
soldier's family. Whether it could be used more generally of
any man's family is not indicated by our evidence.

The senses of the word, then, according to the available
evidence, are:

1. 'baggage';
2. (a) 'the baggage-train of an army, comprising baggage and
persons attached to the army';
    (b) ' a soldier's baggage, family, and other persons
attached to him';
3. 'a soldier's family (wife, children, and other household
members)'.

In the Pentateuch there are some 16 occurrences of

27. See esp. Kiessling's *Archiv* article already cited.

ἀποσκευή, usually as a rendering of קט . Before looking at these there are two points we ought to notice.

'Children', 'little ones', given by BDB, is not the only sense of קט. As BDB themselves note in their Addenda et Corrigenda, the word refers in a number of passages to women as well as children (e.g. *Ge.* 47.12, *Ex.* 10.10,24).[28] It seems clear that the meaning in these places is in fact 'family', 'dependents' (wives and children, and probably others as well).

Secondly, the places where the translators render קט by some other word than ἀποσκευή have something to tell us about their understanding of the Hebrew word. These other renderings are: τέκνα (*De.* 2.34, 3.19), ἔκγονα (*De.* 29.10, 31.12), παιδία (*Ge.* 45.19 and elsewhere), συγγένεια (*Ge.* 50.8), οἰκίαι (*Ge.* 50. 21), ἀπαρτία (*Nu.* 31.17,18; the meaning of this word is uncertain), and in *Ge.* 47.12 קטה יפל is rendered κατὰ σῶμα. It is clear that the translators took קט as having not only the sense of 'children', but also a more general sense, namely 'family', 'household'.

The usage of ἀποσκευή in the Pentateuch closely resembles that found in contemporary Greek. In certain passages the word is clearly used in the sense of 'a man's family (wife, children, and other members of the household)'.[29] Thus in *Ex.* 10.8ff. Pharaoh agrees to let the Israelites go and offer worship, and asks who are to go. Moses replies that they wish to take young and old, sons and daughters, sheep and cattle. Pharaoh objects, saying (10) καθότι ἀποστέλλω ὑμᾶς, μὴ καὶ τὴν ἀποσκευὴν ὑμῶν; ... (11) μὴ οὕτως· πορευέσθωσαν δὲ οἱ ἄνδρες, καὶ λατρεύσατε τῷ θεῷ. The plague of locusts follows; then the three days of darkness. Pharaoh relents, and says: (24) βαδίζετε, λατρεύσατε κυρίῳ τῷ θεῷ ὑμῶν· πλὴν τῶν προβάτων καὶ τῶν βοῶν ὑπολίπεσθε· καὶ ἡ ἀποσκευὴ ὑμῶν ἀποτρεχέτω μεθ' ὑμῶν. (The sing. here is of

---

28. See also Skinner, *Genesis* (*ICC*), on *Ge.* 47.12.
   Cf. KB s.v., who give the basic sense as 'those of a nomadic tribe who are not (or in small extent) able to march'.
29. ἀποσκευή renders קט in all the places cited unless otherwise indicated.
   I leave out of account *Ex.* 27.19, 39.22, *Nu.* 32.16, where the major MSS disagree on the reading.

course used collectively.)

Similarly in *Ex.* 12.37 it is clear that the word refers to all persons apart fom the full-grown men; i.e. the men's families, and all the other persons attached to them:

ἀπάραντες δὲ οἱ υἱοὶ Ισραηλ ... εἰς ἑξακοσίας χιλιάδας πεζῶν οἱ ἄνδρες πλὴν τῆς ἀποσκευῆς (38) καὶ ἐπίμικτος πολὺς συνανέβη αὐτοῖς καὶ πρόβατα καὶ βόες καὶ κτήνη πολλὰ σφόδρα.

Other examples of the same kind are found in *Ge.* 43.8, *Nu.* 32.17,24.

In certain other instances the sense is probably the original one of 'baggage', 'movable property': *Ge.* 15.14 μετὰ δὲ ταῦτα ἐξελεύσονται ὧδε μετὰ ἀποσκευῆς πολλῆς (~ רכש); similarly 31.18 (~ רכש).

In *Ge.* 14.12 ἔλαβον δὲ καὶ τὸν Λωτ ... καὶ τὴν ἀποσκευὴν αὐτοῦ καὶ ἀπῴχοντο (~ רכש) the word seems to have its most general sense of 'baggage and family, etc.' (cf. sense 2.(b) above). Later, when Lot is rescued (vs. 16), mention is made of the recovery also of τὰ ὑπάρχοντα αὐτοῦ καὶ τὰς γυναῖκας καὶ τὸν λαόν. The last-mentioned are presumably the miscellaneous crowd of relatives and slaves which formed part of Lot's ἀποσκευή.

We have finally to notice certain instances in which ἀποσκευή occurs together with αἱ γυναῖκες. E.g.

Ge. 46.5-6 ἀνέλαβον οἱ υἱοὶ Ισραηλ τὸν πατέρα αὐτῶν καὶ τὴν ἀποσκευὴν καὶ τὰς γυναῖκας αὐτῶν ἐπὶ τὰς ἁμάξας ... (6) καὶ ἀναλαβόντες τὰ ὑπάρχοντα αὐτῶν καὶ πᾶσαν τὴν κτῆσιν ... εἰσῆλθον εἰς Αἴγυπτον.

De. 20.13-14 καὶ πατάξεις πᾶν ἀρσενικὸν αὐτῆς [a city] ἐν φόνῳ μαχαίρας, (14) πλὴν τῶν γυναικῶν καὶ τῆς ἀποσκευῆς καὶ πάντα τὰ κτήνη ...

Similar examples are found in *Ge.* 34.29, *Nu.* 31.9, 32.26,30.

What is the meaning of our word here? Is it 'children'?[30]

30. So LSJ Suppl.: 'children, little ones , LXX *Ge.* 46.5, al.' This is plainly based on the supposed meaning of the Hb. word (note the rendering 'little ones').

Clearly this is a possible sense, and at first glance may seem
the right one. I suggest, however, that we are not justified
in taking it in this way. Nothing ought to be based on the
meaning of the Hebrew word. There is no certainty that the
translators intended their rendering in the same sense as ‎טף .
Moreover I do not think it has been satisfactorily established
that ‎טף itself means 'children' here. Despite the tautology,
I think ἀποσκευή in these passages is intended in the sense of
'family'.[31] There is no compelling reason for seeing a new
sense here.

This argument is strongly supported by the one remaining
example, *Nu*. 16.27, where ἀποσκευή is plainly tautological (as
is ‎טף):

καὶ Δαθαν καὶ Αβιρων ἐξῆλθον καὶ εἱστήκεισαν παρὰ τὰς
θύρας τῶν σκηνῶν αὐτῶν καὶ αἱ γυναῖκες αὐτῶν καὶ τὰ
τέκνα αὐτῶν καὶ ἡ ἀποσκευὴ αὐτῶν.

Here the word must be vague and general, and include the women
and children just mentioned. (It cannot, of course, mean
'baggage'.)

We have seen, then, that the usage of ἀποσκευή in the
Pentateuch is closely linked with that in the Greek of the time.
There is, however, a slight difference. As we saw, the word is
used outside the Pentateuch only in reference to soldiers'
families, in some instances as a technical legal term. In the
Pentateuch, on the other hand, it is used in a more general way
of any man's family. It is difficult to tell whether this was
an innovation in the translators' Greek. The extension is such
a slight one that it could easily have occurred already in the
Greek of the time; and it can hardly be due to Hebraism.
Nevertheless there is a possibility that the translators themselves extended the usage of this convenient term. The extension would have been helped by the fact that many of the
contexts in which such a word is needed are quasi-military ones:
see e.g. *Nu*. 31.9, where the Israelites defeat the Midianites
in battle and plunder their property, and *Ex*. 12.37, where the

---

31. In some of them, *Ge*. 46.5, *Nu*. 31.9, 32.30, it might also
be taken as 'baggage', but this seems less likely.

men are actually called πεζοί.

At any rate it is certain that the translators were familiar with the current usage of this term. We have seen moreover that a knowlwdge of the current usage helps considerably in understanding the meaning of the word in the Pentateuch.

In -ών

This suffix, though old, was especially productive in Hellenistic Greek. It was used for forming words that designate places, especially places where plants grow.[32]

ἀμπελών

Surprisingly the word is not attested before the Koine period, except for an uncertain reading in Aeschin. 2.156 (ἀμπελουργεῖον Teubner).[33] It is extremely common in the papyri from iii B.C. onwards, as e.g. *PCair.Zen.* 236.8 (254/3 B.C.) τὸ ἀργύριον παρὰ τῶν οἰνοκαπήλων οἴνου οὗ ἔλαβον ἐκ τοῦ ἀμπελῶνος.[34] In the Pentateuch it occurs some 18 times, mostly rendering כרם. E.g. *Ge.* 9.20 ἐφύτευσεν ἀμπελῶνα, *De.* 6.11 ... ἀμπελῶνας καὶ ἐλαιῶνας, οὓς οὐ κατεφύτευσας.

σιτοβολών ('granary')

This word, along with the related words σιτοβολ-εῖον, -ιον, -ον (all with the same meaning), is attested first in the Koine. To the examples noted by LSJ, *PSI* 358.9 (252-1 B.C.) and an inscription from Delos, also of iii B.C., can now be added *PCol.Zen.* 53.2 (250 B.C.) νυκτὸς ἐκ τοῦ σιτοβολῶνος ἀπόλωλεν σήσαμον. It is used in the Pentateuch in *Ge.* 41.56 καὶ ὁ λιμὸς ἦν ἐπὶ προσώπου πάσης τῆς γῆς· ἀνέῳξεν δὲ Ιωσηφ πάντας τοὺς σιτοβολῶνας καὶ ἐπώλει πᾶσι τοῖς Αἰγυπτίοις.

---

32. See BP 247f., Palmer, *Gramm.* 120, Mayser, *Gramm.* I.iii 86ff., B. Olsson, *Aegyptus* XIII (1933) 327-30, and MM s.v. ἐλαιών.

33. If it had been in use in Class.Gk. we should expect to find at least some examples of it, since the idea is such a common one. Yet it is difficult to discover what word was used instead.

34. For other examples see MM and Kiessling.

108

ἐλαιών

Ex. 23.11, De. 6.11, very commonly in papyri, e.g. PCair. Zen. 157.2 (256 B.C.) τῶν στροβίλων φύτευσον ... περὶ τὸν ἀμπελῶνα καὶ τοὺς ἐλαιῶνας. Deissmann, BS 208ff.

πυλών ('gateway')

Ge. 43.19 ἐλάλησαν αὐτῷ ἐν τῷ πυλῶνι τοῦ οἴκου, often in papyri and inscriptions from iii B.C. onwards: e.g. PCair.Zen 193.9 (255 B.C.) συνετάγη δὲ τῶι ἀρχιτέκτονι ... τὸν πυλῶνα ... μεταθεῖναι, PEnt. 74.3 (iii B.C.). Cf. Moeris 88 αὐλία θύρα Ἀττικῶς, πυλὼν Ἑλληνικῶς.

Various

ἀμνάς ('ewe-lamb')[35]

Often in the Pentateuch, as e.g. Nu. 6.14 προσάξει ... ἀμνάδα ἐνιαυσίαν ἄμωμον μίαν, Ge. 21.28, Le. 5.6. It is attested elsewhere only in PCair.Zen. 576.3 (iii B.C.) ... τὴν χίμαιραν καὶ τὴν ἀμνάδα, 406.6 (iii B.C.), and Theoc. 8.35, J. AJ 7.7.3.

ἐλεημοσύνη ('mercy', 'pity')

De. 6.25 καὶ ἐλεημοσύνη ἔσται ἡμῖν, ἐὰν φυλασσώμεθα ποιεῖν πάσας τὰς ἐντολὰς ταύτας (~ צדקה), Ge. 47.29 (~ חסד). As LSJ and Bauer record, the word is found in Call. 4.152 (iii B.C.); to this can be added PCair.Zen. 495.10 (iii B.C., a letter to Zenon) πρὸς σὲ οὖν καταφυγγάνομεν, ἵνα ἐλεημοσύνης τύχωμεν.

It also occurs in the Pentateuch in De. 24.13, where the sense is not quite clear. It is perhaps 'kind deed', from which comes the later sense, as in NT, of 'alms', 'almsgiving' (cf. Bauer).

μοσχάριον ('calf')

Nine times in the Pentateuch, e.g. Ge. 18.7 ἔλαβεν

---

35. On the formation see esp. BP 411ff. The use of this suffix for names of animals is old.

μοσχάριον ἁπαλὸν καὶ καλόν, and commonly in iii B.C. papyri:
e.g. *PCair.Zen.* 326.141 (c.249 B.C.)'Ισιδώραι τιμὴν μοσχαρίου,
PSorb. 22.6. The older word μόσχος continues to be common in
the Koine (and so also in the Pentateuch).

πυρράκης ('of ruddy complexion')[36]

Ge. 25.25 ἐξῆλθεν δὲ ὁ υἱὸς ὁ πρωτότοκος πυρράκης, ὅλος
ὡσεὶ δορὰ δασύς (~ אדמוני). The word is known, apart from the
LXX, only in iii B.C. papyri, where it is found a number of
times in personal descriptions. Thus e.g. *PPetr.* 3.6(a).9
(237 B.C.), the remains of a will, ὡς LϚ πυρράκης οὐλὴ μ[...,
'about 60 years old, of reddish complexion, a scar ...'.
Similarly 3.1.1.19, *PCair.Zen.* 76.11, 374.5 (all iii B.C.).

Adjective formations

ἀρσενικός and θηλυκός

These two words, which form a pair, are conveniently
treated together. They both appear in the third century B.C.
as synonyms of Classical ἄρσην (ἄρρην) and θῆλυς, and are examples of the tendency towards replacement of third declension
forms by first and second declension. [37] They pass into Modern
Greek as the normal vernacular words.[38] Nevertheless ἄρσην and
θῆλυς are still common in the third century B.C. and remain so
until late in the Koine.[39]

ἀρσενικός occurs about 40 times in the Pentateuch, as e.g.

---

36. For a number of other formations of this uncommon type see
BP 4; cf. Mayser, *Gramm.* I.i 455.
   πυρράκης is strictly a noun (like μανιάκης, ἱππάκης,
ἀττάκης, etc.) used attributively.

37. Cf. Thackeray, *Gramm.* 140.
   On -ικός formations see BP 636ff., Palmer, *Gramm.* 35.
Palmer notes that 'such formations often replace earlier
adjectives of a different type'.

38. Thumb, *Handbook of the Modern Greek Vernacular* 72, Swanson.

39. Examples in MM, Preisigke, and Kiessling. Only the older
words are found in *NT*.

Nu. 3.43 πάντα τὰ πρωτότοκα τὰ ἀρσενικά, *Ge*. 17.10, *Ex*. 13.12,
and θηλυκός twice, *Nu*. 5.3 ἀπὸ ἀρσενικοῦ ἕως θηλυκοῦ
ἐξαποστείλατε, *De*. 4.16. The older words are also common, ἄρσην
occurring some 40 times, θῆλυς 26.

Examples from the translators' time are found in *PCair.
Zen*. 166.2 (255 B.C.) ζεύγη θηλυκὰ καὶ ἀρσενικά, *PLille* 10.5,
PPetr. 3.93.7.11, and often elsewhere in *PCair.Zen*.

The next two words similarly form a pair of parallel
formations related to the same object.

δειλινός ('in the afternoon')[40]

Recorded first in Diocles Med. *Fr*. 141 p.180.12 (iv B.C.
acc. to Bauer), then Men. *Kon*. 7. From iii B.C. papyri can be
quoted an example not noted by LSJ and Bauer: *PCair.Zen*. 207.37
(255/4 B.C.) τὸ γὰρ πρωινὸν θερίζομεν καὶ τὸ διλινὸν
βοτανίζομεν.[41] It is also found in Koine authors (see LSJ).

In the Pentateuch it occurs in *Ge*. 3.8 τοῦ θεοῦ περι-
πατοῦντος ἐν τῷ παραδείσῳ τὸ δειλινόν, *Ex*. 29.39,41, *Le*. 6.13,
all τὸ δειλινόν adv.

πρωινός ('in the morning')[42]

First in Thphr. *CP* 3.24.2, then *PCair.Zen*. 207.36 quoted
above. Otherwise only later examples are known (*NT* and late
writers: see LSJ and Bauer).

The word is found four times in the Pentateuch: (a) adj.
Ex. 29.41 κατὰ τὴν θυσίαν τὴν πρωινήν, *Le*. 9.17, *Nu*. 28.23;
(b) adv. *Ge*. 49.27.

ἑσπερινός, 'in the evening', may also be mentioned here, although
it has not yet been found in early documents. It occurs in X.
Lac. 12.6, *AP* 5.201.4 (Asclep. or Posidipp., both iii B.C.),
papyri of iv/v A.D. (see MM), and in the Pentateuch in *Le*. 23.5.

The remainder are of various types.

---

40. On the suffix see BP 261, Palmer, *Gramm*. 19.
41. διλινόν is of course just an alternative spelling.
42. Cf. Thackeray, *Gramm*. 90.

ἀναφάλαντος

This word, meaning 'bald on the forehead', is common in iii B.C. papyri in personal descriptions. See e.g. *PCair.Zen*. 347.1 (c. 245 B.C.), *PPetr*. 1.19.4,5,7,23 (225 B.C.). The translators use it in *Le*. 13.41.

ἀπερίτμητος ('uncircumcised')

Ge. 17.14, *Ex*. 12.48, *Le*. 26.41, and often elsewhere in the LXX and in the *NT*. Even Deissmann thought it probable that the word was coined by the Alexandrian Jews.[43] But an example has turned up that makes this very unlikely.[44] In *PCair.Zen*. 76 (257 B.C.) Toubias, 'a great hereditary chief in Transjordania',[45] writes to Apollonius that he has sent him a gift of a eunuch and four boy slaves: (1.5) ἀπέσταλκά σοι... παιδάρια... τέσσαρα, ὧν [ἐστὶν] ἀπερίτμητα δύο. A detailed description of the slaves follows (1.14): two are described as ἀπερίτμητος, two as περιτετμημένος. There is no reason to think that Toubias's Greek (or his scribe's) was in any way influenced by Jewish terminology. ἀπερίτμητος is moreover the formation we should expect for expressing this idea: περιτέμνω is old in the sense of 'circumcise' (Hdt.).

κόκκινος ('red', 'scarlet')

This formation appears first in the third century B.C., as a replacement for Classical ἐρυθρός, and continues on into Modern Greek as the normal word for 'red' (Swanson). It has been noted in Herod. 6.19 (iii B.C.), but not again until writers and papyri of i A.D. and later, and *NT*.[46] I now find

---

43. *BS* 153. Deissmann goes uncharacteristically astray here: he suggests that ἄσημος may have been the word for the idea among the Greek Egyptians, then adds: 'the more definite and, at the same time, harsher ἀπερίτμητος corresponded to the contempt with which the Greek Jews thought of the uncircumcised'. How is the latter word 'harsher'? In any case the meaning of ἄσημος is much more general, viz. 'without distinguishing mark'.

44. Recorded by Bauer, s.v.

45. Edgar, *Selected Papyri* no.84 (= *PCair.Zen*. 76).

46. LSJ, MM, Kiessling Suppl.

it also in *Inscr. Del*. 1416 A i 58 (ii B.C.) σαγγαικὸν βεβαμμένον κόκκινον ἐν κιβωταρίῳ, ἀνάθεμα ʿHρακλείας, and *BGU* 1300.24 (iii/ii B.C.) a list of items (combs, ear-rings, and the like) κόκκινα β, 'two scarlet garments', or 'two pieces of scarlet cloth'.

The word is common in the Pentateuch, being the usual rendering of שני and תולעה . (a) adj., e.g. *Nu*. 4.8 ἱμάτιον κόκκινον, (b) subst., e.g. *Ex*. 28.5 λήμψονται ... τὸ κόκκινον καὶ τὴν βύσσον. For the substantival use cf., in addition to the *BGU* example above, the examples in Epict. and *NT* noted by Bauer.

ἐρυθρός in the Pentateuch, as in the Koine generally, is confined to the set phrase ἐρυθρὰ θάλασσα.

μίσθιος

Usually as a substantive, 'hired labourer'. It is found first in papyri of the third century B.C., *PCair.Zen*. 378.14, and now *PCol.Zen*. 75.19 (c. 248-6 B.C., an account of salary expenditures) μίσθιοι β (δραχμαί). For later examples see LSJ, MM. It occurs in the Pentateuch in *Le*. 25.50 ἔσται τὸ ἀργύριον τῆς πράσεως αὐτοῦ ὡς μισθίου.

παρεπίδημος ('temporary resident')

Ge. 23.4, *PPetr*. 1.19.22, 3.7.15 (both iii B.C.): see Deissmann, *BS* 149.

σανιδωτός ('of boards')

Ex. 27.8 κοῖλον σανιδωτὸν ποιήσεις αὐτό [τὸ θυσιαστήριον]. Previously not known elsewhere, but now recorded by LSJ Suppl. in *Inscr.Délos* 1417 A ii 55 (ii B.C.) κλίνας σανιδωτάς, 1403 Bb ii 33 (ii B.C.).

Another formation of the same type is:

δικτυωτός ('net-like', 'latticed')

Ex. 27.4 ... ἐσχάραν ἔργῳ δικτυωτῷ, 38.24. In addition to the examples in D.S. and Plb. (LSJ), cf. now *PMich.Zen*. 38.18 (iii B.C.) τοῦ κοιτῶνος θυρίδας δικτυωτὰς ἦ, 'in the bedroom, 8 latticed windows' (ed.).

Verb formations

ἀροτριάω

This Koine word is one of a whole new group of formations on the stem ἀροτρ- (from ἄροτρον). They tend to replace the words of the older group based on ἀρο-. ἀροτριάω takes the place of Classical ἀρόω,[47] which is rare in the Koine except in literary writers.

ἀροτριάω is attested first in Thphr. *HP* 8.6.3, then in various authors (Call., Babr., see LSJ, Bauer), and in *NT*. In iii B.C. papyri we have *PPetr*. 3.31.7 τοῦ ζεῦγος τῶν βοῶν μου πορευομένου ... ὥστε ἀροτριᾶν, *PCair.Zen*. 729.5, *PSI* 661.5.

The word is found in the Pentateuch in *De*. 22.10 οὐκ ἀροτριάσεις ἐν μόσχῳ καὶ ὄνῳ ἐπὶ τὸ αὐτό. (ἀρόω is not used in the Pentateuch, or at all in the LXX.)

ἐμπυρίζω ('burn', 'set on fire')

Le. 10.6 τὸν ἐμπυρισμόν, ὃν ἐνεπυρίσθησαν ὑπὸ κυρίου, 16. Cf. *PCol.Zen*. 96.2,3 (iii B.C.?) ὁ ἐμπυρίσας τὴν χέρσον ἐνεπύρισεν τῶν παρ' ἡμῶν συκᾶς β, *PCair.Zen*. 387.3 (iii B.C.).

κυριεύω ('be master of', 'rule', 'control')

A common Koine verb, which appears first in X., then Arist., Men. In the translators' time we have e.g. *Sammelb*. 8545.13 κυριεύσας δὲ τῆς τε ἐντὸς Εὐφράτου χώρας πάσης καὶ..., *PRev*. 3.2, 46.9 (all iii B.C.). For further examples, in authors and later papyri, see LSJ and MM.

It occurs in the Pentateuch in *Nu*. 24.7 κυριεύσει ἐθνῶν πολλῶν, 21.18, *Ex*. 15.9, *Ge*. 3.16, 37.8.

---

47. Cf. Moeris 22 ἀροῦν Ἀττικῶς, ἀροτριᾶν Ἑλληνικῶς.

CHAPTER VI

NEW WORDS

In this chapter we have to consider a third type of innovation in the Koine vocabulary, namely new words other than those created by formation on existing stems. These are mainly loan-words from outside Greek, but there are also some words that came into the Koine from dialects other than Attic. We shall see that here too there are links between the Pentateuch vocabulary and that of the time.

βουνός

The word appears first in Hdt. (4.192,199), who says it was Cyrenaean. Phryn. (333) tells us it was used by Syracusan poets. At any rate it seems clear that it was a Doric word, but whether originally borrowed from outside Greek is unknown.[1] It was still a strange word for Philemon (49, 142) at the end of the fourth century. In the Koine it becomes common, and continues on into Modern Greek as the usual vernacular word for 'mountain' (Swanson, Jannaris).

From inscriptions and papyri can be cited e.g. Schwyzer, *DGE* 289.169 (200-190 B.C.) καὶ ἀπὸ τούτου παρὰ τὸν βουνὸν ἔστε καὶ τὰν φάραγγα ἐθήκαμεν ἄλλον ὅρον, *Archiv* I 63.15 (123 B.C.), *PTheb.Bank* I.i.3, 32 (131 B.C.), *BGU* 1216.19 (ii B.C.).[2] It is also used by Plb., e.g. 3.83.1, 5.22.3, and by other Koine writers.

In the Pentateuch the word occurs as follows:

(a) 'hill' or 'mountain', *Ex.* 17.9 ἕστηκα ἐπὶ τῆς κορυφῆς τοῦ βουνοῦ, 10, *Nu.* 23.9, *De.* 33.15 (in all ~ גבעה).

(b) 'mound', 'heap', *Ge.* 31.46 συνέλεξαν λίθους καὶ ἐποίησαν βουνόν, similarly 46 *bis*, 47 *bis*, 48 *ter*, 52 (mostly ~ גל).

---

1. See Mayser, *Gramm.* I.i.8, Bl. DF §126.1b, Thumb, *Hellenismus* 224, Frisk s.v., and most recently Chantraine, *Dictionnaire étymologique de la langue grecque* s.v.
    βοῦνις is found in A. *Supp.* 117,129.

2. Others in MM; and for later pap. exx. see Preisigke and Kiessling.

114

This latter use is paralleled in *PFlor.* 58.12 (iii A.D.) βουνὸν σείτου (LSJ, MM).

γογγύζω

This verb is attested first in the third century B.C., but γογγυσμός in Anaxandr. Comicus 31 (iv B.C.) implies it earlier. According to Phryn. 336, both are Ionic.[3] The etymology of this group of words is uncertain.[4]

In iii B.C. papyri we have *PPetr.* 3.43(3).20 (241 B.C.) τὸ πλήρωμα γογγύζει φάμενοι ἀδικεῖσθαι, 'the gang are grumbling ...'. It is next recorded in *NT* and later Koine writers.[5]

The translators use the word seven times (Rahlfs): *Ex.* 17.3 ἐγόγγυζεν ἐκεῖ ὁ λαὸς πρὸς Μωυσῆν λέγοντες ..., *Nu.* 11.1, 14.27, etc.

θῖβις

The meaning of this loan-word[6] is apparently 'basket', though precisely what kind of basket is unknown. It is attested only in the Pentateuch and Egyptian papyri of iii/ii B.C. In the latter we have *PCair.Zen.* 69.5 (257 B.C.) ἐν θίβει νάρδου μαρσίππια ἐσφρα(γισμένα) ε, *UPZ* 149.21 (iii B.C.) θῆβις τῶν ἄρτων, *PPetr.* 3.51.4,13 (iii B.C.), *PGrenf.* 1.14.10 (ii B.C.).

It is used in the Pentateuch of the basket in which Moses was placed: *Ex.* 2.3 ἔλαβεν αὐτῷ ἡ μήτηρ αὐτοῦ θῖβιν καὶ κατέχρισεν αὐτὴν ἀσφαλτοπίσσῃ, 5,6 (~ תבה).

κάρταλλος

Another word for a kind of basket.[7] It seems not to be a

---

3. Cf. Thumb, *Hellenismus* 215, and Bauer for other refs.
4. Chantraine, *op.cit.*, s.v.: 'Verbe à harmonie imitative qui ne se prête pas à une étymologie précise'. Cf. Frisk for possible cognates in Skr.
5. See Anz, *Subsidia* 368f.
6. From Hb. תבה, Mayser, *Gramm.* I.i 42, LSJ. The Hb. word itself was apparently a loan-word from Egyptian (BDB, KB). Could θῖβις have been borrowed from Egyptian rather than Hb.?
7. 'Basket with pointed bottom', LSJ.

loan-word, and may in fact be old in Greek.[8] At any rate it is
not attested before the third century B.C. It is found in
papyri in *Sammelb.* 6801.4 (iii B.C.) ἔχω παρὰ Θεοδώρου, ἀνθ᾿ ὧν
ἔδωκα Φτηρεῖ τῷ ″Αραβι εἰς καρτάλλους χαλ(κοῦ) ⊢ β, and the
diminutive occurs *ib.* 26; otherwise only in LXX, Ph., and
Hsch. (LSJ).

There are two examples in the Pentateuch: *De.* 26.2 λήμψῃ
ἀπὸ τῆς ἀπαρχῆς τῶν καρπῶν τῆς γῆς σου ... καὶ ἐμβαλεῖς εἰς
κάρταλλον, 4 (in both ~ אנט).

κόνδυ ('cup')[9]

The word appears first in Comedy, Hipparch. Com. 1.6, Men.
Kol. fr. 2.2 (Koerte), then in papyri and inscriptions, e.g.
PPetr. 2.32.1.23 (iii B.C.) κύαθον κόνδυ ∠ ι , *PLond.* 402.II.13
(ii B.C.). It occurs in the Pentateuch seven times in *Ge.* 44:
e.g. vs. 2 καὶ τὸ κόνδυ μου τὸ ἀργύριον ἐμβάλατε εἰς τὸν
μάρσιππον τοῦ νεωτέρου.[10]

κόρος (a dry measure)

A loan-word from Semitic (cf. Hebrew כֹּר),[11] found in the
LXX, *NT* (once), J., and Eupolem. ap. Euseb. *Pr. Ev.* 9.33, where
it is clearly meant as a Semitic term: it occurs in what
purports to be a letter from Solomon, and the writer explains
its meaning.

I find it also, however, in *PSI* 554.14 (259-8 B.C.)
]μένου κόρων κ καὶ β εἰς τὸ συναγαγεῖν ὡς ἐκ τοῦ γενομένου
ἀποτεῖσαι αὐτοὺς ἐκ κόρ<ων> ιβ̄. Whether the writer of this was
Jewish and to what extent this measure was in use in Egypt are
unclear.

---

8. 'Technisches oder volkstümliches Wort aur -αλλος ...,
letzten Endes auf ein Verb 'drehen, flechten' zurückgehend,
aber im einzelnen dunkel', Frisk.

9. 'Wie viele andere Wörter auf -υ ... offenbar entlehnt',
Frisk. Its origin is however unknown.

10. LSJ add, in ref. to this example, 'as a measure': as Caird
notes *JTS* XX (1969) 22, this comment is quite gratuitous. (44.5
shows plainly that a drinking-vessel is meant.)

11. Frisk s.v.

The word occurs in the Pentateuch in *Nu*. 11.32 συνήγαγον
τὴν ὀρτυγομήτραν, ὁ τὸ ὀλίγον συνήγαγεν δέκα κόρους, *Le*. 27.16.
Curiously, in both places κόρος renders חמר, not כר, though
κόρος is the usual rendering of כר elsewhere in the LXX.

No firm conclusion can be drawn from this example, but
there is clearly a possibility that κόρος was not confined to
Jewish circles in Ptolemaic Egypt.

μάρσιππος ('sack')

An old word, but not in Attic.[12] It is found in X. *An*.
4.3.11, and in the diminutive form in Hp. *Acut*. 21, Apollod.
Car. (Comicus) 13 (iv/iii B.C.). It perhaps entered the Koine
from Ionic. It is common in papyri of iii B.C., e.g. *PSI* 427.1
γραφὴ σάκκων καὶ μαρσίππων, *PCair.Zen*. 69.14 (257 B.C.); the
dimin. is found e.g. in *PLille* 6.15 (iii B.C.) μαρσίππιον ἐν ὧι
χαλκοῦ ⊢ ζ.

It occurs some 19 times in the Pentateuch, e.g. *Ge*. 44.2
quoted above under κόνδυ, 44.11, *De*. 25.13 (mostly ~ אמתחת ,
'sack', BDB).

12. 'Fremdwort unbekannter Herkunft', Frisk.
    Moeris 96: βαλλάντιον, Ἀττικῶς. μαρσίππιον, Ἑλληνικῶς.

CHAPTER VII

INNOVATION AND OBSOLESCENCE

In the three preceding chapters we have been considering
innovations in the Koine vocabulary. It is however a well-known
characteristic of language that the intrusion of new words and
uses does not take place in isolation from other words in the
vocabulary.[1] It is frequently the case that the intrusion of
one word is related to the obsolescence of another. As a
certain word for an idea comes into use the existing word for
the idea drops out; or, put the other way, as one word becomes
obsolete another appears and takes its place. The two
processes, the intrusion of one word and the obsolescence of
another, are complementary to each other.

There were many such changes in the Koine vocabulary.
For a variety of reasons, many earlier words and uses had
become obsolete and been replaced by new ones. In this chapter
three examples of this phenomenon will be examined in detail.
We shall consider what changes had taken place in the manner
of expressing certain ideas in the Greek of the third century
B.C., and a comparison will be made with the usage of the
Pentateuch. It will be seen that the translators' vocabulary
is in agreement with contemporary developments in these areas.

'Give a drink to';

'Irrigate'

In Classical Greek ἄρδω, which is first attested early
(*Homeric Hymns*, Pi., etc.; cf. ἀρδμός in Homer), was the normal
word for 'give a drink of water to', 'water' (an animal), and
'water', 'irrigate' (plants, land). It is common in these
senses in Attic up till Arist., and in Hdt. It would appear,
however, that it was not normally used of giving a drink to a

---

1. See e.g. L. Bloomfield, *Language*, London, 1935, 430ff.

human being; the only such example is in the highly poetic
... ὀχέτους, Ἵππαρις [a river] οἷσιν ἄρδει στρατόν, Pi. *O*. 5.12.
It was also not normally used of any liquid other than water
(in Ar. *Eq*. 96 ἐξένεγκέ μοι ταχέως οἴνου χόα, τὸν νοῦν ἵν᾽ ἄρδω
it is of course used to give a comic effect; similarly in 114).
It thus appears to have had much the same range of usage as the
Eng. verb 'water', being applicable to animals, plants and
land, but not human beings. If used with a person as object
it suggests pouring water over him, not giving him a drink: so
Ar. *Lys*. 384 ἄρδω σ᾽, ὅπως ἂν βλαστάνῃς.

Much less usual was ἀρδεύω, 'water', 'irrigate', attested
first in Aeschylus (*Pr*. 852), but not again until Arist. and
Thphr.

The word ποτίζω also appears in Classical times, with the
meaning 'give (a person or animal) water (or something else
specified) to drink'. Liquids other than water are specified
in Pl. *Phdr*. 247 e τοὺς ἵππους ... νέκταρ ἐπότισεν, Hp. *Aph*. 7.46
ἄκρητον ποτίσας, Arist. *Ph*. 199 a 34 ἐπότισεν ... ὁ ἰατρὸς τὸ
φάρμακον, but in X. *Smp*. 2.25 we find it in the sense of 'give
a drink of water to': δοκεῖ μέντοι μοι καὶ τὰ τῶν ἀνδρῶν σώματα
ταῦτα πάσχειν ἅπερ καὶ τὰ τῶν ἐν γῇ φυομένων. καὶ γὰρ ἐκεῖνα,
ὅταν μὲν ὁ θεὸς αὐτὰ ἄγαν ἀθρόως ποτίζῃ, οὐ δύναται ὀρθοῦσθαι
...· ὅταν δ᾽ ὅσῳ ἥδεται τοσοῦτο πίνῃ, καὶ μάλα ὀρθά τε αὔξεται,
'... for when God gives the plants too much water all at once
to drink, they cannot stand up straight ..., but when they drink
only as much as they enjoy, they grow up very straight'. It is
clear that Xenophon uses ποτίζω, πίνω and ἥδομαι metaphorically
here, describing plants in human terms.[2]

These examples give only an incomplete picture of the
usage of ποτίζω in Classical times, but it would seem that
although the word may have been initially used only of liquids
other than water, it was quickly extended to water as well.
The two uses are in any case so close that they are perhaps not
to be distinguished at all. Thus ποτίζω began early to overlap
with ἄρδω. At the same time it had a wider usage in that it
was applicable to human beings as well as animals. It was not
however used of watering plants and land.

---

2. X. still uses ἄρδω for 'irrigate', e.g. *An*. 2.3.13.

In the Koine we find that ποτίζω had developed further in meaning: from the third century B.C. onwards it is common in the sense of 'water', 'irrigate' (plants, land). This extension is to be found already in [Arist.] *de Plantis* 821 a 39 αἱ ῥοιαὶ ('pomegranates') ... δι᾽ ὕδατος γλυκέος καὶ ψυχροῦ ποτιζόμεναι βελτιοῦνται (not noted by LSJ). In the papyri the term occurs frequently: e.g. *PPetr*. 3.44(3).4 (iii B.C.) ἀνοιχθήτω οὖν ἡ θύρα ὅπως ἡ ἐν Θευγένιδι γῆ ποτισθῆι τὸ τάχος, *PCair.Zen*. 155.3, 4 (256 B.C.) εὐθέως πότισον τὴν γῆν ἀπὸ χερός, ἐὰν δὲ μὴ δυνατὸν ἦι, κηλώνεια ἐπιστήσας πλείονα οὕτω πότιζε. (For other examples see MM, Preisigke.)

The earlier sense, 'give (a person or animal) water (or something else specified) to drink' continues in use, though it is not as well attested. Applied to animals it is found in Theoc. 1.121 (iii B.C.) Δάφνις ὁ τὼς ταύρως καὶ πόρτιας ὧδε ποτίσδων, *OGI* 483. 169 (ii A.D.) μηθενὶ δὲ ἐξουσία ἔστω ἐπὶ τῶν δημοσίων κρηνῶν μήτε κτῆνος ποτίζειν μήτε ἱμάτια πλύνειν, but for the application to human beings we have (apart from LXX and *NT*) only *OGI* 200.16 (iv A.D.) ποτίζοντες αὐτοὺς ζύτῳ τε καὶ οἴνῳ καὶ ὑδρεύμασιν.

ἄρδω, on the other hand, has dropped out of ordinary use in the Koine. It is found occasionally in literary writers (Ph., Ath., see LSJ), but no examples are known in the papyri. ἀρδεύω also is mainly confined to the literary Koine (Plb., M. Ant., etc.), though a number of examples are found in papyri of ii-vi A.D. (see Preisigke, Kiessling). Neither word appears in the LXX or *NT*.

ποτίζω continues into Modern Greek as the normal word for 'give a drink to'; 'water', 'irrigate' (*Lex. Pr*., Swanson). ἄρδω has disappeared altogether, and ἀρδεύω is confined to the καθαρεύουσα.[3]

It is clear, then, that in vernacular Greek of the third century B.C. ποτίζω had taken over altogether from ἄρδω (and ἀρδεύω).[4]

---

3. Confirmed by Mr. Papastavrou.
4. It is worth noticing that the incoming word is 'fuller-sounding' than ἄρδω (cf. Bl. DF §126); it is also more 'transparent' (cf. Ullmann, *Semantics* 91).

This development is reflected in the vocabulary of the
Pentateuch, where we find only ποτίζω (28 times), never ἄρδω or
ἀρδεύω. ποτίζω is used in the following ways:

1.(a) 'give (a person) a drink' (of something specified):
wine *Ge*. 19.32 ποτίσωμεν τὸν πατέρα ἡμῶν οἶνον, 33, al.; water
24.17 πότισόν με μικρὸν ὕδωρ ἐκ τῆς ὑδρίας σου, 43, al.;

(b) 'give a drink of water to': a person *Ge*. 21.19 ἔπλησεν
τὸν ἀσκὸν ὕδατος καὶ ἐπότισεν τὸ παιδίον, 24.18,45, *Nu*. 20.8;
animals *Ex*. 2.19 ἤντλησεν ἡμῖν καὶ ἐπότισεν τὰ πρόβατα ἡμῶν, al.

2. 'water', 'irrigate', *Ge*. 2.10 ποταμὸς δὲ ἐκπορεύεται ἐξ
Εδεμ ποτίζειν τὸν παράδεισον, 6, 13.10; *De*. 11.10 ἔστιν γὰρ ἡ
γῆ, εἰς ἣν εἰσπορεύῃ ἐκεῖ κληρονομῆσαι αὐτήν, οὐχ ὥσπερ ἡ γῆ
Αἰγύπτου ἐστίν, ὅθεν ἐκπεπόρευσθε ἐκεῖθεν, ὅταν σπείρωσιν τὸν
σπόρον καὶ ποτίζωσιν τοῖς ποσὶν ὡσεὶ κῆπον λαχανείας.[5]

The translators' use of the word is in close agreement
with current usage, except possibly in one respect: as we have
seen, the sense 'give a drink of water to' applied to human
beings is not directly attested, though it is implied by the
example in Xenophon and the other very similar uses. It may be
that in this the translators have extended the usage of ποτίζω
beyond what was usual. This would have come about readily
through mechanical representation of the Hebrew, the equivalence
שקה - ποτίζω having once been established.

The expression ποτίζειν τοῖς ποσίν in *De*. 11.10 is of
special interest. Although the wording of the Greek of course
derives from the Hebrew original (MT אשר תזרע את-זרעך והשקית
ברגלך), there is reason to think that the translators and their
Egyptian readers would have seen here a reference to a familiar
practice. Compare the similar expressions in *PFlor*. 369.7
(ii A.D.) μέχρι τοῦ ἐσομένου ἀπὸ ποδὸς ποτισμοῦ, and *PRyl*.

---

5. ποτίζω renders שקה *hiph*. in all instances except *Ge*. 24.17,
where it translates גמא *hiph*.
    As far as I know no other words for these ideas are found
in the Pentateuch. שקה is rendered by ποτίζω except *Ge*. 40.13
οἰνοχοέω (~ מֶשְׁקֶה), 40.20 ἀρχιοινοχόος (~ שר השקים), and 24.
18-19, where a literal rendering is abandoned in favour of more
idiomatic Gk.: καὶ ἐπότισεν αὐτόν, ἕως ἐπαύσατο πίνων MT: ותשקהו
ותכל להשקתו . גמא *hiph*. occurs only in the place noted. There
are no compounds of ποτίζω, ἄρδω, or ἀρδεύω in the Pentateuch.

157.20 ff. (135 A.D.) εἰ χρεία γείνοιτο [ποτίσαι ἐ]ν̣ ἀναβάσει
ἀπο ποδὸς τὴν αὐτὴν νοτίνην μερίδα, παρέξει ἡ λαβοῦσα τὴν
βορρίνην μερίδα τὸ ὑδραγωγεῖσθαι δι᾿ αὐ[τῆς].[6] Though these
examples are several centuries later than the Pentateuch, it is
probable that the method of irrigation referred to had been in
use for a very long time (the Hebrew original itself probably
alludes to the same method).[7]

'Send rain', 'it rains'

The way in which the older word for this idea is replaced
in the Hellenistic vernacular has often been noticed.[8] The
Classical word, ὕω, though still found e.g. in Herodas (7.46)
and in writers of the literary Koine (Thphr., Str., Plu., etc.),
is not known to occur in the papyri. It is used in the LXX only
in two instances shortly to be considered, and not at all in
the *NT* .

In its place we find βρέχω, which in Classical times was
normally used only in the sense of 'wet', 'drench'. According
to Phrynichus, βρέχω as a synonym of ὕω occurred early in a
comedy doubtfully attributed to Telecleides (v B.C);[9] and in
X. *Oec.* 17.2 οἱ ἄνθρωποι πρὸς τὸν θεὸν ἀποβλέπουσιν, ὁπότε

---

6. Both examples are noted by MM, LSJ and Suppl., s.v. πούς.
(LSJ's *Stud.Ital.* 13 (1905) 366 = *PFlor.* above).

7. Just what was meant by watering 'with the foot' is not definitely known, but a practice observed in modern times in
Egypt and described by Driver, *Deuteronomy* (*ICC*, 3 ed. 1902),
p.XXI (cf. p.129), suits the case very well: '... each plot of
land is divided into small squares by ridges of earth a few
inches in height; and the water ... is conducted into these
squares by means of small trenches. The cultivator uses his
feet to regulate the flow of water to each part, by a dexterous
movement of the toes raising or breaking down small embankments
in the trenches, and opening or closing apertures in the ridges
(Manning, *The Land of the Pharaohs*, 1887, p.31).' Cf. *HDB* s.v.
'irrigation'.

8. See e.g. Kennedy, *Sources of New Testament Greek* 39,155,
Thackeray, *Gramm.* 262, Bl. DF §129.

9. Phryn.258 (R) βρέχειν ἐπὶ τοῦ ὕειν ἔν τινι κωμῳδίᾳ ἀρχαίᾳ
προστιθεμένη Τηλεκλείδῃ τῷ κωμῳδῷ ἐστὶν οὕτως εἰρημένον. ὅπερ
εἰ καὶ γνήσιον ἦν τὸ δρᾶμα, τὸ ἅπαξ εἰρῆσθαι ἐφυλαξάμεθ᾿ ἄν.
ὁπότε δὲ καὶ νόθον ἐστί, παντελῶς ἀποδοκιμαστέον τοὔνομα. Cf. Th.
Mag. 57.8 βρέχειν οὐδεὶς τῶν ἀρχαίων εἶπεν ἐπὶ ὑετοῦ, ἀλλὰ ὕειν.
These comments by Atticist grammarians of course give a clear
indication that the usual vernacular Koine word was βρέχω, not ὕω.

βρέξας τὴν γῆν ἀφέσει αὐτοὺς σπείρειν it is probable that βρέχω
is to be taken as 'send rain upon' (cf. ὕω with direct object
of the place on which rain falls, LSJ s.v. I.3). But apart from
these isolated examples, βρέχω 'rain' does not appear until the
Koine, and was clearly not established until then. Xenophon
elsewhere uses ὕω (e.g. HG 1.1.16), and in Aristotle ὕω is still
normal (about a dozen examples), while βρέχω is used only in its
ordinary Classical sense (Bonitz, s. vv.).

Instances of the new use of βρέχω from rather late in the
Koine have long been noted,[10] e.g. POxy. 1482.6 (ii A.D.) ὁ
Ζεὺς ἔβρεχε, Arr. Epict. 1.6.26 (ii A.D.) οὐ καταβρέχεσθε, ὅταν
βρέχῃ; NT e.g. Ep. Jac. 5.17 προσηύξατο τοῦ μὴ βρέξαι, καὶ οὐκ
ἔβρεξεν ἐπὶ τῆς γῆς, but it can also be quoted from a papyrus
contemporary with the Pentateuch, PCornell 1.152 (256 B.C.) διὰ
τὸ τὴν νύκτα βρέχειν, 'because it rained during the night'.
This example satisfactorily establishes what might otherwise
have been open to doubt, namely, that the use was current in
the third century B.C.

βρέχει passes into Modern Greek as the ordinary word for
'it rains', ὕω being confined to archaizing Greek (Lex. Pr.).

In the Pentateuch βρέχω occurs as follows, in each place
rendering מטר hiph.:

(a) 'send rain', Ge. 2.5 οὐ γὰρ ἔβρεξεν ὁ θεὸς ἐπὶ τὴν γῆν.

(b) 'cause (something) to fall like rain', Ge. 19.24 κύριος
ἔβρεξεν ἐπὶ Σοδομα καὶ Γομορρα θεῖον καὶ πῦρ, Ex. 9.23 ἔβρεξεν
κύριος χάλαζαν ἐπὶ πᾶσαν γῆν Αἰγύπτου. (For this latter sense
cf. PMag. 36.301 σὺ εἶ τὸ θεῖον, ὃ ἔβρεξεν ὁ θεός. ὕω had
been used in the same way: see LSJ s.v. I.4.)

In regard to βρέχω, then, the translators' usage is in
accordance with the contemporary development. But there are
also, unexpectedly, two examples of ὕω, which as we have seen
is likely to have been unusual in the vernacular Koine. The
examples are:

Ex. 9.18 ἰδοὺ ἐγὼ ὕω ταύτην τὴν ὥραν αὔριον χάλαζαν
πολλὴν σφόδρα.

---

10. See Anz, Subsidia 305f., LSJ, Bauer.

16.4 ἰδοὺ ἐγὼ ὕω ὑμῖν ἄρτους.

In both places ὕω renders מטר *hiph*., the same word as is rendered by βρέχω in three other instances (above). The variation in the renderings therefore cannot be due to a variation in the words used in the original.

A special explanation for the appearance of the obsolescent word in these two places may be put forward. It is noticeable that it occurs only in the first person singular in words spoken by God, and that βρέχω is not so used. This contrast is particularly marked in *Ex*. 9, where God's own words in vs. 18 are ἰδοὺ ἐγὼ ὕω ταύτην τὴν ὥραν αὔριον χάλαζαν, while the narrative a few verses later has (vs.23) ἔβρεξεν κύριος χάλαζαν. The explanation, I suggest, is that antiquated ὕω, having a dignified tone, was deliberately chosen because it was felt to be more appropriate to the speech of God than βρέχω, which no doubt had a colloquial ring.[11]

In view of this it is probably not accidental that in the only other place where מטר *hiph*. is not rendered by βρέχω the words are again spoken by God, with the verb in the first person: *Ge*. 7.4 ἐγὼ ἐπάγω ὑετὸν ἐπὶ τὴν γῆν. The periphrasis has no foundation in the original, which reads אנכי ממטיר על-הארץ Thus it seems that βρέχω has been avoided here, too, though it is twice used elsewhere in *Ge*., in the third person (2.5, 19.24).

---

11. There are a number of parallels to this phenomenon in the *NT*: βοάω, which had been largely replaced by κράζω, is used in the more vernacular gospels only once, of Jesus, *Ev*. *Marc*. 15.34; similarly δακρύω, milder and more dignified than the usual κλαίω, occurs in *NT* only in *Ev*. *Jo*. 11.35 ἐδάκρυσεν ὁ ᾿Ιησοῦς; obsolescent βούλομαι, whose meaning had been taken over by θέλω, is found only occasionally in the gospels, in passages of an official, legal, or otherwise solemn nature. These examples are taken from G.P. Shipp, 'Some Observations on the Distribution of Words in the New Testament', in: *Essays in Honour of G.W. Thatcher*, Sydney, 1967, 135,137f.
I do not know of any parallels in the LXX, but it is likely that there are some to be found. Cf. G.B. Caird, *JTS* XIX (1968) 464: 'The LXX, as I hope to show at a later date, can provide many instances of deliberate archaism'. A curious feature noted by Katz, *Th.Z.* IX (1953) 229f., is possibly relevant in some way: in *De*. 28.7-36 the aor. opt., with,according to K., a future sense, is used when God is subject, the fut. ind. when men are.

'Depart', 'go away'

The developments in the ordinary words for this idea in the early Koine have seldom been noticed, but are of considerable interest. They afford good evidence of the agreement of the Pentateuch vocabulary with the Greek of its time.

The innovation here is the semantic development in ἀποτρέχω. In Classical Greek (Ar., Hdt., Pl., al.) this word normally had the sense of 'run away', 'run off', literally, as e.g. in X. *Oec.* 11.18 ἐγὼ δὲ τὰ μὲν βάδην τὰ δὲ ἀποδραμὼν οἴκαδε ..., but in the third century B.C. and later it is commonly found in the sense of 'depart', 'leave', without any suggestion of running or even haste.[12] This is clearly seen e.g. in *PMich. Zen.* 55.10 (240 B.C.): Philon asks Zenon to settle a certain matter with Philon's brother ἵνα ταχέως πρός με ἀναστρέφηι καὶ μὴ ἐπικωλύωμαι ἐὰν δέηι ἀναπλεῖν· συντόμως γὰρ δεῖ ἀποτρέχειν ἐντεῦθεν ('... I must be off from here shortly', ed.) Similarly *PCair.Zen.* 409.8 (iii B.C.) εἰ δὲ μὴ χρέαν ἔχεις, ἵνα ἀποτρέχω εἰς τὸ τεταγμένον, 'if you do not need me, let me go away to my assignment'.[13]

In its five occurrences in Polybius the word has the same sense, e.g. 21.42.9 τοῖς δὲ Ῥωμαίοις καὶ τοῖς συμμάχοις εἴ τινες εἶεν <ἐκ τῆς Ἀντιόχου βασιλείας>, εἶναι τὴν ἐξουσίαν καὶ μένειν, εἰ βούλονται, καὶ ἀποτρέχειν.[14] Compare also Aristeas 273 ... κἂν ἐκ τοῦ ζῆν ἀποτρέχωσιν.

The use is also seen in a fixed expression familiar in manumissions, ἀποτρέχω ἐλεύθερος, or simply ἀποτρέχω, 'go free'. E.g. *GDI* 2038.9 (Delphi, 186 B.C.) εἰ δέ κα πάθη τι Μενέστας, ἀποτρεχέτω ἐλευθέρα Γνωσιφίλα ὅπαι κα θέληι, 1899.5 (*ib.*, ii

---

12. Signs of this development can be seen already in Xenophon and Comedy. See X. *An.* 7.6.5, Ar. *Av.* 1162, Lysipp. Com. 7.3 (Kock), Men. *Dysc.* 918 . The word is however not used by Arist.

13. Other iii B.C. examples of the word are quotable, but in contexts too broken to be clear: *PCair.Zen.* 563.5, *PEnt.* 78.7 (both pres. tense). In *PEnt.* 23.8 τε]τάχθαι ἀποτρέχειν ἔξω Σαμαρείας the meaning is almost certainly 'had been ordered to leave S.'. Another example is found in *PHal.* 1.179 (iii B.C.), quoted below p.128 n.21.

14. The other examples are at 3.22.7, 3.24.11, 21.42.18, 31.20.3 (all pres. tense).

B.C.) ποιέων ὅ κα θέλη καὶ ἀποτρέχων οἷς κα θέλη. We may note
further the use in the sense of 'decamp', 'abscond', of the
action of workers, e.g. *PSI* 421.8 (iii B.C.), a complaint about
wages, εἰ δὲ μή, ἀποδραμούμεθα. Cf. *PCol.Zen.* 66.11 (iii B.C.).

The change in meaning in ἀποτρέχω is interestingly paralleled later in φεύγω, Classical and Hellenistic 'flee', now in
Modern Greek 'leave', 'go away' (Swanson). Cf. English 'run
away' e.g. in 'run away from home'.

In the Pentateuch ἀποτρέχω is quite clearly used in the
new sense in all ten occurrences. It renders הלך, יצא, and
שוב, never a word meaning 'run away'.

Ex. 3.21 καὶ δώσω χάριν τῷ λαῷ τούτῳ ἐναντίον τῶν Αἰγυπτίων·
ὅταν δὲ ἀποτρέχητε, οὐκ ἀπελεύσεσθε κενοί
MT   כי תלכון לא תלכו ריקם

10.24 βαδίζετε, λατρεύσατε κυρίῳ τῷ θεῷ ὑμῶν· πλὴν τῶν
προβάτων καὶ τῶν βοῶν ὑπολίπεσθε· καὶ ἡ ἀποσκευὴ ὑμῶν
ἀποτρεχέτω μεθ' ὑμῶν
MT   ילך

Similarly *Ge.* 12.19, 24.51. Followed by εἰς:

Ge. 32.10 κύριε ὁ εἴπας μοι ᾿Απότρεχε εἰς τὴν γῆν τῆς
γενέσεώς σου καὶ εὖ σε ποιήσω
MT   שוב לארצך

Similarly *Le.* 25.41, *Nu.* 24.14; cf. 22.13, with πρός. This
construction is common with ἀπέρχομαι in Classical Greek (LSJ
s.v. I.2); in it there is often the suggestion of going away
back to a place (see e.g. Hdt. 1.22,68).

In two places the translators employ the formulaic expression found in manumissions:

Ex. 21.5 ἐὰν δὲ ἀποκριθεὶς εἴπη ὁ παῖς ᾿Ηγάπηκα τὸν κύριόν
μου καὶ τὴν γυναῖκα καὶ τὰ παιδία, οὐκ ἀποτρέχω ἐλεύθερος
MT   לא אצא חפשי

21.7 ἐὰν δέ τις ἀποδῶται τὴν ἑαυτοῦ θυγατέρα οἰκέτιν, οὐκ
ἀπελεύσεται ὥσπερ ἀποτρέχουσιν αἱ δοῦλαι
MT   לא תצא כצאת העבדים

It is to be noted that this must be deliberate. The literal
rendering would have been ἐκπορεύομαι. Only here is אצי
rendered by ἀποτρέχω. These two examples strikingly illustrate
the translators' adherence to contemporary terminology.

ἀποτρέχω, then, has in the Koine the same sense as the
earlier word ἀπέρχομαι. The latter, moreover, is rarely found,
and it is clear that ἀποτρέχω has taken its place.[15] This
applies, however, only to the present (and impf.) tense. In the
other tenses the suppletives remain the same as before, i.e.
ἀπ-ελεύσομαι, -ῆλθον, -ελήλυθα.[16] Thus in iii B.C. papyri I
find ἀπ-ελεύσομαι and -ελήλυθα once each, -ῆλθον 27 times, but
no examples of -έρχομαι. On the other hand, ἀποτρέχω is as we
have seen quite common, but in the present tense. Even in Plb.
there are no examples of -έρχομαι, only -ῆλθον.[17]

Similarly in the Pentateuch ἀπ-ελεύσομαι and -ῆλθον are
common, but there are no examples of -έρχομαι.[18] ἀποτρέχω, which
we have just seen occurs ten times, is present tense in all except one instance, *Le.* 25.41 καὶ ἀπελεύσεται εἰς τὴν γενεὰν αὐτοῦ,
εἰς τὴν κατάσχεσιν τὴν πατρικὴν ἀποδραμεῖται (MT ישׁוב... ושׁב).[19]

---

15. As far as I know this has been observed only by Meecham, *The
Letter of Aristeas* 297: 'ἀποτρέχω takes, in general, the place of
ἀπέρχομαι' in Koine Gk. Thackeray's remark, *Gramm.* 287 , is somewhat astray: 'ἀποτρέχω now replaces ἄπειμι= "depart", especially
in imperat. ἀπότρεχε = ἄπιθε' (sic). (I think it is accidental
that about a third of the LXX examples of ἀποτρέχω are imper.)

16. Cf. the way in which ὁράω is replaced in pres. and impf. by
βλέπω, while ὄψομαι, εἶδον, ἑώρακα remain unchanged (pp.133 ff.).

17. In the *NT* ἀπ-ελεύσομαι, -ῆλθον, -ελήλυθα are still usual, and
-έρχομαι occurs rarely and only in the more literary books: *Evv.
Matt.* 8.19, 25.10, *Luc.* 9.57, *Act. Ap.* 23.32 (in all except the
first there is a v.l. with a different verb). ἀποτρέχω, however,
is not found (Bauer cites in this period only Herm. *Vis.*3.3.1).
One might well ask why this is so. The explanation, I suggest,
is that by *NT* times it had been eclipsed by ὑπάγω, often 'go
away', as well as just 'go'. Cf. Th. Mag. 368.11 τὸ ὑπάγω μὴ
εἴπῃς ἀντὶ τοῦ ἀπέρχομαι. ὑπάγω occurs only in pres. and impf.
(Bauer; cf. Bl. DF §101 s.v. ἄγειν).
    This use of ὑπάγω seems not to have become established until
the time of the *NT* (MM cite no examples earlier than i A.D.). In
the LXX it appears only in *To. S* , e.g. 8.21, and *Je.* 43.19 S*. The
Pentateuch has the word in the older trans. use in *Ex.* 14.21.

18. Nor does -έρχομαι occur elsewhere in the LXX.

19. ἀπο-δραμεῖται B, -θανεῖται A, but A's reading is scarcely
possible (Grabe emends it).

It is noteworthy that in this one place where ἀποδραμοῦμαι occurs it follows ἀπελεύσομαι, and may therefore have been resorted to for reasons of style.[20] Clearly the normal use of ἀποτρέχω is as present to ἀπ-ελεύσομαι, -ῆλθον, as is well illustrated by *Ex*. 3.21, 21.7 quoted above (see also *Ge*. 31.13 ἄπελθε compared with 32.10 ἀπότρεχε).

Other verbs do not seriously affect this pattern. ἄπειμι, like other compounds of εἶμι, is of course rare in the Koine. In the Pentateuch it appears once, in the participial form, *Ex*.33.8 κατενοοῦσαν ἀπιόντος Μωυσῆ (see above p.86 n.4.). ἀποίχομαι is found occasionally, especially in the impf. So e.g. *PCair.Zen*. 753.66 (iii B.C.); *Ge*. 14.12, 26.31, 28.6. ἀποβαίνω usually has the senses of 'disembark' and 'turn out' (of events), and is therefore not involved.

The changes in words for 'go away' form part of a whole series of developments in words for 'go out, in, towards', etc. In the present and imperfect the older compounds of ἔρχομαι tend to drop out. In their place, as was noticed earlier (p.85), new compounds of πορεύομαι generally appear, while in the other tenses the earlier suppletives continue unchanged. In the case of words for 'go away', however, the πορεύομαι compound is comparatively uncommon.[21] The reason is clearly that the place it would have occupied has already been filled by ἀποτρέχω. There are no examples of ἀποπορεύομαι in the Pentateuch (or elsewhere in the LXX, or in the *NT*).

---

20. For other instances of stylistic variation see above pp.71,80 n.35, and cf. Gooding, *The Account of the Tabernacle* 8f.

21. The examples are: X. *HG* 4.1.15 αὐτὸς ἐπὶ Δασκυλείου ἀπεπορεύετο ('he himself set off for D.'; perhaps πορεύομαι in its sense of 'march', 'travel'' is intended here, and the meaning would not have been the same if X. had written ἀπῄειν). Arist. *Oec*. 1350a 33 τῶν στρατιωτῶν ... πρὸς τοὺς ὑπεναντίους φασκόντων ἀποπορεύεσθαι. *SIG* 546 B. 18 (Melitaea, iii B.C.)... καὶ ἔχοντες ἀποπορευέσθων βουλευτὰν ἕνα. Plb. 24.7.6 ὁ δὲ Χαίρων ... τοῦτον ἀποπορευόμενον ἡμέρας ἐκ βαλανείου προσπέμψας τινὰς ἐξεκέντησεν (for no reason that I can see LSJ give the meaning here as 'go back' 'return').

In the papyri the only example so far known is *PHal*. 1.177 (iii B.C.), where it occurs in the same context as ἀποτρέχω: Ptolemy instructs that when soldiers leave their billets they are not to make improper use of them, καθάπερ νῦν ἀκούομεν γίνεσθαι, ὅταν ἀποπορεύωνται, ἀπομισθοῦν αὐτοὺς καὶ ἀπο[....]μένους τὰ οἰκήματα ἀποτρέχειν (for possible restorations see ed., and David & van Groningen, *Papyrological Primer,* no.5).

Quite separate is the technical use, of machinery (zurückfahren', ed.), in Hero *Aut*. 6.3, 19.5.

CHAPTER VIII

LEXICAL EVIDENCE FOR
THE DATE OF THE
PENTATEUCH TEXT

The major importance in LXX studies of the problem of
establishing the text is well known. The great complexity of
the textual history of the LXX and subsequent recensions creates
difficulties which have occupied scholars' attention for several
generations and are even now only in the process of solution.
These difficulties have also given rise to two fundamentally
opposed types of approach to the study of the text. Kahle, on
the one hand, maintained the impossibility of recovering an
original LXX version, since in his view there arose, in the same
way as the Aramaic Targums, not one but a number of Greek translations, and the 'LXX' as we know it was the end product of a
long process of assimilating different versions and isolated
fragments of translation.[1] The opposite view, represented
notably by Rahlfs and other Göttingen editors and by Katz and
Orlinsky, is that an original, 'official', LXX version does lie
behind the Christian recensions and that by analysing the mass
of variants and isolating secondary recensions it is possible to
recover it.[2]

Kahle's view now finds few supporters. Indeed, as Jellicoe
has put it, 'the very data adduced by Kahle have been increas-
ingly turned against him in vindication of the Lagardian
hypothesis'.[3] In particular, Kahle's claim that the recently
discovered Dodekapropheton fragments support his position has

1. See especially *The Cairo Geniza*, 2 ed., Oxford, 1959.

2. See e.g. P. Katz, 'Septuagintal Studies in the Mid-Century',
in *The Background of the NT and its Eschatology,*ed. W.D. Davies
and D. Daube, Cambridge, 1956, 205f.; J.W. Wevers, 'Proto-
Septuagint Studies', in *The Seed of Wisdom. Essays in honour of
T.J. Meek*, ed. W.S. McCullough, Toronto, 1964, 58-77.

3. *SMS* 62.

been strongly contested by Barthélemy,[4] who has argued, in the opinion of many scholars convincingly,[5] that these fragments represent not an independent translation but a recension of the LXX text bringing it into closer agreement with MT.

The general opinion today, then, is that there is every hope of recovering an original Alexandrian LXX. Nevertheless this task remains a difficult one. It is clear that most if not all of our MSS contain some recensional elements, which the textual scholar must attempt to analyse. In some books the MS tradition presents a number of quite different texts deriving from different recensions, and to identify and evaluate these recensions can be a complex matter. In *Kingdoms* βγ for example, if Barthélemy is right the so-called 'Lucianic' text of certain minuscules often alone preserves the original LXX translation, and the whole of the rest of the MS tradition represents a text that has undergone revision.[6] Similar problems arise with the task of identifying the recensions witnessed to by *OT* quotations in ancient authors[7] and by daughter versions of the LXX.[8]

Although the Pentateuch raises fewer problems than other books, it is still of some interest to look for confirmation, outside of purely textual evidence, that the text presented by the major MSS does date from the time when it is generally agreed the translation of the Pentateuch was made, i.e. about the middle of the third century B.C. If this could be found, though it would of course not disprove Kahle's view, it would at least demonstrate the reliability of these MSS as witnesses to an early text of the Pentateuch, and increase our confidence in the possibility of establishing the elusive LXX *Urtext*.

---

4. *Les Devanciers d'Aquila* (Vet.Test.Suppl.X), Leiden, 1963.

5. See e.g. F.M. Cross, *HTR* LVII (1964) 383, S.P. Brock, *Studia Evangelica* V (1968) 176.

6. Barthélemy, *Devanciers* 126ff.; cf. Brock, *op.cit.* 177. Cross, *op.cit.* 295, disagrees, however; in his opinion the 'Old Gk.' of *Ki.* βγ is lost.

7. See e.g. P. Katz, *Philo's Bible. The Aberrant Text of Bible Quotations in some Philonic Writings and its Place in the Textual History of the Greek Bible,* Cambridge, 1950.

8. Cf. Jellicoe, *SMS* 243ff., 341.

In the present chapter an attempt will be made to obtain an indication of this kind from an examination of certain features of vocabulary. It is of course already clear, from the evidence examined in the preceding chapters, that the vocabulary of the Pentateuch would suit very well a date in the third century B.C. But that evidence is of little value for establishing such a date, since it consists of words and uses which for the most part continued in use in the language long after the third century B.C. What I shall attempt to assemble here is evidence that points to an early *terminus ante quem* for the text of the Pentateuch.

The features of vocabulary which will be considered are the everyday words for the ideas of 'see' and 'donkey'. I hope to show that in vernacular Greek certain developments in the ways of expressing these ideas took place not long after the third century B.C. and thus provide us with the evidence we require. It must be emphasized, however, that linguistic changes of this kind are by their nature incapable of being accurately dated. They are gradual developments which take place over a fairly long period of time. At best, therefore, we cannot expect to date our text more accurately than to within a century.

It is a prerequisite for our investigation that the vocabulary of the Pentateuch should be known to be predominantly that of vernacular rather than literary Greek. The reason for this is that the literary vocabulary tends to retain features obsolete in the living language, and these would vitiate any attempt at dating by the method proposed here. I take it that the generally vernacular character of our text has been sufficiently demonstrated by the evidence already considered.

We begin with the examination of developments in words for 'see'.

In Classical Greek the ordinary word for 'perceive visually', trans., was ὁράω pres., ἑώρων impf., ἑώρακα perf., with aor. supplied by εἶδον, and the other tenses by the root ὀπ- (ὄψομαι, etc.).

βλέπω was used chiefly in the sense of 'look' (in a

specified direction).[9] It also had the sense of 'have the power
of sight'; and a further use is found in the set phrase βλέπειν
φάος (with φάος sometimes omitted), equivalent to 'be alive'.
It does occur a number of times as a synonym of ὁράω in the
sense of 'perceive visually', but investigation shows this use
to be confined mainly to poetry. There are some twenty examples
in Sophocles,[10] e.g. *Tr.* 594 τόνδε γὰρ βλέπω θυραῖον ἤδη, *Ph.*
357, and a smaller number in Euripides, e.g. *Ion* 925 οἴκτου
σὸν βλέπων ἐμπίπλαμαι πρόσωπον, *Hec.* 681. It occurs once in
Aristophanes, *Pax* 208 ἵνα μὴ βλέποιεν μαχομένους ὑμᾶς ἔτι, but
not at all in Demosthenes, Herodotus, Xenophon, Andocides,
Lycurgus, or Aristotle. In Plato there are three examples:[11]
Ti. 51c ταῦτα ἅπερ καὶ βλέπομεν ὅσα τε ἄλλα διὰ τοῦ σώματος
αἰσθανόμεθα, *Lg.* 875d τάξιν τε καὶ νόμον, ἃ δὴ τὸ μὲν ὡς ἐπὶ τὸ
πολὺ ὁρᾷ καὶ βλέπει, τὸ δ' ἐπὶ πᾶν ἀδυνατεῖ, 921a οὐδὲν τῷ νῷ
βλέπων.

In all these authors ὁράω is the normal word for the idea.
Even in those in which βλέπω 'see' is found, ὁράω is by far the
commoner word.

We may conclude, therefore, that in the Classical period
βλέπω in the sense of 'see' was a poetic variant of ὁράω, somewhat like Eng. 'behold' compared with 'see', but was not usual
in prose, either Attic or Ionic, and, as its absence especially
from Xenophon and Aritotle suggests, had spread little or not at
all into everyday language. That it had, however, begun to
appear occasionally in ordinary speech by about the end of the
fourth century is a probable conclusion to be drawn from what we
can learn of Menander's usage.[12] In what survives of his plays
I find three examples: *Epit.* 612 τί σ'αὖ βλέπω 'γώ; *Fr.* 641
μέγιστόν ἐστιν ἄρα τοῖς ἐπταικόσιν τὸ παρόντας ἐγγὺς τοὺς
συναλγοῦντας βλέπειν, 683.12 ὁ γὰρ θεὸς βλέπει σε πλησίον παρών.

---

9. A good illustration of the difference is seen in Ar. *Eq.* 162-3
δευρὶ βλέπε. τὰς στίχας ὁρᾷς τὰς τῶνδε τῶν λαῶν; cf. e.g. D. 19.87.

10. Information about the usage of Class. authors is derived from
the standard indexes and lexicons to individual authors (see
Bibliography).

11. I.e. among the occurrences of the word noted by Ast, *Lexicon
Platonicum*; but Ast does not claim completeness.

12. Index in Koerte (2 ed.) and *OCT* of *Dysc* .

The present tense of ὁράω, on the other hand, occurs more than
fifty times, the imperfect twice, so it is clear that ὁράω was
still the usual word.

θεάομαι and θεωρέω, though to some extent overlapping the
uses of ὁράω etc., had special applications which can usually be
discerned in their Classical occurrences.[13]

Other old words which could be used in this sense, such as
δέρκομαι, λεύσσω, are irrelevant for our purpose, as being poetic
or dialectal.

Going forward to the first century A.D. we find that a
number of developments have occurred in the manner of expressing
this idea. Our main evidence for this period is the *NT*, whose
length and subject-matter require the expression of the idea
often enough to make it a fairly reliable representative of
first century A.D. usage. Moreover the usage of the *NT* is fully
supported by the evidence of the papyri.[14]

The *NT* usage of the words concerned has often been observed
and need not be demonstrated in detail here.[15] The main points
are as follows.

ὁράω in the pres. and impf. has almost, though not entirely,
fallen out of use. Twenty occurrences of the pres. are found,
but of these twelve are the imper. (ὅρα, ὁρᾶτε) in the sense of
'take care' (that, not to, etc.); in the remaining eight ὁράω
has its normal older sense of 'see', but it is probably significant that all except one of these instances are found in the
more literary books, viz. Luke, Acts, and the Epistles.[16] The
one remaining example is *Ev. Marc.* 8.24 βλέπω τοὺς ἀνθρώπους,
ὅτι ὡς δένδρα ὁρῶ περιπατοῦντας, a passage not without certain
difficulties.[17] In any case this one example in a predominantly

13. See e.g. A. Prévot, *Rev.Phil.* IX (1935) 266-9.
14. See esp. MM s.vv. βλέπω, θεάομαι, θεωρέω, ὁράω.
15. See Bl. DF §101 s.vv. βλέπειν, ὁρᾶν; Bauer s.v. ὁράω; MM;
TWNT V 316ff. (Michaelis); H. Reinhold, *De Graecitate Patrum
Apostolicorum Librorumque Apocryphorum NTi Quaestiones
Grammaticae* (Diss.Phil.Hal. XIV.i) 1898, 97-100.
16. *Ev. Luc.*16.23, 23.49, *Act.Ap.* 8.23, *Epp.Hebr.* 2.8, 11.27,
Jac. 2.24, 1 *Pet.* 1.8.
17. See e.g. C.E.B. Cranfield, *St. Mark* (Cambridge Gk.Test.Comm.),
ad loc.

vernacular book does not affect the general picture. The impf. is found only once, *Ev. Jo.* 6.2, with v.l. ἐθεώρουν.

The pres. and impf. are normally provided by βλέπω, whose use in the sense of 'perceive visually', trans., is now fully established in ordinary usage, occurring over 100 times in *NT*.[18]

The other tenses are normally expressed as before by εἶδον, ἑώρακα, ὄψομαι, etc.

In addition to βλέπω, two other contenders have appeared, θεάομαι and θεωρέω. The former (20 or so times in *NT*) is now practically synonymous with βλέπω, ὁράω.[19] It is used mostly in aor., never pres., thus competing to a small extent with the much commoner εἶδον. θεωρέω (over 50 times), although its fuller sense as in Classical Greek may often be felt, is also nearly synonymous with βλέπω, ὁράω, θεάομαι in many contexts.[20] It, too, tends to be restricted to certain tenses, viz. pres., and, less often impf., rarely aor., fut.

The uses of βλέπω, εἶδον established by *NT* times are maintained into Modern Greek, in which 'see' is normally expressed by pres. βλέπω, aor. εἶδα. In the δημοτική ὁράω has disappeared altogether.

Of the changes in words for 'see' which had occurred in the Koine vernacular by the time of the *NT*, the most important was that βλέπω had almost completely taken the place of the pres. and impf. tenses of ὁράω. It is clear that this development, just beginning at the end of the fourth century B.C., had more or less reached completion by the first century A.D. It is

---

18. It continues to be used in its other senses as well, and, invading the territory of ὁράω still further, is also used in the sense of 'take care' (Bauer, s.v. 6).

19. Cf. examples in Bauer and MM s.v.
   Ammonius, *Diff.* 30, maintains the difference between βλέπω and θεάομαι, an indication that the popular tendency was to use them without differentiation of meaning. Similarly Th.Mag. 60.7.

20. C.C. Tarelli, *JTS* XLVII (1946) 175f.; *TWNT* V 319: 'θεωρέω then became a synon. of θεάομαι and ὁράω and largely replaced ὁράω in the *koine*' (forgetting βλέπω).
   MM s.v. θεωρέω however maintain that θεωρέω 'was hardly a synonym of ὁράω'. *Ev. Jo.* 16.16, among other evidence cited in support, is particularly unconvincing.

reasonable to assume that the process of replacement was a
gradual and continuous one during that period; that, in other
words, as time went on, βλέπω was used more as ὁράω was used
less. There is a possibility, therefore, of using these words
to obtain an indication of the approximate date of a given text.

The evidence which we have already considered could by
itself be applied in this way to the text of the Pentateuch, but
what we must next endeavour to do is to trace the course of the
replacement of ὁράω by βλέπω in the period between the end of
the fourth century B.C. and the middle of the first century A.D.
If that can be done with success it may be possible to narrow
down the indication of date to within a century.

The evidence at our disposal for this period is, as might
be expected, far from adequate, and is for practical reasons
not easy to assemble. An attempt will be made, however, to
collect such evidence as is available and to draw the conclusions
it warrants, tentative though they may be.

For the third century B.C. a survey was made of the main
collections of iii B.C. papyri.[21] The pres. tense of ὁράω in
the sense of 'see' is found some 24 times in these documents,
the impf. three times. βλέπω occurs only in the sense of 'face'
(towards).[22]

The papyrus evidence of the first and second centuries
B.C. is very meagre. In addition, some has to be sought among
publications of documents of other periods, so that a survey of
all the evidence is difficult. The main collections[23] were
examined, however, and gave the following result. Eight examples
of the pres. of ὁράω 'see' are found, none of the impf. βλέπω,
on the other hand, is twice found clearly in this sense:

21. *PCair.Zen.*, *PHib.* i,ii, *PMich.Zen.*, *PCol.Zen.* i,ii, *PLille* i,
PMagd., *PPetr.*, *PGurob*, *PEleph.*, *PRev.*, *PHamb.* ii, *PSorb.*, and
portions of *PSI* iv-vii.

22. Three times, *PCair.Zen.* 847.7,42,50. In one other occurrence
of the word, *ib.* 639.5, the meaning is unclear, and since the
preceding letters are lost the original reading could have been
a compound of βλέπω (so ed., suggesting διαβλέπω as a possibility).

23. *PTeb.* i, iii.1 and 2, *PAdler*, *BGU* vi, viii, *UPZ* i, ii,
PStrassb. ii, and parts of *PRyl.* ii, iv, *PSI* ix, *PAmh.* ii.

UPZ 68.6 (152 B.C.) ἐγὼ γὰρ ἐνύπνια ὁρῶ πονηρά, βλέπω
Μενέδημον κατατρέχοντά με.

BGU 1747.24 (64/3 B.C.) τοὺς δ' ἵππους εἰς ἀσθένειαν [...
διὰ τὴν] ὑποδεικνυμένην αἰτίαν βλέποντες προσ [...

Some further information about this period may be gained
from Polybius (c. 202-120 B.C.). The transitive use of βλέπω
in the sense of 'see' occurs fifteen times in his writings,[24]
e.g.

18.46.8 βουλομένων τῶν ἀνθρώπων μὴ μόνον ἀκούειν, ἀλλὰ
καὶ βλέπειν τὸν λέγοντα

18.20.7 ... ὥστε ... μήδε τοὺς ἐν ποσὶ δύνασθαι βλέπειν.

The word is however still most often used in its earlier sense
of 'look' (at, towards), with preposition following. Unfortunately no information is available from the lexicons for
Polybius' use of ὁράω,[25] but we can almost certainly assume that
he used it more often than βλέπω.[26]

Finally, we can add from the inscriptions an example of
βλέπω 'see' from the first century B.C.:

SIG 1104.42 (c. 37/6 B.C.)... ἵνα ... πολλοὶ ζηλωταὶ γίνωνται
(τοῦ) τὴν σύνοδον ἐπαύξειν, βλέποντες τὸν κτίσαντα
τυγχάνοντα τῆς πρεπούσης εὐνοίας τε καὶ μνήμης.

This is the only example in the inscriptions collected in
Dittenberger, *SIG*.

It seems likely that in the third century B.C. ὁράω was
still the normal word in the pres. and impf. Although not as
many as we should like, the comparatively large number of its
occurrences, 27, as against none of βλέπω, makes that conclusion
probable. βλέπω may, however, have been used occasionally, as

---

24. Mauersberger, *Polybios-Lexikon*, s.v.

25. Mauersberger's lexicon is still in progress, and the earlier
lexicon of Schweighäuser does not note any occurrences of the
word.

26. Examples of ὁράω noted at random are at 5.26.14, 6.2.7,
6.5.8.

we should expect judging from the evidence of Menander noticed
earlier, and that possibility is of course not ruled out by the
fact that no examples are found in iii B.C. papyri.

For the next two centuries the papyri fail us almost completely, providing too few examples of the two words for a
satisfactory comparison of one with the other. But the examples
that are found would support the tentative conclusion that
during the second century B.C. βλέπω 'see' became more common,
so that by the end of the century, perhaps earlier, the two
words were equally common; and that in the first century B.C.
βλέπω became more and more the usual word, with ὁράω beginning
to be obsolete. Additional information from another source
helps towards this conclusion. That βλέπω 'see' appears at all
in Polybius, whose Greek tends towards the literary language, is
I suggest an indication that it had become fairly well established in everyday language by his time.

I am suggesting, then, that it was during the second
century B.C. that βλέπω began to compete seriously with ὁράω.
Clearly the evidence does not permit a positive conclusion on
this point. We do know, however, that by about the middle of
the first century A.D. βλέπω had all but ousted ὁράω. It is
highly probable, therefore, that βλέπω began to be common some
time earlier. Naturally it is difficult to estimate the rate at
which a development of this kind would progress, but it is
certain to have taken place gradually. Therefore we may say
with some certainty that at the latest βλέπω would have been in
fairly common use by 100 B.C. And, if the evidence of Polybius
in particular is kept in mind, an earlier date, around 150 B.C.,
can reasonably be inferred. An even earlier date is of course
quite possible, but we have insufficient evidence to attempt to
establish it. Around the middle of the century is suggested
here as the earliest at which it can be put with any safety.

Turning at last to the Pentateuch, we find 25 occurrences
of the pres. of ὁράω and three of the impf. (Rahlfs' text).
These may be classified as follows:[27]

---

27. Some of the examples are difficult to classify satisfactorily, but these do not affect the main point.
    For an analysis along different lines see *TWNT* V 324-8.

1. 'take care', *Ex*. 33.5 ὁρᾶτε μὴ πληγὴν ἄλλην ἐπάξω ἐγὼ ἐφ'
ὑμᾶς, and probably also 31.13.

2. 'look', *Ge*. 29.2 καὶ ὁρᾷ καὶ ἰδοὺ φρέαρ, *Ex*. 14.10
ἀναβλέψαντες ... τοῖς ὀφθαλμοῖς ὁρῶσιν, καὶ οἱ Αἰγύπτιοι
ἐστρατοπέδευσαν ...[28]

3. 'have the faculty of sight': (a) *Ge*. 27.1 ἠμβλύνθησαν οἱ
ὀφθαλμοὶ αὐτοῦ τοῦ ὁρᾶν, (b) of prophetic vision, 'have the
power of perception', *Nu*. 24.3,15 ὁ ἄνθρωπος ὁ ἀληθινῶς ὁρῶν.

4. 'perceive visually', trans., fourteen times in the pres.,
e.g. *Ge*. 13.15 τὴν γῆν, ἣν σὺ ὁρᾷς, 31.5, *Ex*. 2.6, 32.19, *Nu*.
14.22; three times impf., *Ex*. 5.19, 20.18, 33.10.

5. ὅρα exclamatory, 'look!' or 'see!': *Ge*. 31.50 ὅρα οὐθεὶς
μεθ' ἡμῶν ἐστιν, *Ex*. 4.23, 25.40, *Nu*. 1.49.

Thus ὁράω in the sense that concerns us occurs in the
Pentateuch fourteen times in the pres., three times in the impf.
As we shall see in a moment, this number considerably outweighs
the number of occurrences of βλέπω in the same sense.

Tenses other than pres. and impf. are supplied by εἶδον,
ἑώρακα, ὄψομαι (with passives ὤφθην, ὦμμαι, ἑώραμαι, ὀφθήσομαι).

θεάομαι and θεωρέω do not occur at all.

βλέπω is used in the following ways:

1. (a) 'look' (at), *De*. 28.32 οἱ ὀφθαλμοί σου βλέψονται
σφακελίζοντες εἰς αὐτά, (b) 'face' (towards), of aspect, *Nu*.
21.20 ἀπὸ κορυφῆς τοῦ λελαξευμένου τὸ βλέπον (sic) κατὰ πρόσωπον
τῆς ἐρήμου.

2. 'watch', 'look on', abs., *De*. 4.34 ὅσα ἐποίησεν ...
ἐνώπιόν σου βλέποντος.

3. 'have the faculty of sight', *Ex*. 4.11 τίς ἐποίησεν ...
βλέποντα καὶ τυφλόν; 23.8, *Ge*. 48.10, *De*. 29.3.

---

28. This example might also be regarded as an instance of sense
4, since the καί clause is in effect the object of ὁρῶσιν. Cf.
M. Johannessohn, *Zeitschr. f. vergleichende Sprachforschung*
LXIV (1937) 198, and, for examples of this paratactic construction in Mod.Gk., Thumb, *Handbook of the Modern Greek Vernacular*
185.

4. 'perceive visually, trans., *Ge.* 45.12 ἰδοὺ οἱ ὀφθαλμοὶ ὑμῶν βλέπουσιν καὶ οἱ ὀφθαλμοὶ Βενιαμιν τοῦ ἀδελφοῦ μου ὅτι τὸ στόμα μου τὸ λαλοῦν πρὸς ὑμᾶς,[29] *De.* 28.34 καὶ ἔσῃ παράπληκτος διὰ τὰ ὁράματα τῶν ὀφθαλμῶν σου, ἃ βλέψῃ.[30]

In the Pentateuch, then, there are only two examples of βλέπω in the sense of 'perceive visually', trans. Of these, it is important to note, one is the future tense, competing not with ὁράω or ἑώρων but with ὄψομαι (which occurs about 50 times). Thus the numbers to be compared are: ὁράω 14, βλέπω 1; ἑώρων 3, ἔβλεπον 0. It is clear that the normal word in the pres. and impf. is still ὁράω.

It is worth adding that the four examples of exclamatory ὅρα (above, ὁράω 5) might also be taken into account in this comparison. If at the time our text was written βλέπω was displacing ὁράω, it would probably have been used in those places also.[31]

What conclusion, then, is to be drawn? If my interpretation of the evidence is correct, βλέπω as a synonym of ὁράω had begun to be fairly common at latest by about the middle of the second century B.C., so that in a vernacular text dating from that time or later we could expect βλέπω to be used more than occasionally for the idea of 'perceive visually', trans. Since ὁράω is still the usual word in the Pentateuch, it can be concluded that our text must be dated earlier than 150 B.C., and that a date in the third century B.C. would be quite

---

29. βλέπουσιν A; no. v.11. (BS are lacking here).

30. βλέψῃ AB etc., βλέπεις Gkx, ὄψῃ Θgnpt.
According to Thackeray, 'the last few chapters of Dt. seem to occupy a position by themselves in the Pentateuch' (*Gramm.* 8 n.2), and 'in Dt. some new elements in the vocabulary begin to make their appearance ..., particularly in the closing chapters' (14). Thackeray did not elaborate on this, beyond noting two examples of novel renderings. If correct, the observation could be of some significance here.
F. Baumgärtel, 'Zur Entstehung der Pentateuchseptuaginta' 77 (in: Herrmann and Baumgärtel, *Beiträge zur Entstehungsgeschichte der Septuaginta,*Berlin, 1923) considers evidence for dividing *De.* into two halves by different translators, but does not add to Thackeray's observation.

31. Cf. 1 *Ki.* 25.35 βλέπε ἤκουσα τῆς φωνῆς σου, 3 *Ki.* 17.23 βλέπε, ζῆ ὁ υἱός σου.

consistent with the evidence.

The fact that θεάομαι and θεωρέω are not used in the Pentateuch also points to an early date. As we saw, by the first century A.D. these two words had become current as near synonyms of the other words for 'see' (θεάομαι usually in the aor., θεωρέω pres. and impf.). I have not attempted to trace the course of this development in the centuries between the end of the Classical period and the first century A.D., but it is likely that it took place gradually during that time. Therefore a text in which the words are not used for the idea is almost certainly to be dated early in that period rather than late.

An examination of the words used for 'donkey' gives a similar result. Here we have the case of an incoming word competing for a time with the older word for an idea and then falling out of use, leaving the older word in possession again.

ὄνος, ὁ, ἡ, the normal word since Homer, continues in use in post-Classical Greek right up to Byzantine times, when it begins to be eclipsed by γάϊδαρος (γαϊδούρι), the Modern Greek word. It is fully attested in papyri throughout this period (examples in MM).

In the third century B.C. and later in the Ptolemaic period ὑποζύγιον, originally any 'beast of draught or burden' (Theogn. +), is frequently used, as Mayser shows,[32] to mean 'donkey'. Thus e.g. in *PHib*. 34.3 (243-2 B.C.) ... ἐν ὧι ἐγέγραπτο ἐπαναγκάσαι τὸν Καλλίδρομον ἢ τὸ ὑποζύγιον ἀποδοῦναι τῶι κυρίωι ἢ τιμὴν τοῦ ὄνου (δραχμὰς) κ, and see the other examples quoted by Mayser. It may be true that in some contexts ὑποζύγιον still had the more general reference (cf. MM s.v.), but there can be no doubt that it mostly meant 'donkey' specifically.[33]

---

32. *Gramm.* II.i 31, cf. Deissmann, *BS* 161.

33. According to Mayser this restriction in meaning is already beginning to appear in Arist., and is fully established in Thphr. LSJ also find it as early as Hp. *Aph*. 4.70 τὰ οὖρα ἀνατεταραγμένα οἷον ὑποζυγίου, but it does not seem necessary here, or in the similar example in *Epid*. 1.26.123.
The semantic development seen in this word incidentally tells us that the donkey was the beast of burden *par excellence* at the time when the development occurred. On the donkey in Ptolemaic Egypt see Schnebel, *Landwirtschaft* 335ff.

The important point for our purpose is that, according to
the evidence of the papyri, ὑποζύγιον in the sense of 'donkey'
was very common in the third century B.C., but in the second or
first century B.C. began to disappear from use and by the first
century A.D. had fallen out more or less completely.[34]

In the collections of iii B.C. papyri examined earlier for
ὁράω, βλέπω, there occur a total of 72 examples of ὄνος, 86 of
ὑποζύγιον. It is clear, then, that the two words were equally
common at this time.

For the next two centuries the evidence is meagre once
again, but nevertheless points to the conclusion that at some
time in ii B.C. ὑποζύγιον began to be less common than
previously.

In ii B.C. papyri I find 3 examples of ὄνος in its normal
use, and, perhaps to be left out of account, over 50 examples in
the sense of 'donkey-load' in *PTeb*. 848, 849, etc. ὑποζύγιον is
found twice, viz. *PTeb*. 92.13 = 161.8 (late ii B.C.) καὶ ἐντεῦθεν
κατάγεται δι᾽ ὑποζυγίων, *PStrassb*. 93.5 (120 B.C.) ἁλωτικὰ
ὑποζύγια. In both these instances there is a possibility,
though it is not to be pressed, that the less specific sense is
intended. The editors translate the *PTeb*. example by 'beasts
of burden'.

In the papyri of i B.C. I find ὄνος 5 times, ὑποζύγιον not
at all.

By i A.D. ὑποζύγιον in the sense of 'donkey' had quite
definitely fallen out of normal use. In the papyri of i A.D.
and later in *BGU* i, ii, and iii there are 50 or more examples of
ὄνος, in *POxy*. i-iv, vi-x there are 18, and none of ὑποζύγιον in
either collection. In this period the only examples of the
latter word known to me, apart from *NT*, are *Sammelb*. 3924.12,27
(an edict of Germanicus, 19 A.D.) τὰ δὲ διὰ τῆς πόλεως δια-
τρέχοντα ὑποζύγια τοὺς ἀπαντῶντας πρὸς βίαν περιαιρεῖσθαι κωλύω,

---

34. 'Seit der Kaiserzeit kommt das Wort nicht mehr vor, ὄνος
herrscht wieder allein', Mayser, *ib*.
    In Mod.Gk. ὑποζύγιον has only the meaning 'beast of burden',
and that too only in learned or archaistic Gk. (Jannaris, s.v.
burden).

Berichtigungsliste I p.102.18 = *PMasp*. 279.18 (vi A.D.) ζῷα
ἐννέα καὶ ὑποζύγια δύο. In these cases it seems probable that
the word is intended in its general sense, especially in the
official language of the edict.[35]

The *NT* has two examples of ὑποζύγιον, one of which, *Ev.
Matt.* 21.5, is in a quotation from the LXX. The other is at
2 *Ep.Petr.* 2.16, in a reference to the story of Balaam and the
ass: ... Βαλαὰμ τοῦ Βεώρ, ὃς μισθὸν ἀδικίας ἠγάπησεν, ἔλεγξιν
δὲ ἔσχεν ἰδίας παρανομίας· ὑποζύγιον ἄφωνον ἐν ἀνθρώπου φωνῇ
φθεγξάμενον ἐκώλυσεν τὴν τοῦ προφήτου παραφρονίαν. Although in
the LXX description of this incident, in *Nu.* 22.28, ὄνος, not
ὑποζύγιον, is the word used, it is possible, I suggest, that
ὑποζύγιον was used by the author of the Epistle as a deliberate
reminiscence of LXX language.[36] ὄνος, on the other hand, occurs
five times in *NT* (twice in quotations of LXX).

In the Pentateuch ὑποζύγιον is found 14 times altogether
(Rahlfs' text). Although the context does not always give a
decisive indication of the meaning, there can be no doubt that
the translators used it in the sense of 'donkey'. In all
instances where there is a word corresponding to it in MT it
renders Hebrew חמור , 'he-ass', BDB, and there are numerous
examples of its use in the same kind of context as ὄνος: e.g.
Ex. 22.9 ὑποζύγιον ἢ μόσχον ἢ πρόβατον ἢ πᾶν κτῆνος, *Ge.* 12.16
πρόβατα καὶ μόσχοι καὶ ὄνοι, ... ἡμίονοι καὶ κάμηλοι; *Ex.* 13.13
πᾶν διανοῖγον μήτραν ὄνου ἀλλάξεις προβάτῳ, 34.20 καὶ πρωτότοκον
ὑποζυγίου λυτρώσῃ προβάτῳ.

ὄνος occurs a total of 43 times (Rahlfs), rendering חמור

---

35. The slight evidence afforded by the inscriptions in *SIG* and
OGI accords with the above. ὑποζύγιον occurs only in an inscription of iv B.C., *SIG* 243 D. 55 (whether it means 'donkey' or not
it is impossible to tell); one example of ὄνος is from iii B.C.,
the rest (3) A.D.

36. The unusual style of this Epistle has been remarked on. '1
Peter is written in straightforward Hellenistic Greek, whereas 2
Peter affects a style that is almost literary, replete with
quite uncommon words', Sidebottom, *James, Jude & 2 Peter* (Century
Bible) 96; cf. Bigg (*ICC*) 224f. It is worth mentioning also that
the Epistle is generally agreed to be late: certainly later than
100 A.D., and for some as late as 140 A.D. It is unlikely that
the writer reflects the living speech of his time in using
ὑποζύγιον in this way.

and אתון ('she-ass', BDB). In 17 instances, most of which are
in *Nu*. 22, it is found with the feminine article. In these
places ὑποζύγιον, giving no indication of sex, could not have
been used. The discrepancy between the numbers of occurrences
of the two words is therefore not as great as at first appears
and is hardly enough to be significant. It seems clear that in
the translators' vocabulary both words were in full use. Both
are to be found within the space of two or three chapters, as
e.g. *Ge*. 34.28 ὄνος, 36.24 ὑποζύγιον, *Ex*. 20.10 ὑποζύγιον,
21.33 ὄνος, and on one occasion within the same chapter: *Ex*.
22.3 ὄνος, 8,9,29 ὑποζύγιον.

It is true that whereas ὄνος occurs in all books ὑποζύγιον
is not found in *Le*. and *Nu*. But it would be hard to see significance in this. *Le*. and *Nu*. could scarcely be separated from
the other books on this basis, since the evidence of the
vocabulary as a whole points overwhelmingly to the homogeneity
of the Pentateuch. Moreover, in the case of *Le*. a word for the
idea is required only once (15.9). Notice also that in one
book, *Ex*., ὑποζύγιον outnumbers ὄνος 11 to 3. In short, the
distribution of the two words appears to be random.

Clearly, then, in regard to words for 'donkey', the
vocabulary of the Pentateuch text as we know it fits very well
with a date in the third century B.C. Owing to the unsatisfactory nature of our evidence for the second century B.C., it
cannot be said with certainty whether a date in that century is
also possible. It is reasonable to argue, however, that since
ὑποζύγιον, like ὁράω, must have dropped out gradually, and
appears to have become obsolete by the first century B.C., a
text exhibiting ὑποζύγιον as often as the Pentateuch could not
be much later than about the middle of the second century B.C.
It can at any rate be stated with confidence that a date in the
first century B.C. or later is quite improbable.

The two groups of words we have examined, then, support
each other in indicating that our text of the Pentateuch is
older than about the middle of the second century B.C. The
evidence does not permit us to conclude definitely that our text
is as old as the third century B.C., but it does show that our
MSS preserve, essentially unchanged, an early text. It is a

reasonable supposition that that text is in fact the ancient
LXX version of the third century B.C.

There are a number of other groups of words that might be
used to support this result. It has not been possible to
examine these in detail for the present study, but it is worth
while noticing them because even without a full examination it
can be seen that they point to an early date for our text. It
is however uncertain whether they would agree with the lower
limit of 150 B.C. suggested by the words for 'see' and 'donkey'.

In the later Koine βούλομαι tends to be replaced by θέλω
(which alone passes into Modern Greek).[37] In the more vernacular
books of the *NT* the former occurs only in special contexts,[38]
the latter being the usual word. In the Pentateuch, however,
βούλομαι is still in full use (14 times; θέλω c. 20 times).

Much the same situation is found with βοάω and κράζω. In
the Pentateuch the former is the usual word for 'cry out' (c. 13
times). κράζω appears to be just coming into use. It is found
5 times, in somewhat different contexts from βοάω, viz. in
descriptions of a body of people raising a cry, not of a single
person. In the *NT*, on the other hand κράζω is the usual word;
βοάω is rare, occurring occasionally in more literary books, in
quotations from the LXX, and once in Mark for a special reason.[39]

Words for 'go (away)' also indicate the earliness of the
Pentateuch. The common later use of ὑπάγω in this sense was
apparently not established until the first century A.D. It
does not occur in the Pentateuch. On the other hand ἀποτρέχω,
which appears to have dropped out later, is common in the
Pentateuch and in iii B.C. Greek.[40]

---

37. Cf. Bl. DF §101 s.v. θέλειν.
38. See above p.124 n.11.
39. See above p.124 n.11.
40. See above pp.125 ff., and esp. 127 n.17.

CHAPTER IX

CONCLUSION

The vocabulary of the Pentateuch has many close links with
the vocabulary of contemporary vernacular Greek. It has been
shown that the translators' vocabulary includes a large number
of uses, formations, and words that had recently become current
in the language. Some instances in which an old word became
obsolete in the Koine and was replaced by a new one have also
been examined. Here too we have found agreement between the
Pentateuch and the Greek of the time.

The examples that have been studied in detail here are of
course only a section of the vocabulary. But it can hardly be
doubted that what has been shown for these examples is also
true of the greater part of it. Attention has been concentrated
on new words and uses attested in documents close in date to the
Pentateuch. But these are only the most obvious illustrations
of the connexion between the translators' vocabulary and that of
the time. As we saw in the general survey in Chapter III there
are many other new words and uses that are less well attested
but are nevertheless sure to have been normal Greek of the third
century B.C. In addition we saw that old words and uses are an
important element in the translators' vocabulary. Moreover, a
large number of these are attested in papyri of the third
century B.C. It is also clear that the translators were familiar
with many idiomatic Greek expressions and uses. Words for
'wash' (pp.36ff.) are a case in point.

Some of the examples studied give an especially good
indication of the translators' familiarity with the vocabulary
of their time. Words like τοπάρχης (p. 98), παρεπίδημος (112),
and πάροικος (60), and uses such as χρυσοῦς as the name of a
measure of weight and value (63ff.), ἀπέχω 'I have received'
(61f.), and ἀποτρέχω 'go free', of slaves (127), were part of
the technical terminology of the day. It seems unlikely that
speakers of an isolated form of Greek would employ such terms
at all.

145

It is worth pointing out, too, that in regard to subject-
matter the words and uses examined are a cross-section of the
vocabulary.

As to words and uses unattested outside Biblical and
related literature, the survey in Chapter III suggested that
these are actually a small proportion of the whole vocabulary.
Moreover, there are strong indications that a number of them
are in fact normal Greek. They are unattested because of the
incompleteness of our evidence. If more evidence were available
their currency in normal Greek would almost certainly be established. We have seen a number of instances in which a word or
use apparently peculiar to Biblical Greek has now been shown to
be normal Greek by evidence recently made available or previously overlooked.[1] It can hardly be doubted that there are
others of the same kind.

In short, the conclusion to which this examination leads
is that the bulk of the Pentateuch vocabulary is the same as
that of contemporary Greek.

It has also been shown that the case for regarding the
Greek of the LXX as a 'Jewish-Greek' dialect is a weak one.
Especially detrimental to this theory is the observation that
the Pentateuch translators frequently avoid reproducing the
Hebrew idiom of their original. There are undoubtedly numerous
Hebraisms in the version, but advocates of 'Jewish-Greek' have
emphasized them to the exclusion of instances in which Hebraism
is avoided.

These findings strongly support the view that the Greek of
the LXX is to be regarded as essentially the Greek of the time
and that its peculiarites are to be explained chiefly as a
result of the translation process. A final conclusion on this
question will of course not be possible until the remainder of
the LXX and syntax as well as vocabulary have been fully
examined. Nevertheless this study has shown that there are
strong grounds for reaffirming Deissmann's view.

---

1. See ἀπερίτμητος (111), κόρος (116f), μέρος 'side' (72ff.),
and examples on p.44f.

This study is also offered as a contribution to LXX lexicography. The detailed examination of individual words and uses will, it is intended, form part of the preliminary study for the much-needed LXX lexicon. In addition there are certain general points to be noticed.

It has been clearly shown that lexical study of the LXX cannot afford to neglect the evidence of contemporary Greek, in particular the evidence of the Egyptian papyri. The LXX vocabulary must not be studied in isolation from its linguistic context. This is not to say that it will always be found to agree with the Greek of the time. Undoubtedly the opposite will be the case in many instances. But it must not be assumed, before the evidence is thoroughly investigated, that LXX usage in a given instance is independent of current usage.

It has been shown that the evidence of the papyri does contribute to the understanding of LXX usage. We have seen instances in which it throws considerable light on the meaning of a word in the LXX.[2] Indeed in some cases the meaning could hardly be understood correctly without the knowledge of contemporary usage.[3]

Furthermore, there are clearly many discoveries yet to be made about the LXX vocabulary. The treatment of it in the existing lexicons is seldom satisfactory and must not be relied on. Much investigation is needed before a satisfactory lexical treatment of LXX word can be given.

It may be added that in the present study I have given most attention to the evidence of papyri and little to that of inscriptions, the editions of which are poorly indexed. But it is certain that the latter, if thoroughly investigated, would have much relevant information to offer.[4]

---

2. E.g. ἀποτρέχω (125ff.), ἐνοχλέω (66), παράδεισος (53ff.), προσπορεύομαι (89 ff.).

3. E.g. ἀποσκευή (101ff.), τοπάρχης (98), χρυσοῦς (63ff.).

4. Cf. the attestation provided by the inscriptions in the case of ἐκδανείζω (93), κόκκινος (111f.), σανιδωτός (112), and other words noticed on p.45.
   The evidence for βλέπω and ὁράω (pp.135ff.) in iii-i B.C. could, I feel sure, be supplemented from this source.

In regard to the dating of our text of the Pentateuch, it has been possible only to show that our text is probably older than the middle of the second century B.C. This nevertheless is a useful indication that our MSS witness to an early text.

Moreover, the method of dating used here could be applied in other parts of the LXX. An illustration of this may be noticed. In the two texts of *Judges* as printed by Rahlfs, A and B, there are a number of differences in vocabulary that must be significant for dating. They are as follows: 9.36, 19.30 ὁράω A, βλέπω B; 13.23 βούλομαι A, θέλω B; 5.10, 19.3,10,21,28 ὑποζύγιον A, ὄνος B (in 1.14, however, B has ὑπ. once, where A has it twice). In each place (apart from 1.14) the reading of B is likely to be more recent than that of A: where A has the word in use early in the Koine B has the word which later replaced it.[5] The textual history of *Judges* is very complicated, involving a good deal more than just the two major texts A and B. And these texts themselves no doubt contain recensional elements. It would therefore be unwise to draw any firm conclusion here about the age of A or B as a whole. It may however be said that the features of vocabulary mentioned suggest that the text witnessed to by A is older than that witnessed to by B. At any rate it is clear that these features have something to contribute to the study of the text of *Judges*.

In conclusion two other points may be mentioned.

Some have found evidence to suggest that more than one translator worked on the Pentateuch.[6] This view is very likely correct, but it is worth noticing that the evidence examined here does not provide any support for it. This study suggests that both in age and level of language the vocabulary of the Pentateuch is homogeneous. That is to say, all parts of it employ on the whole the everyday vocabulary of the third or second century B.C.

---

5. I have noted here only words discussed in Chapter VIII. Others pointing in the same direction might be added.

6. See F. Baumgärtel's study already cited (above p.139 n.30), and O.J. Baab, *JBL* LII (1933) 239-43.

The other point is one of interest for the study of
Hellenistic Greek generally. It is clear that the Pentateuch
itself is likely to be a good witness to the vocabulary of
early Koine Greek. It must of course be used with caution.
Any possibility of Hebraism would naturally vitiate its evidence.
But there are many instances in which it could be of value. It
frequently provides early attestation for a word or use known
only from late in the Koine. There are also many words and uses
unattested elsewhere that could be accepted as normal Greek on
its evidence.

APPENDIX   I

FURTHER EXAMPLES OF
AVOIDANCE OF HEBREW IDIOM

Here are collected some other examples of the same kind as
those discussed in Chapter II. I note each as briefly as
possible, giving only the information necessary to identify it.
The references cited in each case are not meant to be exhaustive.

I.   A Hebrew word is not rendered by the literal equivalent

<table>
<tr><td>(i)</td><td>כרת</td><td>διατίθημι</td><td>Ge. 15.8 and often elsewhere</td></tr>
<tr><td></td><td></td><td>ἐξολεθρεύω</td><td>Le. 17.9 and often elsewhere</td></tr>
<tr><td></td><td></td><td>καταγράφω</td><td>Ex. 17.14, 32.15, Nu. 11.26</td></tr>
<tr><td></td><td></td><td>τίθημι</td><td>Ex. 34.10,27</td></tr>
<tr><td>(ii)</td><td>בוא</td><td>πάρειμι</td><td>Nu. 22.20</td></tr>
<tr><td>(iii)</td><td>יצא</td><td>ἀποτρέχω</td><td>Ex. 21.5,7</td></tr>
<tr><td>(iv)</td><td>מצא</td><td>τυγχάνω</td><td>De. 19.5</td></tr>
<tr><td></td><td></td><td>ἁλίσκομαι</td><td>De. 24.7</td></tr>
<tr><td></td><td></td><td>ἀρκέω</td><td>Nu. 11.22   bis</td></tr>
<tr><td>(v)</td><td>שים</td><td>περιτίθημι</td><td>Ge. 24.47, 41.42</td></tr>
<tr><td>(vi)</td><td>שלח</td><td>ἐπιφέρω</td><td>Ge. 37.22</td></tr>
<tr><td></td><td></td><td>ἀνίημι</td><td>Ge. 49.21</td></tr>
</table>

II. A Hebrew idiomatic expression is not rendered literally

<table>
<tr><td>(i)</td><td>involving</td><td>רב</td><td>Ex. 9.28, Nu. 16.3,7, De.1.6, 2.3</td></tr>
<tr><td>(ii)</td><td>involving</td><td>מעט</td><td>Ge. 30.15</td></tr>
<tr><td>(iii)</td><td>involving</td><td>כפי, לפי</td><td>Ge. 47.12, Ex. 16.21, Le. 25.52 27.16, Nu. 7.5, 35.8</td></tr>
</table>

150

(iv)   מי־יתן   *Ex.* 16.3

(v)   בין הערבים   *Ex.* 12.6, 29.39,41

(vi)   Other examples of various kinds may be seen in:
          Ge. 18.1, 21.20, 27.20, 43.23, *Ex.* 23.1, 36.4,
          Nu. 4.19, 21.4, 32.19, *De.* 2.37.

III. A Hebrew construction is not rendered literally

      A noun in the construct followed by another noun is
      rendered by noun and adjective

      מצבת אבן   στήλη λιθίνη   *Ge.* 35.14
      לחת אבן   πλάκες λίθιναι   *Ex.* 31.18, etc.

      Other examples may be seen in the translators' use of the
      following adjectives: ἀργυροῦς, βρώσιμος, πατρικός,
      πολεμικός, πτερωτός, σιδηροῦς, στιππύινος, στυράκινος,
      τεκτονικός, χαλκοῦς, χρυσοῦς, χωνευτός.

APPENDIX II

SOME OLD WORDS AND USES

ATTESTED ALSO IN iii B.C. PAPYRI

This list has been compiled on the basis of the papyrus
evidence recorded by LSJ, Bauer, and MM, in which the exact
references may be seen. I have not personally confirmed the
references given there.

ἀμάω	δεσμωτήριον
ἀνδρίζομαι 'act courageously'	δεσμώτης
ἀντιλαμβάνομαι 'help'	διαμαρτάνω
ἀξίνη	διασαφέω
ἀπάγω 'arrest'	διατηρέω
ἀπειθέω	δίδραχμον
ἀπολύομαι 'depart'	διέρχομαι of time, 'elapse'
ἀποσοβέω 'scare away'	δικαστής
ἀποτίθημι 'stow away'	διῶρυξ
ἀποτίνω	δρέπανον
ἀρεστός	δρυμός
ἀρραβών	δωρεάν
ἀρχιτεκτονέω	ἐγκαταλείπω
ἀσέβεια	ἐγχώριος
ἀσεβέω	ἐκδύνω
ἀσεβής	ἐκθερίζω
ἀσκός	ἐκλείπω 'fail'
ἀτιμάζω	ἐκχωρέω
αὐλή	ἐλέγχω pass. 'be convicted'
ἄχυρον	ἐμπίμπλημι
βοηθός	ἐμπόριον
βόσκω	ἔμπορος
βύσσινος	ἐναντίον + gen.'in the presence of'
γραμματεύς	ἐνδεής
δάνειον	ἔνδεια
δεκάτη 'tithe'	ἐνέχυρον
δέρμα	ἐντολή

ἐξαιρέω 'rescue'
ἐξέρχομαι of time, 'expire'
ἐξετάζω
ἐξοδία
ἐπέχω 'wait'
ἐπιλανθάνομαι
ἐπιλέγω
ἐπίλοιπος
ἐπιμελέομαι
ἐπιτελέω
ἐπιτιμάω 'rebuke'
ἐπιφαίνω pass. of a god
ἐρεοῦς
ἐρευνάω
ἔριον
ἑτοιμάζω
ἕτοιμος
εὐθύς adv.
ἐφόδιον
ἐχόμενος 'next to'
ζώνη
ἡγεμών
θεμέλια, τά
θερίζω
θήρα 'hunt'
θηρεύω
θυσία
ἶβις
ἱερεύς
ἱππεύς
καθαιρέω 'demolish','dismantle'
καθαίρεσις 'demolition'
καθίζω intrans.
καθίστημι 'appoint'
καλάμη
κάμινος
κάρυον
καταλαμβάνω 'detect'
κατακλυσμός 'inundation'

καταλύω 'pass the night'
κατέχω 'detain'
κείρω 'shear'
κιννάμωμον
κλέπτης
κλῆρος 'block of land'
κλίβανος
κοιλία 'belly'
κομίζω med. 'recover' (money)
κόραξ
κόσμος 'adornment'
κραυγή
κριθή
κρίθινος
κρόκη
κύαθος
λίθινος
λιμός
λοιδορέω
λοιδορία
λυχνία
λύχνος
μαρτυρέω 'give evidence'
μαρτυρία
μάρτυς
μεταπέμπομαι
μέτωπον
νουμηνία
οἰκέτης
ὀκνέω
ὄλυρα
ὁμοθυμαδόν
ὀρύσσω
ὀρφανός
ὀφείλημα
ὀφρῦς
παραγίγνομαι 'come'
παραδίδωμι 'hand over into custody'
παραθήκη

154

παρακρούομαι 'cheat'
παρατίθημι 'deposit'
πατρικός
πάχος
πενθερός
πενιχρός
περιτέμνω 'circumcize'
πῆχυς measure of length
πλινθεύω
ποικίλος of cattle
πρᾶσις
προσεύχομαι
προσπίπτω 'prostrate oneself'
πρόσταγμα
προστάσσω
προχειρίζω 'select', 'appoint'
πυγμή
ῥαθυμέω
ῥαντός
ῥόα
σιτοποιός
σκόρδον
σταφίς
στέαρ
στερεός
στήμων
στολή
στῦλος '(tent-)pole'
συμβαίνω
συμπορεύομαι
συναγωγή of gathering harvest
συναναβαίνω
συναντάω 'meet'
συναποστέλλω
σύνεγγυς
σύνοιδα
συνοικέω 'live in wedlock with'
σφραγίζω
σφραγίς 'seal'; 'signet-ring'

σῶμα 'person'
τελευτάω 'die'
τέλος 'tax'
τετράπουν
τιμάομαι 'assess value'
τόκος 'interest'
τράγος
τράπεζα cultic term 'table for
offerings'
τρίμηνον 'period of three months'
τρίχινος
τροφή
τροφός
τρυγάω
τρύγητος
τύμπανον
ὑδροφόρος
ὑπερέχω 'outdo'
ὕσσωπος
ὑφάντης
ὑφαίνω
φιάλη
φυλακή period of time, 'watch'
χῖδρον
χίμαιρα
χόρτος
χοῦς (measure)
χωρέω 'have room for'
ὡσαύτως
ὡσεί 'as if'; with numbers,
'about'

BIBLIOGRAPHY

This bibliography is supplementary to the list of abbreviations, where the major reference books have been listed. It includes works already referred to in the body of the dissertation, as well as other works consulted.

Abel F-M., 'Coup d'oeil sur la Koine', *Revue Biblique* XXXV (1926) 5-26.

Allen J.T. & Italie G., *Concordance to Euripides*, Berkeley & Los Angeles; London, 1954.

Ast F., *Lexicon Platonicum*, Lipsiae, 1835-6.

Auerbach M., *De vocibus peregrinis in Vetere et Novo Testamento Graeco obviis* (Eus Suppl. 7), Leopoli, 1930.

Baab O.J., 'A Theory of Two Translators for the Greek Genesis', *JBL* LII (1933) 239-43.

Barr J., *Biblical Words for Time* (Studies in Biblical Theology 33), London, 1962.

Barr J., 'Common Sense and Biblical Language', *Biblica* XLIX (1968) 377-87.

Barr J., *Comparative Philology and the Text of the Old Testament,* Oxford, 1968.

Barr J., 'Vocalization and the Analysis of Hebrew among the Ancient Translators', *VT Suppl.* XVI (Festschr. W. Baumgartner) (1967) 1-11.

Barthélemy D., *Les Devanciers d'Aquila* (*VT Suppl.* X), Leiden, 1963.

Bell H.I., *Egypt*, Oxford, 1948.

Bertram G., 'Der Sprachschatz der Septuaginta und der das hebräischen Alten Testaments', *ZAW* LVII (1939) 85-101.

Bickerman E.J., 'The Septuagint as a Translation', *PAAJR* XXVIII (1959) 1-39.

Billen A.V., 'The Classification of the Greek Manuscripts of the Hexateuch', *JTS* XXVI (1924-5) 262-77.

Black M., 'Second Thoughts IX. The Semitic Element in the New Testament', *ET* LXXVII (1965-6) 20-3.

Blau J., 'Zum Hebräisch der Übersetzer des AT, *VT* VI (1956) 98-100.

Bonitz H., *Index Aristotelicus*, Berlin, 1870.

Bowman R.A., 'Aramaeans, Aramaic, and the Bible', *JNES* VII (1948) 65-90.

[Brenton L.C.L.], *The Septuagint Version of the Old Testament, with an English Translation*, Bagster, London, n.d.

Brock S.P., 'The Phenomenon of Biblical Translation in Antiquity', *Alta* II.8 (1969) 96-102.

Brockington L.H., 'Septuagint and Targum', *ZAW* LXVI (1954) 80-6.

Browning R., *Medieval and Modern Greek*, London, 1969.

Büchsel F., 'Die griechische Sprache der Juden in der Zeit der Septuaginta und des Neuen Testaments', *ZAW* n.s. XIX (1944) 132-49.

Caird G.B., 'Towards a Lexicon of the Septuagint', I, *JTS* XIX (1968) 453-75; II, XX (1969) 21-40.

Chantraine P., *Dictionnaire étymologique de la langue grecque: histoire des mots*, Paris, 1968- (in progress).

Cleef F.L. van, *Index Antiphonteus*, Cornell Univ., 1895.

Colwell E.C., 'The Greek Language', *Interpreters' Dictionary of the Bible* II 479-87.

Conybeare F.C. & Stock St.G., *Selections from the Septuagint*, Boston, 1905.

David M. & Groningen B.A. van, *Papyrological Primer*, Leyden, 1965.

Debrunner A., *Geschichte der griechischen Sprache*, Berlin, 1953-4.

Deissmann G.A., 'Hellenistisches Griechisch', *Realencyklopädie für protest. Theol. und Kirche* VII 627ff.

Deissmann G.A., *The New Testament in the Light of Modern Research*, Haskell Lectures, 1929.

Deissmann, G.A., *Philology of the Greek Bible*, (transl. L.M. Strachan), London, 1908.

Delekat L., 'Ein Septuagintatargum', *VT* VIII (1958) 225-52.

Dieterich K., *Untersuchungen zur Geschichte der griechischen Sprache von der hellenistischen Zeit bis zum 10 Jahrhundert n. Chr. (Byz. Archiv I)*, Leipzig, 1898.

Ellendt F., *Lexicon Sophocleum*, Regimontii Prussorum, 1835.

Elliott J.H., *The Elect and the Holy (Novum Testamentum Suppl. XII)*, Leiden, 1966.

Essen M.H.N. von, *Index Thucydideus*, Berolini, 1887.

Forman L.L., *Index Andocideus, Lycurgeus, Dinarcheus,* Oxford, 1897.

Fuchs L., *Die Juden Ägyptens in ptolemäischer und römischer Zeit,* Wien, 1924.

Gautier L., *La langue de Xénophon,* Geneva, 1911.

Gehman H.S., '"Αγιος in the Septuagint, and its Relation to the Hebrew Original' *VT* IV (1954) 337-48.

Gehman H.S., 'Adventures in Septuagint Lexicography', *Textus* V (1966) 125-32.

Gehman H.S., 'The Hebraic Character of Septuagint Greek', *VT* I (1951) 81-90.

Gehman H.S., 'Hebraisms of the Old Greek Version of Genesis', *VT* III (1953) 141-8.

Geldart E.M., *The Modern Greek Language in its Relation to Ancient Greek*, Oxford, 1870.

Gingrich F.W., 'The Greek NT as a Landmark in the Course of Semantic Change', *JBL* LXXIII (1954) 189-96.

Glaser O., *De ratione quae intercedit inter sermonem Polybii et eum qui in titulis saeculi III, II, I apparet*, Diss. Giessen, 1894.

Gooding D.W., *The Account of the Tabernacle. Translation and Textual Problems of the Greek Exodus* (*Texts & Studies* n.s. VI), Cambridge, 1959.

Gooding D.W., *Recensions of the Septuagint Pentateuch* (Tyndale O.T. Lecture, 1954), London, 1955.

Grobel K., 'Σῶμα as "Self, Person", in the LXX', *ZNW Beiheft* XXI 52-9.

Gundry R.H., 'The Language Milieu of First-Century Palestine. Its Bearing on the Authenticity of the Gospel Tradition', *JBL* LXXXIII (1964) 404-8.

Herrmann J., & Baumgärtel F., *Beiträge zur Entstehungsgeschichte der Septuaginta*, Berlin, 1923.

Hill D., *Greek Words and Hebrew Meanings*, Cambridge, 1967.

Holmes D.H., *Index Lysiacus*, Bonnae, 1895.

Huber K., *Untersuchungen über den Sprachcharakter des griechischen Leviticus*, (Diss. Zürich), Giessen, 1916.

Italie G., *Index Aeschyleus*, Leiden, 1964.

Jannaris A.N., *An Historical Greek Grammar*, London, 1897.

Johannessohn M., 'Der Wahrnehmungssatz bei den Verben des Sehens in der hebr. und griech. Bibel', *Zeitschr. f. vergleichende Sprachforschung* LXIV (1937) 145-260.

Joüon P., 'Quelques hébraïsmes du Codex Sinaiticus de Tobie' *Biblica* IV (1923) 168-74.

Katz P., 'Septuagintal Studies in the Mid-Century', in: *The Background of the New Testament and its Eschatology. Studies in Honour of C.H. Dodd*, ed. W.D. Davies & D. Daube, Cambridge, 1956, pp. 176-208.

Katz P., 'Zur Übersetzungstechnik der Septuaginta', *Die Welt des Orients* II.3 (1956) 267-73.

Kennedy H.A.A., *Sources of New Testament Greek*, Edinburgh, 1895.

Kilpatrick G.D., 'Πορεύεσθαι and its Compounds', *JTS* XLVIII (1947) 61-3.

Knopf R., Lietzmann H., Weinel H., *Einführung in das Neue Testament*, 5 ed., Berlin, 1949.

Ledogar, R.J., 'Verbs of Praise in the LXX Translation of the Hebrew Canon', *Biblica* XLVIII (1967) 29-56.

Lefort L.-Th., 'Pour une grammaire des LXX', *Le Muséon* XLI (1928) 152-60.

Lesky A., *A History of Greek Literature* (transl. by J. Willis & C. de Heer), London, 1966.

Lys D., 'The Israelite Soul according to the LXX', *VT* XVI (1966) 181-228.

Maidhof A., *Zur Begriffsbestimmung der Koine, besonders auf Grund des Attizisten Moiris* (Beiträge zur historischen Syntax der griech. Sprache 20), Würzburg, 1912.

Mandelkern S., *Veteris Testamenti Concordantiae Hebraicae atque Chaldaicae*, Tel Aviv, 1967.

Marcus R., 'Jewish and Greek Elements in the Septuagint', in: *Louis Ginzberg Jubilee Volume* I, New York, 1945, pp. 227-45.

Margolis M., 'Complete Induction for Identification of the Vocabulary in the Greek Versions of the Old Testament with its Semitic Equivalents: Its Necessity and the Means of Obtaining it', *JAOS* XXX (1910) 301-12.

Martin R.A., 'Some Syntactical Criteria of Translation Greek', *VT* X (1960) 295-310.

Mauersberger A., *Polybios-Lexikon,* Berlin, 1956- (in progress).

Meecham H.G., *The Letter of Aristeas: A Linguistic Study with Special Reference to the Greek Bible*, Manchester, 1935.

Meister R., 'Prolegomena zu einer Grammatik der LXX', *Wiener Studien* XXIX (1908) 228-59.

Montevecchi O., 'Continuità ed evoluzione della lingua Greca nella *Settanta* e nei papiri', *Actes du Xe Congrès Internat. de Papyrologues* 1964, pp. 39-49.

Montevecchi O., 'Quaedam de graecitate Psalmorum cum papyris comparata', *Proceedings of the IXth International Congress of Papyrology* 1958, pp. 293-310.

Morenz S., 'Aegyptische Spuren in den Septuaginta', *Festschr.Th. Klauser: Jahrb. f. Antike u. Christentum*, Erg.-Bd. I, 1964, pp. 250-8.

Munck J., 'Les sémitismes dans le NT. Réflexions méthodologiques', *Class. et. Med.*VI (1944) 110-50.

Nida E.A., *Toward a Science of Translating: With Special Reference to Principles and Procedures Involved in Bible Translating*, Leiden, 1964.

Nock A.D., 'The Vocabulary of the New Testament', *JBL* LII (1933) 131-9.

Orlinsky H.M., 'Current Progress and Problems in LXX Research', in: *The Study of the Bible Today and Tomorrow*, ed. H.R. Willoughby, Chicago, 1947, pp.144-61.

Ottley R.R., *Handbook to the Septuagint*, London, 1920.

Pernot H., 'Grec d'Égypte et grec des Écritures', *REG* XLIV (1931) 167-204.

Pernot H., 'Observations sur la langue de la Septante', *REG* XLII (1929) 411-25.

Powell J.E., *Lexicon to Herodotus,* Cambridge, 1938.

Préaux C., *Les Grecs en Égypte, d'après les archives de Zénon,* Bruxelles, 1947.

Preuss S., *Index Aeschineus,* Lipsiae, 1896.

Preuss S., *Index Demosthenicus,* Lipsiae, 1892.

Preuss S., *Index Isocrateus,* Lipsiae, 1904.

Prévot A., 'Verbes grecs relatifs a la vision et noms de l'oeil', I, *Rev. Phil.* IX (1935) 133-60; II, 233-79.

Pring J.T., *The Oxford Dictionary of Modern Greek,* Oxford, 1965.

Rabin C., 'The Translation Process and the Character of the Septuagint', *Textus* VI (1968) 1-26.

Reinhold H., *De Graecitate Patrum Apostolicorum Librorumque Apocryphorum NTi Quaestiones Grammaticae* (Diss. Phil. Halenses XIV.1), Halle, 1898.

Riddle D.W., 'The Logic of the Theory of Translation Greek', *JBL* LI (1932) 13-30.

Riesenfeld H. & B., *Repertorium Lexicographicum Graecum: A Catalogue of Indexes and Dictionaries to Greek Authors* (Coniectanea Neotestamentica XIV, 1953).

Rife J. Merle, 'The Mechanics of Translation Greek', *JBL* LII (1933) 244-52.

Robinson, R., *Definition,* Oxford. 1954.

Schmidt J.H.H., *Synonymik der griechischen Sprache,* Leipzig, 1876-86.

Sevenster J.N., *Do You Know Greek?* (*Novum Testamentum Suppl.* XIX), Leiden, 1968.

Shipp G.P., 'Some Observations on the Distribution of Words in the New Testament', in: *Essays in Honour of G.W. Thatcher,* ed. E.C.B. MacLaurin, Sydney, 1967, pp. 127-38.

Soisalon-Soininen I., *Die Infinitive in der Septuaginta,* Helsinki, 1965.

Sturz F.G., *De dialecto Macedonica et Alexandrina,* Lipsiae, 1808.

Sturz F.G., *Lexicon Xenophonteum,* Lipsiae, 1801-4.

Tabachovitz D., *Die Septuaginta und das Neue Testament,* Lund, 1956.

Tarelli C.C., 'Johannine Synonyms', *JTS* XLVIII (1946) 175-7.

Thiersch H.G.J., *De Pentateuchi versione Alexandrina libri iii,* Erlangae, 1841.

Thomson C., *The Septuagint Bible,* revised by C.A. Muses, 2 ed., Indian Hills, 1960.

Thumb A., *Handbook of the Modern Greek Vernacular* (transl. by S. Angus), Edinburgh, 1912.

Todd O.J., *Index Aristophaneus,* Cambridge Mass., 1932.

Torrey C.C., *Aramaic Graffiti on Coins of Demanhur* (Numismatic Notes & Monographs 77), New York, 1937.

Turner E.G., *Greek Papyri: An Introduction*, Oxford, 1968.

Turner N., *Grammatical Insights into the New Testament*, Edinburgh, 1965.

Turner N., 'Second Thoughts — VII. Papyrus Finds', *ET* LXXVI (1964) 44-8.

Turner N., 'The "Testament of Abraham": Problems in Biblical Greek', *NTS* I (1954-5) 219-23.

Turner N., 'The Unique Character of Biblical Greek', *VT* V (1955) 208-13.

Ullmann S., *Semantics: An Introduction to the Science of Meaning*, Oxford, 1967.

Vergote J., 'Grec biblique', *Dictionnaire de la Bible*, Suppl. III, pp. 1320-68.

Wevers J.W., 'Proto-Septuagint Studies', in: *The Seed of Wisdom. Essays in honour of T.J. Meek*, ed. W.S. McCullough, Toronto, 1964, pp. 58-77.

Wevers J.W., 'Septuagint', *Interpreter's Dictionary of the Bible* IV, pp. 273-8.

Wevers J.W., 'Septuaginta Forschungen seit 1954', *Theologische Rundschau* XXXIII (1968) 18-76.

Ziegler J., *Untersuchungen zur Septuaginta des Buches Isaias* (Alttestamentliche Abhandlungen XII.3), Münster, 1934.

Ziegler J., 'Zur Septuaginta-Vorlage im Deuteronomium', *ZAW* XXXI (1960) 237-62.

INDEXES

GREEK

See also Appendix I (150f.), and II (152ff.)

ἐξαποστέλλω	93f.	θῖβις	115
ἐξέρχομαι	92	θυσιαστήριον	52
ἐπαίρω πρόσωπον	51		
ἐπαύριον	95	ἰδού	51
ἐπέρχομαι	88f.	ἱλαστήριον	30,52
ἐπιβάλλω	70	ἵλεως γίνομαι	34
ἐπικαταράομαι	48	ἱματισμός	101
ἐπιπορεύομαι	88f.	ἵππος	35
ἐπωμίς	51	ἴσον ἴσῳ	35
ἐργοδιωκτέω	97	ἴχνος	42
ἐργοδιώκτης	96f.		
ἔργον	91	καθαίρω	48
ἐρυθρός	111,112	καθαρίζω	48
ἔρχομαι	85	κάθημαι	40,51
-έρχομαι	85f.,128	καί	51
ἑσπερινός	110	καιρός	83
ἐτασμός	44f.	καλύπτω	77
ἑτερόζυγος	97	κάρταλλος	115f.
-ετής	26	κατὰ μόνας	35
εὐδοκέω	97	κατὰ χώραν μένω	35
εὑρίσκω	51	καταβοάω	29
ἐχθρία	43	καταγίνομαι	95
ἔχω	32	καταγώγιον	99
		καταδυναστεία	48
ζητέω τὴν ψυχήν	51	κατακλίνω	28
ζύμη	46	κατάλυμα	99
		καταπενθέω	42
ἡγεμονία	83	καταπρονομεύω	48
		κατατείνω	71f.
θαυμάσιος	33	κατατρέχω	83
θεάομαι	133,134,138,140	καταφεύγω	28
		καταφυτεία	58
θέλω	124,144,148	καταφύτευσις	58
θεραπεία	33	καταφυτεύω	45,57f.
θεωρέω	133,134,138,140	κατάφυτος	58
		καταχέω	34
θηλυκός	109f.	καταψύχω	50
θῆλυς	109	κερατίζω	42
θηριάλωτος	52	κῆπος	54,55

χόρτασμα	100
χρόνος	83
χρυσοῦς	63ff.,145
	147
ὧδε	81f.

HEBREW AND ARAMAIC

אורים	51	לי	17
אם	17	לבדו	35
אתון	143	לקח	29
		לריק	35
בד בבד	35		
בוא	87	מגרשים	80
בן	11,24,26	מום	51
בנה	51	מטר	123f.
		מצא	51
גיורא	16	מקרא	51
גמא	121	מרד	36
גן	55f.	משקל	63
גר	16		
		נגש	91
דרך	51	נוס	28
		נטש	69f.
הגה	51	נטע	58
		נתן	11
זהב	65		
		סור	36
חגרה	95		
חזה	51	עברי	52
חלה	66	עין	26
חלל	71	עלה	36
חמור	142	ערב	60
חמר	117	עשה	51
		עתק	36
טף	104ff.		
		פסחה	16
יצא	127	פקיד	98
יקום	51	פתכרא	16
ישב	40,51	פתר	78
כבס	39f.		
כלי	39	צפן	77
כסף	64f.		
כר	116,117	קרב	91
כרם	107